6s
11.2.04

DESTINATION BENCHMARKING
CONCEPTS, PRACTICES AND OPERATIONS

CABI Publishing is a division of CAB International

CABI Publishing
CAB International
Wallingford
Oxon OX10 8DE
UK
Tel: +44 (0)1491 832111
Fax: +44 (0)1491 833508
E-mail: cabi@cabi.org
Website: www.cabi-publishing.org

CABI Publishing
875 Massachusetts Avenue
7th Floor
Cambridge, MA 02139
USA
Tel: +1 617 395 4056
Fax: +1 617 354 6875
E-mail: cabi-nao@cabi.org

A catalogue record for this book is available from the British Library,
London, UK.

Library of Congress Cataloging-in-Publication Data
Kozak, M. (Metin), 1968-
    Destination benchmarking: concepts, practices and operations / M. Kozak
        p. cm.
Includes bibliographical references (p.   ).
    ISBN 0-85199-745-7 (alk. paper)
    1. Tourism--management. 2. Benchmarking (Management) I. Title.
    G155.A1K68 2004
    910'.68'4--dc21
                                                            2003011297

ISBN 0 85199 745 7

Typeset in 10/12pt Optima by Columns Design Ltd, Reading
Printed and bound in the UK by Biddles Ltd, King's Lynn

Contents

Preface

The review of past benchmarking literature shows that there are a sub-stantial number of both conceptual and empirical attempts to formulate a benchmarking approach, particularly in the manufacturing industry. However, there has been limited investigation and application of bench-marking in tourism businesses and particularly in tourist destinations. The purpose of this book is to evaluate approaches to benchmarking and their application within tourist destinations, to show the ways to develop the concept of benchmarking further for application within tourist destinations and to evaluate its potential impact on destination performance. As an introduction to the book, this preface briefly discusses the development of the destination benchmarking concept and its rationale, along with setting the aims, objectives and methodological procedures. Brief information about each of the succeeding chapters is also given.

The Study

In recent years, tourism has become a highly competitive market. The development of the tourism industry reflects the wider development of tourist destinations, which are becoming more important than individual businesses. A number of factors contribute to this trend. Tourists are more familiar with the practicalities of travel – booking their holidays, making the journey, learning other languages and making return visits to a favourite destination. New destinations have emerged in the international market, e.g. the Caribbean and the eastern Mediterranean. The media and tour operators are having an increasing impact on the market. Tourists, suppliers and intermediaries are all becoming more concerned about the environment. Finally, the contribution of tourism to the local economy is increasing significantly. As the expansion of holiday destinations around the world makes the competition more fierce, each destination could establish goals and objectives to attract the type of tourists who are relevant to what it has to offer. To achieve this, priority might be given to identifying major tourist motivations and needs and whether they are likely to return. An examination of how other destinations, particularly competitors, perform is also the subject of this category of research.

The concepts of benchmarking and competitiveness are strongly related. Success in the former brings success in the latter. Perhaps this is why benchmarking has been applied increasingly by many individual and governmental organizations. Benchmarking has become a significant tool for total quality improvement in manufacturing and service industries. There are a number of benchmarking examples in the literature, but very few are concerned with the tourism industry. A lot of work has been carried out in relation to the measurement of destination performance through image and customer satisfaction measurement research, either comparatively or individually. Although the potential benefits of benchmarking in tourism have already begun to be recognized by practitioners and authorities, an extensive review of the literature has demonstrated that there is still a clear gap in the benchmarking literature relating to tourist destinations. Organizations such as the European Commission and regional tourist boards in Britain recently have begun to carry out destination benchmarking research, particularly focusing on external benchmarking, which is applicable for practical uses, rather than developing a research methodology.

Until very recently, efforts to apply benchmarking to tourism have been confined to individual organizations such as hotels. These studies have several weaknesses in terms of the use of research methods and choosing approaches. These weaknesses also exist in the general benchmarking literature. It has been observed in such literature that there are far more conceptual papers with an emphasis on the advantages or disadvantages of benchmarking and potential ways of using it than on empirical research focusing on methodological concerns such as how to generate and assess data, how to measure one's own performance and possible gaps compared with others. The literature suggests several stages in a benchmarking study. Priority, however, should be given to the proposition of a relevant and accurate methodology to investigate how to measure performance gaps and who needs to be involved in the study, rather than listing the necessary practical procedures.

Such weaknesses of previous research into methodology have brought another dimension to this book. On starting this project, the prime purpose was to develop a specific concept of destination benchmarking by following the guidelines of previous benchmarking literature. Then, it became apparent that the existing benchmarking literature does not pay sufficient attention to the development of an effective benchmarking model. The term 'benchmarking' has been used incorrectly by both practitioners and academic researchers. There are many questionable research projects into 'benchmarking'. Excluding quantitative measures, the previous research lacks the proper investigation and the use of qualitative measures. For example, there are limited applications with respect to statistical test assessment, the consideration of cross-cultural differences between nationalities and differences between demographic, economic and psychographic characteristics of individuals. Very little research has been carried out on how one organization can learn from another and apply the lessons learned to its own organization. This book therefore attempts to fill this generic gap while at the same time applying the benchmarking concept to tourist destinations.

The literature suggests two main components of benchmarking studies: performance benchmarking (elements of quality and customer satisfaction and qualitative measures) and process benchmarking (discrete work, processes and operating systems). Performance benchmarking compares performance levels between organizations on the basis of ranking (outcomes), whereas process benchmarking seeks to investigate how others achieve their aims (drivers). In its preliminary research aims and objectives, this book investigates the performance benchmarking approach since this would make it easier to examine the reasons for the superiority or deficiency in the performance indicators. A supplementary objective is to achieve the process benchmarking.

In terms of the performance measurement of destinations, competitiveness could be evaluated both quantitatively and qualitatively. Quantitative performance of a destination could be measured by looking at such data as tourist arrivals and income from tourism (hard data). There is also a need to take into account the relative qualitative aspects of destination competitiveness (soft data), as these ultimately drive quantitative performance. Dimensions contributing to qualitative competitiveness include those attributes or items that tourists most liked or most disliked during their vacation. A further assumption here is that in arriving at a positive or negative view, tourists compare these attributes in terms of their experience of the same or other destinations. Some of the elements of qualitative measures included in the book are tourist satisfaction, tourist comments, tourist motivations, image and attitude perceptions, and repeat tourists' opinions. The quantitative measures include the volume of tourist arrivals, volume of repeat tourists, volume of tourism receipts, tourist expenditure and length of stay. In terms of supply, measures could be given from the analysis of quality grading and eco-label systems, the number and the type of accommodation available, other tourist attractions, and so on.

In general, the benchmarking literature has focused on the development of external benchmarking procedures. Thus, attention should also be paid to understanding whether external benchmarking is the only solution or whether there could be any other method for identifying performance gaps and accelerating continuous performance improvement, e.g. internal and generic benchmarking. Internal benchmarking refers to monitoring the performance objectives released by the tourism authorities (tourism officers, destination managers, and so on) during the planning stage. Generic benchmarking looks at national or international standards in order to find effective solutions for their particular problems by reviewing best practices. This book examines the possible applications of internal, external and generic benchmarking methods to tourist destinations.

A number of research studies have examined the strengths and weaknesses of different tourist destinations on the basis of various quantitative and qualitative measures generated through primary and secondary sources of information. However, no particular benchmarking methodology was employed and a more comprehensive investigation was not provided in these studies. Whilst useful, such studies did not deal with destination performance in the comprehensive and systematic way that would result from a benchmarking approach. Because the contribution of benchmarking to comparative analysis is that 'lessons are learned', the enabling performance is observed and the enablers are then used as a model for changes in the host organization (or in the host destination).

The relevant literature on benchmarking, customer and tourist satisfaction/dissatisfaction, tourist perceptions and their experiences, service quality, destination image, destination competitiveness and positioning has been explored, and textbooks, unpublished theses and reports and statistical bulletins consulted. Only a small number of benchmarking classifications have been produced. The majority of these classifications are basically related to reflecting the features of organizations, rather than tourist destinations and tourism and travel services (e.g. process benchmarking and performance benchmarking). Excluding some minor contributions that date back to the middle of the 1990s, the application of benchmarking in the tourism and travel industry is scant. Specifically, an extensive literature review has failed to reveal any academic research conducted on developing a destination benchmarking methodology.

Tourism has been defined as a multi-disciplinary field of study borrowing heavily from other related fields (Graburn and Jafari, 1991). As a result, the aims of this study have been defined as: (i) to evaluate the relevance of the benchmarking method, basically as a management concept, to overseas tourist destinations, their development and management; (ii) to investigate and demonstrate how benchmarking can be used to identify required performance improvements within destinations; (iii) to propose, as a result, a specific tourist destination benchmarking model and make recommendations regarding its operation; and (iv) to make a contribution to the general organization benchmarking literature through its further improvement by analysing its strengths and weaknesses. The proposed model is built up in three stages: measuring performance; carrying out a certain type of benchmarking; and taking action. Although both methods are sometimes used in tandem, the literature review shows that benchmarking methodologies in the manufacturing industry are largely dominated by the assessment of quantitative measures such as profits, time scales, production and sale units (New and Szwejczweski, 1995) as opposed to the service industry, which has been largely dominated by qualitative measures such as customer satisfaction with the delivery of services or image (Zairi, 1998). The reason could be the difficulty in quantifying components of services (Shetty, 1993).

Brief Overview of Chapters

The published literature on benchmarking mainly concentrates on individual organizations operating in the manufacturing industry. Its operationalization in the service industry has only been addressed recently. There is too little empirical research focusing on the development of a specific benchmarking methodology referring to tourism organizations and tourist destinations. Despite its limited application for tourism organizations and destinations, a broad range of resources reflecting the characteristics of the terms of benchmarking and destination management is utilized, drawing on previous research in many areas such as management, marketing, economics, planning, and so on. A brief resumé of each subsequent chapter is given below.

Before moving on to evaluating the relevance of the benchmarking theory to international tourist destinations, and their development and management, a brief introduction to the general theory of benchmarking needs to be provided. Chapter 1, therefore, aims to review the concept of benchmarking and methods by which it can be applied. In this context, several approaches to the definition of benchmarking and its development are presented. The perceived benefits and costs of benchmarking and the process of its implementation are examined. Methods used to identify gaps are examined on the basis of qualitative and quantitative research. Several weaknesses of benchmarking models are also addressed.

Chapter 2 analyses the development of benchmarking within the tourism industry together with some examples. So far, there has been a very limited use of benchmarking in the tourism industry, and it is still in its infancy and has been restricted to the study of operational units and businesses, rather than destinations. It is significant that the limited examples of benchmarking carried out within the tourism industry almost all involve the benchmarking process being carried out by third parties external to the organizations being benchmarked. There are a limited number of benchmarking studies in tourism focusing solely on measuring the performance of tourist destinations and providing methods to improve it. The weaknesses of the benchmarking research noted in Chapter 1 also apply to the context of benchmarking in the tourism and hospitality industry.

As a first step towards preparing and performing destination benchmarking research and therefore indicating where and how to be competitive, Chapter 3 attempts to discuss the possible scope of destination management, identify the main reasons for establishing a destination benchmarking study, provide an overall model for those wishing to exploit their performance levels and then analyse its main components. The performance measurement theory is briefly reviewed, along with its application to tourist destinations and the potential use of internal, external and generic benchmarking. Moreover, in line with the theoretical background presented earlier, this part of the study along with the next four chapters will therefore examine the applicability of the benchmarking concept to tourist destinations as a performance measurement, improvement and competitive advantage tool.

Chapter 4 aims to develop further the context of quantitative and qualitative measures, as the primary sources of destination benchmarking research. This encompasses a number of measures specifically related to the measurement of overall destination performance and suggests how to evaluate each in the context of internal and external benchmarking procedures. This chapter provides the basis for what kind of measures can be developed and how they can be applied to tourist destinations from the perspective of internal and external benchmarking. The proposed measures in the book, referring to the assessment of both internal and external performance of tourist destinations, are believed to foster the overall performance of destinations by identifying their own performance, gaps with others and competitive positions.

Based on the model of destination benchmarking presented in Chapter 3, Chapter 5 aims to extend the context of information relating to the practice of internal benchmarking by presenting methods on what and how to benchmark. This part is devoted to the discussion of the practical procedures of internal destination benchmarking and the potential methods that can be used to collect and analyse data and present the benchmarking findings, in comparison with earlier studies in the field of benchmarking. This chapter discusses in detail the content of the benchmarking model basically related to the development of destination benchmarking. The chapter ends with an overview of its strengths and weaknesses.

Chapter 6 aims to extend the context of information relating to the practice of external benchmarking by presenting methods on what, how and who to benchmark. The necessity of developing an external destination benchmarking approach emerges from the fierce competition among international tourist destinations and rapid changes in customer needs, wants and expectations. It seems obvious that destinations need to benchmark their facilities and service levels against those of their counterparts. In conducting external benchmarking, current performance levels in terms of the competition are measured. Without benchmarking no comparison can be made and therefore the performance gap cannot be established.

Chapter 7 introduces the existing quality grading and accommodation classification systems, as well as eco-labels, as a form of generic benchmarking for tourist destinations. This chapter aims to argue their importance in performance measurement and improvement. How benchmarking, linked to external awards and grades, can offer advantages and bring about improvements in competitiveness for destinations is also discussed. The chapter ends with an overview of strengths and weaknesses of generic destination benchmarking.

Chapter 8 provides a discussion of the methodology, research design and procedures to be employed in the investigation of destination benchmarking research in accordance with the proposed qualitative and quantitative measures. General guidelines for the application of qualitative and quantitative data collection methods have been provided and a structured approach to the formulation, estimation and interpretation of data analysis presented. The chapter begins with a brief overview of the literature on designing research methods. Then, it moves on to the operationalization of the destination benchmarking methodology. The chapter concludes by examining how data derived from such methods can be used to produce an overall picture from the destination benchmarking perspective, and to observe and document changes in the market structure.

As emphasized earlier, this book considers two categories of benchmarking in terms of their applications: organization benchmarking and destination benchmarking. The former deals with the performance evaluation of only a particular organization and its departments. In contrast, the latter draws a broader picture including all elements of one destination such as transport services, airport services, accommodation services, leisure and sport facilities, hospitality and local attitudes, hygiene and cleanliness, and so on. The purpose of Chapter 9 is to identify the main differences between organization benchmarking and destination benchmarking and also to consider the limitations arising from the structure of the travel and tourism industry and influencing the successful development and implementation of destination benchmarking practices.

Chapter 10, the concluding chapter, summarizes the main arguments and considers some of the potential contributions and implications in light of the context of previous discussion. The chapter begins by giving an overview of the proposed model of destination benchmarking built upon internal and external benchmarking approaches. Contributions to the benchmarking literature are then pointed out explicitly. It then moves on to the discussion of the practical application of destination benchmarking. The chapter ends with the provision of a brief summary emphasizing both the theoretical and practical contributions the book has provided.

This book is intended to provide an invaluable tool for practitioners, students and lecturers in the service business fields. It therefore assumes an understanding of both the technical and empirical sides of benchmarking operations and a basic knowledge of quality management and improvement in the context of destination management and marketing. It has included examples of current industry practice and case studies of benchmarking where appropriate. It is my hope that practitioners in the industry will find the book both challenging in the way the ideas, concepts and methods are presented, and rewarding in that it will contribute to the continued success and growth of their units and the tourism industry.

Acknowledgements

I would like to express grateful thanks to all those individuals who have helped in the preparation of this book including: Dr Chris Gratton (Sheffield Hallam University, UK), Dr Muzaffer Uysal (Virginia Tech and State University, USA) and Dr Jay Beaman (Auctor Associates, USA) for making a contribution to improving this study with their very useful comments and support; Mike Rimmington (Oxford Brookes University, UK) and Kevin Nield (Sheffield Hallam University, UK) for their guidance and comments to improve the context of the research on which this book is based; Iris Walkland for her great assistance and patience in reading the drafts of all chapters and correcting the language; Tulay Kozak, my wife, for her assistance in producing the final drafts and, most importantly, for her continual love and support. I have no doubt that this book would have never been in your hands without their contribution and support. Finally, my love goes to Çağdaş Miray, our little daughter, for having been so quiet, calm and understanding since she was born.

Metin Kozak
Mugla, 2003

Overview of Benchmarking Theory

Introduction

Before moving into evaluating the relevance of the benchmarking theory to international tourist destinations, and their development and management, a brief introduction to the general theory of benchmarking needs to be provided. This chapter therefore aims to review the concept of benchmarking and methods by which it can be applied. In this context, several approaches to the definition of benchmarking and its development are presented. The perceived benefits and costs of benchmarking and the process of its implementation are examined. Methods used to identify gaps are examined on the basis of qualitative and quantitative measures.

Overview of Benchmarking Theory

The benchmarking theory is simply built upon performance comparison, gap identification and changes in the management process (Watson, 1993). A review of the benchmarking literature shows that many of the benchmarking methodologies perform the same functions as performance gap analysis (e.g. Camp, 1989; Karlof and Ostblom, 1993; Watson, 1993). The rule is first to identify performance gaps with respect to production and consumption within the organization and then to develop methods to close them. The gap between internal and external practices reveals what changes, if any, are necessary. This feature differentiates benchmarking theory from comparison research and competitive analysis. Some researchers make the mistake of believing that every comparison survey is a form of benchmarking (e.g. Zhao et al., 1995). Competitive analysis looks at product or service comparisons, but benchmarking goes beyond just comparison and looks at the assessment of operating and management skills producing these products and services. The other difference is that competitive analysis only looks at characteristics of those in the same geographic area of competition, whilst benchmarking seeks to find the best practices regardless of location (Walleck *et al.*, 1991).

A benchmarking method consists of two parties: benchmarker and benchmarkee. The former is the organization carrying out a benchmarking procedure whereas the latter refers to the organization being benchmarked (see Table 1.1 for the list of definitions of the selected concepts related to benchmarking). Several authors have discussed the extent to which benchmarking is appropriate and its positive and/or negative results affecting the success of performance improvement within the organization (e.g. Cox and Thompson, 1998). It may be appropriate to understand what other organizations are doing and adapt these to the organization's specific problems. In contrast, it might be inappropriate if one is unaware of direct copying of what other organizations are doing and makes general inferences from subjective experiences, and hardly understands the most appropriate methods or applications. The authors also attempted to state the major reasons that make benchmarking still popular despite the fact that it has some risks. Some reasons include being subjective and the ease and quickness of copying what other organizations are doing. By reviewing a more extensive selection of the literature (e.g. Camp, 1989; Zairi, 1992; Smith *et al.*, 1993; Rogers *et al.*, 1995), it seems obvious that benchmarking:

- Helps organizations to understand where they have strengths and weaknesses depending upon changes in supply, demand and market conditions
- Helps to better satisfy the customer's needs for quality, cost, product and service by establishing new standards and goals
- Motivates employees to reach new standards and to be keen on new developments within the related area, and improves the motivation of employees
- Allows organizations to realize what level(s) of performance is really possible by looking at others, and how much improvement can be achieved
- Documents reasons as to why these differences exist
- Helps organizations to improve their competitive advantage by stimulating continuous improvement in order to maintain world-class performance and increase competitive standards
- Promotes changes and delivers improvements in quality, productivity and efficiency, which in turn bring innovation and competitive advantage.
- Is a cost-effective and time-efficient way of establishing a pool of innovative ideas from which the most applicable practical examples can be utilized.

Despite these benefits, time constraints, competitive barriers, cost, lack of both management commitment and professional human resources,

Table 1.1. Definition of benchmarking-related terms.

Terms	Definitions
Benchmarking	Action discovering the specific practices responsible for high performance, understanding how these practices work and are achieved, and adapting them to one's organization.
Benchmarks	A reference or measurement standard for comparison, e.g. how many?, how quickly?, how satisfied?
Benchmarker (the host)	Those doing the benchmarking.
Benchmarkee (the partner)	Those being benchmarked.
Benchmarking gap	The difference in performance scores between the benchmark for a particular activity and other businesses taking part in the comparison.
Business practices	Methods or approaches that help to facilitate the execution of business processes
Critical success factors	A list of variables directly influencing customers' satisfaction with the output, e.g. cost, service quality, image.
Core competencies	Strategic business capabilities that provide a business with a competitive advantage.
Strategy	Plans and means to achieve the goal for a particular objective.
Effectiveness	Doing the right job.
Efficiency	Doing the job in the right way.
Metrics	The quantified effect of implementing the practices.
Performance benchmarking	An activity of comparing one's performance level against other businesses on the basis of ranking, e.g. the speed of computer processing, reliability, and so on.
Process benchmarking	An activity of investigating how others achieve and identifying root causes as to why they are better.
Strategic benchmarking	Benchmarking the critical components of an organization's success that lead to competitive advantage.
Non-competitive benchmarking	Involves comparison of a related process in a non-competitive organization, a related process in a different industry and an unrelated process in a different industry.
Industry benchmarking	Conducting research only in a whole industry to obtain baseline information, e.g. hotel industry.
Reverse engineering	A part of benchmarking activity including the observation of a sample product or practice to discover how it is to be achieved.
Strengths	Those attractions, facilities and operations that match up to the customer's needs.
Weaknesses	Lack of those attractions, facilities and operations that match up to the customer's needs.

Continued

Table 1.1. *Continued.*

Terms	Definitions
Opportunities	Arise both from elements under the control of the industry and from changes in external factors that can be credited to the organization's advantage.
Threats	Arise from both internal and external factors.
Internal benchmarking	Monitoring the performance objectives released and developments in a particular period.
External benchmarking	The converse of internal benchmarking, which requires a comparison work with external organizations in order to discover new ideas, methods, products and services.
Generic benchmarking	A performance improvement process by looking at best practices, recognized nationally and internationally, or world-class organizations.
Best-in-class benchmarking	Identifying the best processes regardless of the industry. For example, a hotel's accounting department looking at that of a manufacturing business may identify it as having the fastest accounts receivable turnover.
Functional benchmarking	Identifying competitors or industry leaders not only in the same but also in different industries.
Operational benchmarking	Attempting to exceed the best practice organizations at a specific activity, function or operation.
Business management benchmarking	Benchmarking support functions such as human resources, research and development, order-processing, or management information systems.
Input	Internal resources to produce goods and services.
Output	What the customer buys.
Enablers	Processes, practices or methods leading to performance improvement and facilitating the implementation of a best practice.
Outcomes	Performance outcomes yielded by utilizing and implementing benchmarking findings.
Process	A series of interrelated activities that convert inputs into outputs.
Re-engineering	Redesigning business processes, organizational structures and management systems to achieve progress in business performance.
Process re-engineering	Rethinking of all aspects of a business process, including its purpose, tasks, structure, technology and outputs and then redesigning them to deliver value-added process outputs.

Source: own elaboration from various sources.

resistance to change, poor planning and short-term expectations are regarded as the main problems affecting successful benchmarking research (Bendell *et al.*, 1993). A poorly executed benchmarking exercise will result in a waste of financial and human resources, as well as time. Ineffectively executed benchmarking projects may have tarnished an organization's image (Elmuti and Kathawala, 1997). Moreover, there is no single 'best practice' because it varies from one person to another and every organization differs in terms of mission, culture, environment and technological tools available. Thus, there are risks involved in benchmarking others and in adopting new standards into one's own organization. The 'best practice' should be perceived or accepted to be among those practices producing superior outcomes and being judged as good examples within the area. Finally, benchmarking findings may remove the heterogeneity of an industry since standards will themselves become globally standardized and attempts to produce differentiation may fail (Cox and Thompson, 1998). For these reasons, Campbell (1999) suggests that organizations should spend little time on benchmarking, instead focusing on their own planning procedures with regard to their own needs.

Definitions

As a quality management and improvement theory, benchmarking basically stems from Deming's quality management theory, which aims to enhance quality and check its sustainability by following several stages in order. Despite this, benchmarking has been given many different definitions by different organizations and authors even though each aims to reach the same conclusion (see Table 1.2). Webster's Dictionary defines benchmark as 'a *standard* by which something can be measured or judged' (Camp, 1989, p. 248; emphasis added). On a similar note, Zairi (1996, p. 35) defines a benchmark as 'something that serves as a *standard* by which others may be served' (emphasis added). The most widely accepted and referenced text on the subject of benchmarking is the definition by Xerox and Robert C. Camp at the end of the 1980s, which is 'the *continuous process* of measuring our products, services and practices against the toughest competitors or those companies recognised as industry leaders' (Camp, 1989; emphasis added). Benchmarking has been defined by Camp (1989) simply as 'the search for industry *best practice* that leads to *superior performance*' (emphasis added). In other words, benchmarking is a process of finding what best practices are and then proposing what performance should be in the future. The three principles of benchmarking are maintaining quality, customer satisfaction and continuous improvement (Watson, 1993).

The American Productivity and Quality Center (1999) has contributed to the definition of benchmarking by stating that it is 'the process of *continuously* comparing and measuring an organisation against business leaders

Table 1.2. What is benchmarking?

Authors	Definitions
Camp (1989)	The continuous process of measuring products, services and practices against the toughest competitors or those companies recognized as industry leaders.
Geber (1990)	A process of finding the world-class examples of a product, service or operational system and then adjusting own products, services or systems to meet or beat those standards.
Codling (1992)	An ongoing process of measuring and improving products, services and practices against the best.
Vaziri (1992)	A continuous process comparing an organization's performance against that of the best in the industry considering critical consumer needs and determining what should be improved.
Watson (1993)	The continuous input of new information to an organization.
Evans and Lindsey (1993)	Measuring own performance against best-in-class organizations to determine how they achieve their performance levels and using the knowledge to improve own performance.
Lu et al. (1994)	A way of collecting information about customers and other businesses within the industry.
Kleine (1994)	An excellent tool to use in order to identify a performance goal for improvement, identify partners who have accomplished these goals and identify applicable practices to incorporate into a redesign effort.
Cortada (1995)	A method for finding how to improve processes quickly by learning from others dealing with similar issues.
Cook (1995)	A kind of performance improvement process by identifying, understanding and adopting outstanding practices from within the same organization or from other businesses.
APQC (1999)	The process of continuously comparing and measuring an organization against business leaders anywhere in the world to gain information that will help the organization take action to improve its performance.

APQC, American Productivity and Quality Center.

anywhere in the world to gain information that will help the organization take action to *improve* its *performance* (emphasis added). Similarly, Vaziri (1992) states that benchmarking is 'a continuous process comparing an organization's performance against that of the best in the industry considering *critical consumer needs* and determining what should be improved' (emphasis added). Watson (1993) defines benchmarking in terms of its continuity feature referring to the continuous input of *new information* to an organization. Geber (1990, p. 36) focuses on the significance of looking at best practices in his definition of benchmarking as follows: 'a process of *finding the world-class examples* of a product, service or operational system and then adjusting your products, services or systems to *meet or beat those standards*' (emphasis added).

The words in italic are especially significant in these definitions as benchmarking studies are perishable and time-sensitive. What is a standard of excellence today may be the expected performance of tomorrow. Improvement is a continuous process, and benchmarking should be considered as a part of that process. As a result, although different authors have defined benchmarking in different ways, as is demonstrated in Table 1.3, all these definitions have a common theme, namely: the continuous measurement and improvement of an organization's performance against the best in the industry to obtain information about new working methods or practices in other organizations.

As Watson (1993) has already stated, it should be 'a process of adaptation, not adoption'. It is not just a question of copying what others are

Table 1.3. Approaches to definitions of benchmarking.

Authors	Features of benchmarking			
	Ongoing process	Against the best	Performance improvement	Gaining new information
Camp (1989)	X	X	X	
Geber (1990)			X	X
Vaziri (1992)	X	X	X	
Balm (1992)	X	X	X	X
Spendolini (1992)	X	X	X	
McNair and Leibfried (1992)	X		X	
Codling (1992)	X	X	X	
Evans and Lindsey (1993)		X	X	X
Watson (1993)	X			X
Kleine (1994)			X	X
Lu *et al.* (1994)				X
Cook (1995)			X	X
Cortada (1995)			X	X
Watson (1997)		X	X	X
APQC (1999)	X	X	X	

Source: own elaboration derived from the related literature review.

doing; the power in benchmarking comes from sharing ideas. Considering benchmarking as a process of learning from the best practices and experiences of others, some authors have used the term *benchlearning* (e.g. Karlof and Ostblom, 1993). Benchmarking is not different from the principle of learning from others' better or worse experiences, but it puts the learning experience into a structured framework. In addition, one should also bear in mind that benchmarking is not the same as benchmarks (American Productivity and Quality Center, 1999). Benchmarking is an action discovering the specific practices responsible for high performance, understanding how these practices work and are achieved, and adapting them to one's organization, while benchmarks represent performance measures such as how many, how fast, and so on. In other words, benchmarking aims to provide real improvement, whereas benchmarks refer to facts.

The benchmarking approach is considered as a significant tool of quality improvement in organizations within the context of total quality management (TQM) (Karlof and Ostblom, 1993; Hutton and Zairi, 1995). As indicated in Fig. 1.1, a link between benchmarking and TQM has already been established since both are regarded as a commitment to the continuous improvement of customer satisfaction (Balm, 1992; Codling, 1992; Zairi, 1992, 1996; Barsky, 1996). Given this, a number of examples can be given from the practical applications of a TQM and benchmarking relationship. International businesses such as AT&T, Alcoa (Zairi, 1996) and Rover Group (Bendell *et al.*, 1993) benchmarked themselves against others by

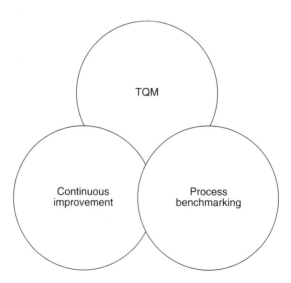

Fig. 1.1. Relationship between total quality management (TQM), performance and benchmarking. Source: Zairi and Hutton (1995).

initially adopting a TQM programme within their organizations. Research findings indicate that the majority of leading US businesses undertake benchmarking and link it to their TQM efforts (Balm, 1992). The implementation of TQM is also a factor in applying for and winning the Baldrige Award, e.g. Motorola and Xerox (Nadkarni, 1995).

Background

With regard to the development of benchmarking, it is believed that Japanese businesses began benchmarking studies in the 1950s by visiting their western counterparts in order to transfer their technology and business practices to themselves (Bendell *et al.*, 1993). With reference to the chronological order presented by Cook (1995) for the systematic development of benchmarking, benchmarking was first applied during the 1950s to measure business performance in terms of cost/sales and investment ratios. This stimulated businesses to identify their own strengths and weaknesses by comparing them with those of their counterparts within the industry. However, it was unable to provide alternatives as to how further performance improvements could be achieved.

In the 1960s and 1970s, the growth of computer technology increased the application of benchmarking. In the USA in the 1980s, benchmarking became a recognized tool in the development of continuous improvement. The other reason for the spreading use of benchmarking in the USA at that time was the Malcolm Baldrige Quality Award. It spread into the UK in the late 1980s. Benchmarking, as a management tool, gained momentum in 1979 when Xerox decided to observe what its competitors were doing. Before 1979, benchmarking was understood as a comparison of various elements of a business with its previous year's performance. Measures were mostly related to economic indicators such as profits, sales volume and expenses (Swift *et al.*, 1995). Businesses would use traditional methods to compare themselves with each other. Site visits, the first method, referred to visiting other businesses to observe what was being done and collecting new ideas that could be adapted. Reverse engineering, the second method, involved the comparison of products. Businesses would buy other businesses' products to analyse how they were made and what kinds of ingredients were used. Competitive analysis, the last method, examined strategies and tactics employed by the competition.

The quantity of benchmarking literature has increased tremendously since 1989 when the first textbook published by Camp appeared. Since then, benchmarking has exploded into other major industries such as telecommunication, health, automotive, transport, medicine, tourism and disciplines such as education. It has been widely used in the manufacturing industry, particularly by US and Japanese businesses, e.g. nearly half of the Fortune 500 businesses conduct benchmarking (Cortada, 1995). It has been reported that most US businesses believe that the amount of bench-marking in their field has increased (Bendell *et al.*, 1993). They also believe that businesses must benchmark themselves to stay in the market (Balm, 1992). Benchmarking is now recognized internationally as a quality improvement tool (Hutton and Zairi, 1995). Benchmarking examples in the international arena have also been recorded (Ohinata, 1994; Roberts, 1995). For example, some US, Japanese and European manufacturing and service businesses have conducted benchmarking studies against each other.

Types of benchmarking

Although several classifications of benchmarking are recorded in the rele-vant literature, the main categorizations are internal, competitive and func-tional benchmarking (Camp, 1989; Zairi, 1992). The benchmarking literature can be mainly separated into two parts: internal and external benchmarking. In this context, competitive and functional benchmarking will be classed under external benchmarking. As will be seen, the process is essentially the same for each category. The main differences are what is to be benchmarked and with whom it will be benchmarked.

Internal benchmarking

Internal benchmarking covers two-way communication and sharing opin-ions between departments within the same organization or between orga-nizations operating as part of a chain in different countries (Cross and Leonard, 1994; Breiter and Kline, 1995). Franchising contracts can also be considered to be within the categorization of internal benchmarking. Once any part of an organization has a better performance indicator, others can learn how this was achieved. Findings of internal benchmarking can then be used as a baseline for extending benchmarking to include external orga-nizations (McNair and Leibfried, 1992; Karlof and Ostblom, 1993). There is a consensus among researchers in the field of benchmarking that all benchmarking processes should start by dealing with internal benchmark-ing because this requires an organization to examine itself, and this pro-vides a baseline for comparison with others (Breiter and Kline, 1995). Among advantages of internal benchmarking are the ability to deal with partners who share a common language, culture and systems, having easy access to data, and giving a baseline for future comparisons (Breiter and Kline, 1995). Therefore, the outcomes of an internal benchmarking can be presented quickly. However, it is claimed that this type of benchmarking study is time-consuming because competitors could be busy increasing their market share while the sample organization is busy measuring its internal performance (Cook, 1995).

External benchmarking

As it is the converse of internal benchmarking, external benchmarking requires a comparison of work with external organizations in order to discover new ideas, methods, products and services (Cox and Thompson, 1998). The gap between internal and external practices displays the way in which to change and if there is any need to change. The objective is continuously to improve one's own performance by measuring how it performs, comparing it with that of others and determining how the others achieve their performance levels. This type of benchmarking provides opportunities for learning from the best practices and experiences of others who are at the leading edge. Consistent with an extensive review of the literature on benchmarking, external benchmarking is divided into three major subcategories: competitive, generic and relationship benchmarking. Each is briefly explained below.

COMPETITIVE BENCHMARKING. Competitive benchmarking refers to a comparison with direct competitors only. This is accepted as the most sensitive type of benchmarking activity because it is very difficult to achieve a healthy collaboration and cooperation with direct competitors and reach primary sources of information. Banks and building societies often apply competitive benchmarking to identify standards of customer satisfaction. As a result, this type of benchmarking is believed to be more rational for larger organizations than smaller ones, as they have the infrastructure to support quality and continuous improvement (Cook, 1995). For example, as a result of the entrance of new competitors, Xerox's market share began to decline. The Xerox management decided to benchmark its own performance with competitors within the same industry. Through benchmarking, it improved its financial position, stabilized its market share and increased the satisfaction level of its customers (Cook, 1995). The benefits of using competitive benchmarking include creating a culture that values continuous improvement to achieve excellence, increasing sensitivity to changes in the external environment and sharing the best practices between partners (Vaziri, 1992). As to the disadvantages of its application, it may become difficult to obtain data from competitors and to apply lessons to be learnt from them. A further risk may include the tendency to focus on the factors that make the competitors distinctive instead of searching for the factors contributing to excellent performance (Karlof and Ostblom, 1993).

FUNCTIONAL BENCHMARKING. Functional benchmarking refers to comparative research and attempts to seek world-class excellence by comparing business performance not only against competitors but also against the best businesses operating in similar fields and performing similar activities or having similar problems, but in a different industry (Davies, 1990; Breiter and Kline, 1995). For instance, British Rail Network South East employed a benchmarking process to improve the standard of cleanliness on trains. The survey results indicated that cleanliness was the most sensitive dimension for customers. British Airways was selected as a partner because a team of 11 people cleans a 250-seat Jumbo aircraft in only 9 min. After the benchmarking exercise, a team of ten people were able to clean a 660-seat train in 8 min (Cook, 1995). Moreover, giving an example from the manufacturing industry, Rover, a car manufacturing company, not only selected Honda, another car manufacturing company, as a partner for benchmarking but also benchmarked itself with IBM and British Airways although these are in a totally different industry. This means that a hotel organization's accounting department would look at the accounting department of a manufacturing organization that has been identified as having the fastest operations. It is believed to be easier to obtain data in such arrangements as best-in-class organizations are more likely to share their experiences. However, generic benchmarking can take a long time to complete, and research outcomes may need a lot of modification in order for organizations to set their own standards. These are disadvantages for the benchmarker (Cook, 1995). This type of benchmarking is also defined as non-competitive benchmarking.

RELATIONSHIP BENCHMARKING. Andersen (1995) introduces relationship benchmarking as a further type of external benchmarking. This refers to benchmarking against an organization with whom the benchmarker already had a relationship in advance of a benchmarking agreement. This method potentially may provide some benefits to organizations since less time is required and the trust established between the two parties will help break down confidentiality barriers. Cox *et al.* (1997) call this 'collaborative benchmarking'. Introducing 'collaborative benchmarking' as an alternative option to 'competitive benchmarking', they suggest that the purpose should be to study what collaborative organizations can gain from benchmarking together, rather than focusing on the benefits only a single organization will gain.

Analysis of benchmarking models

Although benchmarking theory has been derived from Deming's four stages: *plan*, *do*, *check* and *act*, numerous benchmarking process models have been proposed by researchers in both industry and academia. About 40 different models have been identified originating from individual organizations, consulting agencies and individual researchers. The number of phases and process steps in these models is variable. While some specify five phases consisting of a total of 14 steps (e.g. Camp, 1989; Karlof and Ostblom, 1993), some have just four phases with the same number of steps (e.g. Watson, 1993). Having reviewed all the major models, the following steps can be outlined as the main categorization: planning, data collection, analysis, action and review. As widely mentioned in the literature (Camp, 1989; Spendolini, 1992; Vaziri, 1992), the benchmarking process should begin in the host organization in order to be able to specify areas that need to be measured. Further steps are collecting data, examining gaps between partners to identify strengths and weaknesses, taking action and reviewing the future performance level of the host organization. The review stage helps the organization understand whether the process has achieved its objectives.

In reference to the statement given above, the traditional benchmarking approach refers to the notion that there must be a gap between the host and the partner. The gap analysis model considers the differences between performance levels of businesses. The standard is to be set considering the highest value as the best practice. When the score is greater than zero, it is a strength for business A and a weakness for business B. This is regarded as a positive gap. On the other side, when the score is less than zero, this means that the specific attribute performs better in business B (strength) than business A (weakness). This is regarded as a negative gap. A large negative gap could be an indicator that means that radical change is required (McNair and Leibfried, 1992). Depending upon these results, the final decision on whether benchmarking research needs to be carried out is made. Answers to the following questions can be helpful in deciding whether any benchmarking process is conducted (Spendolini, 1992; Vaziri, 1992).

- What is the most crucial factor for the organization?
- What factors are causing the problem?
- What products or services are provided to customers?
- What factors account for customer satisfaction?
- What are the major costs in the organization?
- Which functions have the opportunity for improvement?
- Which functions have the greatest potential for differentiating between competitors?

Based on a gap analysis, Watson (1993) proposes a benchmarking model, as shown in Fig. 1.2. Step 1 identifies the performance measures. Step 2 identifies one's own performance and the performance of the partner to be involved in the study. Step 3 presents the consequence of the performance between the two at the present time, as well as the projected performance trend of the partner. Step 4 includes the goals set by the organization for improvement and its targeted performance. Point A represents the border where the performance of both the host and the partner equal each other. In Watson's model, the host organization initially has a negative gap compared with the partner. As a result of the scheduled managed change, the gap is expected to become positive.

Nevertheless, this model has several weaknesses. A performance gap can not only be negative or positive but can also be neutral, indicating no

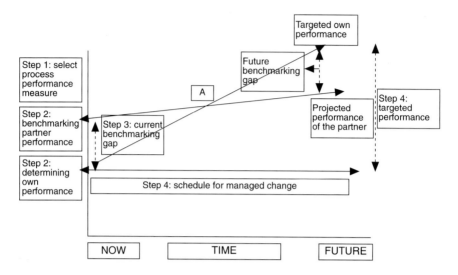

Fig. 1.2. A benchmarking gap analysis model. Source: Watson (1993).

identifiable difference between compared attributes (Karlof and Ostblom, 1993). The partners can go further than the estimated or projected future performance or, since the business environment is so dynamic, an organization may be affected by changes in internal or external factors. The gap exists as a result of differences in performance. Only past and present gaps can be known or measured. In the early stages of benchmarking, most gaps are supposed to be negative. When progress is recorded, the gap begins to decrease. Targeted future performance must be greater than the partner's. However, partners are more likely to increase their performance levels even without benchmarking as they gain greater industry experience and infrastructure (Codling, 1992). Hence, the benchmarker needs to record a significant improvement initially towards their targets and then to close the gap.

As an attempt to represent gap analysis graphically, the matrix chart (M^2, spider charts or radar charts) was developed by Madigan (1993). Although it seems to be visually similar to standard gap analysis representation, the main difference is in the ability to calculate the benchmark value. In the matrix chart, all collected numerical data are brought together to select the best value as a sample. Each numerical value is divided by the best value. If the score is closer to the value '1.0', this means that this attribute is closer to the centre of the chart and performs better. If the score is much closer to the value '0.0', this means that this attribute is far from the centre and needs to be benchmarked (Madigan, 1993). In short, this chart allows users to visualize where they are doing well and where they have opportunity to improve, especially when there are more than two businesses to be compared. The weakness of this method is that it assumes that customers of two organizations have the same characteristics or are homogeneous. A modified version of the matrix chart, called the 'profile accumulation method', has been applied to point out the benchmark elements of small hotel businesses and the results obtained (Johns *et al.*, 1996).

Like the matrix chart, the spider chart is also a method used to represent graphically the performance of an organization for specific attributes in comparison with a partner(s) (Balm, 1992). The achieved performance measurement data are represented by current performance (baseline), the performance of the partner(s) by the best practice (benchmark) and the level of performance a customer expects for total satisfaction (see Fig. 1.3). The latter can be represented, for example, by '7' on a 7-point scale. The centre of the chart represents the lowest performance score of two sample organizations. Though benchmarking between a host and a partner can help to close the gap between current performance and best practice, this method fails to explain what it offers to close the gap between current performance and total customer satisfaction unless a perfect sample or practice is found.

The organization of a benchmarking exercise

Benchmarking literature demonstrates that there are two main approaches to carrying out benchmarking. It can be self-administered or conducted by a third party or research group. In a self-administered benchmarking

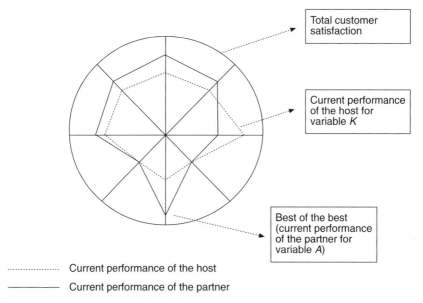

Total customer satisfaction

Current performance of the host for variable *K*

Best of the best (current performance of the partner for variable *A*)

.... Current performance of the host

———— Current performance of the partner

Fig. 1.3. A visual example of a spider chart.

approach, businesses benchmark their performance levels against others and learn about the best practices for their operations, e.g. competitive benchmarking. In a third-party benchmarking approach, research groups and national and international benchmarking organizations (or consultants) such as the European Foundation for Quality Management (EFQM), the Confederation of British Industry (CBI), the UK Department of Trade and Industry (DTI) and the US Benchmarking Clearinghouse measure the performance of a business individually or of an industry as a whole.

Selected businesses are included in the process, and the best and worst performance indicators are ranked respectively. On the basis of these results, experts or organizations present their recommendations and action plans. A few organizations such as the US Benchmarking Clearinghouse and the UK DTI have launched a network for organizations who want to compare their performance levels (on the basis of different indicators) against that of similar organizations. Clearinghouse services include networking, information, partner identification, training and databases of past research. Small businesses may also need the support of consultancy organizations who are experts in benchmarking. Research-based benchmarking studies in academia can also be considered within the category of third-party benchmarking methodology.

This type of classification may also illustrate the boundaries of time when a benchmarking research project is conducted. When benchmarking projects are done by third-party professional organizations, the benchmarking research will be defined as a singular activity, start on a specific date and have a specific completion date. As far as a self-administered benchmarking is concerned, businesses do not have to limit themselves to particular time periods. They can self-administer benchmarking projects as a continuous activity in order to keep up to date with developments in relevant areas (Spendolini, 1992). Research findings show that some US businesses are repeating benchmarking studies every 2–5 years (Bendell *et al.*, 1993).

Overview of Performance Measurement Theory

The traditional approach regards benchmarking as a tool to discover or adopt innovative ideas. Nevertheless, these ideas are not completely original and already exist in other organizations or destinations. It is important to consider benchmarking as a way to achieve innovation through external information practices. In this respect, different methods for measurement will appear as a significant complementary tool to evaluate one's own and others' performance levels and reach objectives. Camp (1989, p. 42) points out that the reason for undertaking benchmarking research is 'to develop a standard or measure against which to compare'. The main idea of benchmarking or continuous improvement is that if something cannot be measured it cannot be managed either (Zairi, 1996; Goh and Richards, 1997). Thus, as long as benchmarking seeks to identify gaps as a preliminary stage in the process, performance measurement based on feedback from customers about the outcome obtained will be necessary because their opinion is the ultimate test, rather than what organizations think or assume. In addition, performance measurement will help to investigate how resources are used in a productive, effective and efficient manner (Karlof and Ostblom, 1993). Undertaking benchmarking will confirm the extent to which the organization's performance results are valid and competitive.

Both benchmarking and methodology literature suggest two categories of performance measures as 'qualitative' and 'quantitative'. In addition, combining both measures, the balanced score card forms the third method. Each measure is briefly explained in this section, but will be examined in more detail in Chapter 4.

Short review of quantitative measures

To consider any value or measure as quantitative, it must be capable of being denoted in a numerical form that falls within a uniform mathematical scale. Examples of performance measures in quantitative terms are financial indicators such as revenues, costs, profitability, number of production and consumption units, and so on. These measures are also accepted as outputs (Walleck *et al.*, 1991). It is argued that most benchmarking researchers prefer using quantitative rather than qualitative measures due to the ease of measurement and the simplicity of identifying gaps (Holloway *et al.*, 1998). Nevertheless, such measures do not give any insight into why the sampled areas perform well or poorly, they only produce values in absolute numbers.

Short review of qualitative measures

Qualitative measures (inputs) indicate the performance of an organization in relation to its operating practices based on perceptual evaluation by assigning a numerical value to each perceptual degree (Walleck *et al.*, 1991). To quantify continuous improvement, it is necessary to transform qualitative data into the quantitative form of soft numbers (Wetzel and Maul, 1996). Measures such as quality and customer satisfaction differ from quantitative measures such as productivity and finance. These types of measures are often used by undertaking research with Likert-type scales and percentage values to obtain feedback from customers or suppliers. The earlier cases of benchmarking were applied to measure particularly the quantitative performance and improve it, e.g. efforts to decrease costs at Xerox. Then, qualitative measures have begun to appear as the recognition

of customer-driven quality measurements, as quality has become more crucial than quantity for both customers and service providers (Zairi, 1996).
For instance, results indicate that reasons for improving customer satisfaction, as a qualitative measure, are to improve business performance and
increase customer loyalty (Zairi, 1996).

Short review of the balanced scorecard

As a performance measurement method, the balanced scorecard presents
an overall performance analysis of organizations by using the combination
of both quantitative and qualitative measures. It helps organizations look
and move forward, become market-orientated and look at their performance levels through different perspectives, namely at customer, internal,
innovation and learning, and financial perspectives (Kaplan and Norton,
1992). It has been mentioned that the balanced scorecard is useful for
organizations to become market-oriented, improve quality, shorten the
response time, emphasize teamwork, reduce new product development
times and manage long-term practices (Kaplan and Norton, 1992). Ritz-
Carlton Hotel chains are an example of using the type of generic benchmarking that works with a balanced scorecard and pays attention to
customer priorities as the main attributes for benchmarking.

How a business is performing from its customers' perspective has
become a vital element in both the manufacturing and service industries.
In other words, the image of a business is shaped by customer perceptions
of all products and services offered within the business. Customers are
likely to be concerned more about time, quality, service and cost.
Customer surveys or comment cards can be used extensively to obtain
feedback from customers. The feedback can be helpful in deciding those
features that are of great importance to both customers and businesses.

Upon completing customer-based measures, processes, decisions and
actions should be established within the business. These internal operations will enable managers to focus on critical or vital elements or operations to satisfy customer needs and reduce customer complaints. Cost,
productivity and quality have recently become major issues in hospitality
businesses. Among methods to be used are meetings and training courses.
The main purpose of innovation and learning through taking different perspectives is to sustain the performance level of the business with respect to
customer satisfaction and internal business processes. Measures can be
regarded as the level of sales, the level of customer satisfaction or the level
of repeat business. The financial perspective examines the profitability,
sales growth and cash flow of the business, all of which are measures of
quantitative performance (see Table 1.4).

Though the balanced scorecard has been criticized as being a kind of
management system, as opposed to just a measurement system, it has been

Table 1.4. Measures in the balanced scorecard.

Type of perspective	Measures
Customer perspective	Time, quality, service, cost.
Internal perspective	Cost, productivity, quality.
Innovation and learning perspective	The percentage of sales, the level of customer satisfaction, the level of repeat business.
Financial perspective	Profitability, sales growth, cash flow.

used particularly in the manufacturing industry (Kaplan and Norton, 1993). It has been claimed that the difference between benchmarking and the balanced scorecard system is that the former can be used for process measurement and the latter only for the measurement of outputs (Kaplan, 1993). Despite this, benchmarking exercises recently have started to consider outputs such as customer satisfaction and repeat business, as well as net profits. This shows that both methods are vital to the measurement process. The results of a balanced scorecard system could be helpful in deciding on or conducting a benchmarking study. Using balanced scorecards, a report on the performance of any business could be easily prepared and a partner who has similar reports be chosen. The comparison of these reports may help both businesses be aware of their strengths and weaknesses and they might need a far shorter time for benchmarking.

Summary

This chapter is an overview of benchmarking theory and its implications for performance improvement and competitive advantage. It has also addressed several weaknesses in past studies of benchmarking. There is little experience of putting benchmarking theory into practice. Bearing this in mind, the following chapters will focus on developing a conceptual destination benchmarking approach. As a first step towards preparing and executing destination benchmarking research and therefore indicating where and how to be competitive, the next chapter will attempt to explore the main reasons as to why a particular destination benchmarking approach is necessary, and then present its main elements.

Evaluating Benchmarking Studies in Tourism

2

Introduction

Before moving into evaluating the relevance of the benchmarking theory to international tourist destinations, and their development and management, this chapter provides a brief introduction in order to have an overview of past tourism-based benchmarking studies relating to the effective management of both businesses and destinations. The emergence of benchmarking as a quality management and improvement concept in both tourist businesses and destinations is discussed, commencing from the mid-1990s. Several weaknesses of past benchmarking research in tourism are also addressed from both the theoretical and practical perspective.

Overview of Benchmarking Studies in Tourism

Although benchmarking has been adapted to a variety of national and international businesses in order to improve their performance levels, it is a new concept in the tourism and hospitality industry. Therefore, either large or medium and small businesses can have difficulties in conducting benchmarking and implementing findings themselves. They will also need further technical knowledge about the application and operation of benchmarking. On the other hand, compared with medium and large businesses, small businesses can be more reluctant to adapt themselves to new ideas or operations that will occur as a result of internal or external adjustments.

It is obvious that small and large businesses in the manufacturing industry are implementing benchmarking in an attempt to become one of the best in the industry. This should be one indication as to why tourism businesses and tourist destinations need to use this technique with respect

© M. Kozak 2004. *Destination Benchmarking: Concepts, Practices and Operations* (M. Kozak)

to maintaining a certain level of service quality they should deliver and customer satisfaction they should achieve. Although benchmarking has become established in the culture of both the manufacturing and service industries, only a small amount of benchmarking research has been carried out among hospitality businesses in order to analyse the competitive position of such businesses by considering the strengths and weaknesses of operations. Some of these studies specifically focused only on individual businesses (e.g. Barksy, 1996; Cheshire, 1997) whereas others focused on the hospitality industry overall (e.g. CBI News, 1995; Department of National Heritage, 1996).

As already emphasized, this book considers two categories of benchmarking in terms of its micro- and macro-applications: organization benchmarking and destination benchmarking. Organization benchmarking deals with the performance evaluation of only a particular organization and its departments. In contrast, destination benchmarking draws a broader picture including all elements of one destination such as transport services, airport services, accommodation services, leisure and sport facilities, hospitality and local attitudes, hygiene and cleanliness, and so on. Thus, the following sections follow this categorization while providing an overview of past benchmarking studies carried out solely in tourism, hospitality, leisure and recreation.

Organization benchmarking studies in tourism

The few examples of benchmarking from within the tourism industry are those involving hotels (Canon and Kent, 1994; CBI News, 1995; Department of National Heritage, 1996). The benchmarking approach was used further in visitor attractions. HMS *Victory* was benchmarked with other well-known organizations such as the Tower of London and Dover Castle (Cheshire, 1997). The majority of these studies focused on the assessment of customer satisfaction as a qualitative measure of performance in identifying strengths and weaknesses of businesses (Morey and Dittmann, 1995; Johns *et al.*, 1996, 1997). There are also several examples of research relating to supply using quantitative measures such as occupancy rates, cost, revenues and capital investment (Breiter and Kline, 1995; Morey and Dittmann, 1995). Some hotel chains (e.g. Ritz-Carlton) not only benchmark other businesses but are also benchmarked themselves by other service or manufacturing businesses (Canon and Kent, 1994; Struebing, 1996). They work with a balanced scorecard system, and customer priorities are the main attributes for benchmarking.

An example was given from an anonymous hotel business's benchmarking applications (Codling, 1992). A large well-known hotel group who decided to make an investment in a country sent a benchmarking team to analyse the strengths, weaknesses and opportunities of the country's tourism industry. Following benchmarking research, the hotel was established and yielded an occupancy rate which 1 year later was 10% higher than the rest of the industry.

A further study benchmarked seven hotel businesses to measure the success of their TQM programme (Breiter and Kline, 1995). A questionnaire survey was mailed to the person in charge of the quality programme in sample hotel businesses. Gaps between importance and performance levels of all businesses were identified. Customer focus, vision, values and training were found to have the greatest gaps. This indicated that those hotel businesses were not best at what was important to their customers. One conclusion of this benchmarking study was that the benchmarking model needed further development. This study was not a full benchmarking research project since the objective was only to recommend to hotel businesses where their benchmarking study should start. The small sample size ($n = 7$) was another critical issue to be considered.

The Department of National Heritage (1996) conducted a benchmarking survey among 70 small hotels, guesthouses and bed and breakfasts in England by employing qualitative research methods to compare their performance levels and to pinpoint the areas that need to be focused on to improve customer satisfaction and increase their own profitability. A standard marking system was developed to measure the performance of hotel businesses on each aspect of operation on a scale of '1–5', with a score of '5' representing the industry best practice. The cumulative marks were calculated to give a total score for each hotel business expressed as a percentage. The highest total score was 82% and the lowest 45%. This study identified strengths and weaknesses of tangible and intangible aspects of units on the basis of customer satisfaction. Areas considered as strengths included satisfaction with service, facilities, operational procedures and control, direction of the business and its marketing. Overall standards of cleanliness, bedroom decor and furnishings, and the quality of beds were among the common weaknesses identified in the study.

The performance of general managers of 54 hotels in the USA was benchmarked to examine whether the manager employed the optimum level of resources for the annual income yielded and the service standards achieved (Morey and Dittman, 1995). The authors calculated efficiency scores indicating each manager's performance level on several quantitative and qualitative measures such as occupancy rates, average daily room rate, energy cost, total room revenues and customer satisfaction levels. The one with the highest efficiency score was selected as the benchmarker or the best practice.

Having designed a typical model of organization benchmarking and primarily used qualitative measures, the Confederation of British Industry carried out a benchmarking survey among UK, German and French hotel businesses. Findings revealed that the UK hotels were more competitive in quality and value for money than their German and French counterparts.

Lower levels of training skills and capital investment were the threats to the continued success of the UK hotels (CBI News, 1995).

A profile accumulation model was developed and applied to small hospitality businesses to identify specific aspects and attributes. These were classed as strengths (satisfaction factors) and weaknesses (dissatisfaction factors) (Johns *et al.*, 1996, 1997). Findings revealed that small business customers identified aesthetics, cleanliness, comfort and friendliness as the most important attributes of the service. It was concluded that dissatisfaction factors tend to be tangibles and satisfaction factors intangibles. Such information is very worthwhile in correcting faults and focusing staff on customers' existing and potential needs. Findings can be used as a benchmark to enable a comparison between businesses.

Min and Min (1997) followed the principles of the gap analysis model. Based on the findings of a questionnaire survey, the hotel business with the highest mean scores was chosen as the benchmark and then compared with those of other sample businesses. Mean differences were accepted as performance gaps of competitive benchmarking for each attribute. The calculation of significance levels of differences by means of a series of statistical tests makes this study distinctive from others, but it is still within the realms of comparison research.

In another study, by carrying out third-party benchmarking research among managers, Phillips and Appiah-Adu (1998) paid attention to the value of benchmarking for the qualitative assessment of business processes. The authors examined the role of benchmarking in evaluating strategic planning processes in the UK hotel industry. The study underlined the importance of benchmarking as a catalyst for maintaining continuous improvement in the 21st century.

A most recent example of organization benchmarking consists of the one on conference and convention centres. Gardini and Bernini (2002) attempted to measure the performance of a total of 47 convention centres by selecting the best practices in some particular geographical areas as well as in the world. A best-in-class organization was nominated by choosing the one performing with the best score. This was then compared with the rest of the other convention centres. The level of their performance was evaluated on the basis of several best performing indicators such as structure (capacity), production (events), organization (capacity utilization), selling performance, demand segmentation, service and accessibility. This study is a typical example of traditional gap analysis, and therefore has several methodology-based weaknesses.

Destination benchmarking studies in tourism

Tourism has been defined as a multi-disciplinary field of study borrowing heavily from other related fields (Graburn and Jafari, 1991). Thus, the rele-

vant literature on benchmarking, customer and tourist satisfaction/dissatis-
faction, tourist perceptions and their experiences, service quality, destination image, destination competitiveness and positioning has been explored,
and textbooks, unpublished theses and reports and statistical bulletins consulted. Only a small number of benchmarking classifications have been
produced. The majority of these classifications are basically related to
reflecting the features of organizations, rather than tourist destinations and
tourism and travel services (e.g. process benchmarking and performance
benchmarking). It seems that destination benchmarking was neglected until
the second half of the 1990s because the application of benchmarking to
tourism and hospitality is quite new. In this section, the status of existing
benchmarking studies dealing with destinations is examined from both
practical and theoretical perspective.

From the practical point of view, Seaton (1996) attempted to apply a
traditional benchmarking study to tourist destinations just by comparing
the performance of Scotland with six other countries during the period of
1984–1994 with respect to the following quantitative measures: tourist
arrivals, number of bed-nights, occupancy trends, balance of payment
trends, proportion of tourism income in Gross Domestic Product (GDP),
seasonality trends, market dependence trends, tourism employment trends
and the National Tourist Organization's (NTO's) total budget and marketing expenditure trends. The practical recommendations have been established for the Scottish tourism industry. On the other hand, although this
can be regarded as a benchmarking study in theory, it would be weak in
practice because a more in-depth investigation has not been provided and
any area with respect to future performance has not been examined. Thus,
it would not be difficult to claim that the study primarily aimed to accomplish a comparison study of destination performance rather than conducting destination-specific benchmarking research. Some other factors might
also be taken into consideration, e.g. weather, relative prices and the
growth of competitive destinations targeting similar tourist-generating
markets.

Several organizations recently have directed their attention towards
carrying out destination benchmarking research that is applicable primarily
for practical uses. Of these, in order to highlight the importance of tourist
satisfaction with destinations and to encourage the improvement of the
competitive advantage of European tourist destinations, the European
Union initiated a project in 1997 called 'An Integrated Quality
Management of Tourist Destinations'. This project aims to develop several
measurable quality standards with respect to different components of
coastal, rural and urban destinations and implement them among the
member countries of the European Economic Area. The project includes
the assessment of both demand and supply indicators such as the activities
of tourism professionals, tourists, local residents and natural, cultural and
economic environmental resources. The study includes 15 destination-

based case studies. The feedback is obtained through local residents, businesses and visitors. The limitation of this project is that the research methods used and approaches chosen are not yet clear.

At the regional level, several regional tourist boards in England have begun modelling destination benchmarking surveys by considering visitor satisfaction as the best value for gaining competitive advantage (Thomason *et al.*, 1999a,b). The overall objective is to produce a national benchmarking database by repeating similar surveys in different parts of the country. Destinations are categorized into historic towns, cities and seaside resorts. Among the attributes used for the measurement and comparison processes are attractions, food and beverage facilities, shopping facilities, accommodation facilities, parking services, public transport, signposting, cleanliness, hospitality and tourist information services. In 2001, the regional tourist boards carried out surveys in 36 destinations throughout England to obtain visitors' opinions of a wide range of indicators. Scores for similar types of domestic destinations were then compared to identify relative performance and best practice. In all these empirical studies, a 5-point Likert scale (ranging between 'very poor' and 'very good') is the approach usually employed to measure the visitor experience. Comparisons are also available in terms of other quantitative indicators including average length of stay and visitor expenditure.

From the academic point of view, there appears to be an increasing interest in recommending how to benefit from benchmarking in today's highly competitive tourism market. For example, in developing a conceptual framework of destination benchmarking, the role of benchmarking within the small hospitality sector was examined in the context of tourist destinations (Kozak and Rimmington, 1998). It is clear that there has been limited application among small hospitality businesses while benchmarking activity is growing in large organizations. This study examines reasons for this and how benchmarking, linked to external awards and grades, can offer advantages and bring about improvements in competitiveness for both small hospitality businesses and tourist destinations. Benchmarking through such schemes brings benefits to destinations and guests as well as to individual businesses. Destinations can measure the extent and quality of the small business component of their offering and plan strategically to develop it effectively, while tourists are likely to experience greater levels of satisfaction. The study finally argues that external benchmarking needs to be directed by local authorities, so that it matches the destination's planned strategic development.

As the frontier in tourism benchmarking research, a holistic model for destination benchmarking was developed using the three main types of benchmarking: internal, external and generic (Kozak, 2000). Internal benchmarking aimed to improve a destination's internal performance by evaluating quantitative and qualitative measures. External benchmarking used tourist motivation, satisfaction and expenditure scores to investigate how one destination may perform better than another. Generic benchmarking aimed to evaluate and improve a destination's performance using quality and eco-label standards. This research provides a discussion of findings and their implications for benchmarking theory and practitioners. The relevance of benchmarking to tourist destinations was examined through the measurement of performance, types of destination benchmarking and taking action. Findings suggest that both internal and external benchmarking can be applied to benchmarking of destinations. However, in the case of external benchmarking, this research indicated that each destination might have its own regional differentiation and unique characteristics in some respects. Cross-cultural differences between tourists from different countries also need to be considered. Given these factors, this research makes a fresh and innovative contribution to the literature not only on tourism but also on benchmarking.

The objective of a more recent study is to develop a model of destination benchmarking. This study initially discusses weaknesses of the 'The Tourism Barometer', developed by the German Federal States, as an existing benchmarking concept for destinations. The proposed benchmarking model focuses on the integration of the related tourism supply and demand forces in the form of both destination-specific resource use and perceived customer value (as an indicator of customer satisfaction). The model encompasses various indicators employed in a data envelopment analysis, regarded as a useful method of data collection for benchmarking tourist destinations. The study also reflects the findings of an empirical survey carried out in the Austrian winter resorts.

Recently, a special issue of the *Journal of Quality Assurance in Hospitality and Tourism* (2/3–4) was devoted to the practice of benchmarking in the tourism and hospitality industries. The issue encompasses papers on benchmarking concepts, practices and operations in the form of case studies worldwide. One study discusses the limitations of past benchmarking studies in tourism and hospitality (Kozak and Nield, 2001). Two papers deal with its application from the perspective of environmental management (Leslie, 2001; Meade and Pringle, 2001). Two studies are about how benchmarks can be used to improve service quality and customer satisfaction in a continuous and systematic way (Matzler and Pechlaner, 2001; Vrtiprah, 2001). One paper focuses on the data-gathering process by developing a benchmarking tool (Fuchs and Weiermair, 2001). In another study, the author introduces a heuristic procedure for the identification of benchmarking partners in an interactive database environment on the Internet (Wober, 2001). The last study identifies best practice case examples relating to a variety of different areas of hotel front office operations and training of employees (Baum and Odgers, 2001). Despite the fact that these studies are not directly related to the principles of destination benchmarking, there is no doubt that they can be expanded to include a wide range of its perspectives.

Finally, the first comprehensive book with particular reference to the application of benchmarking in tourism and hospitality industries has been published (Wober, 2002). This study focuses solely on one phase of the benchmarking process, e.g. recommending alternative methods that are supposed to be helpful while selecting benchmarking partners for tourism businesses (who to benchmark). These methods are related to the use of various mathematical and statistical techniques in order to evaluate best practices among the potential candidates for benchmarking operations and select the most appropriate comparison partner(s). Although this study is a very good example of hotel-oriented organization benchmarking research and of recommending optimistic techniques in the process of partner selection, it might create some problems for both academics and practitioners to apply such techniques in practice and test their reliability in a real benchmarking study. Furthermore, despite the fact that there is little information about how to apply benchmarking to tourist destinations, Wober's book indicates that some information can still be used in the context of nominating partners in destination benchmarking.

Limitations of Past Benchmarking Research in Tourism

Table 2.1 provides an overview of the key features and summarizes the most critical conceptual and methodological issues for benchmarking research in the field of tourism and hospitality. For each study, the table provides information on sampling choice, types of industry, types of benchmarking, use of quantitative or qualitative measures, considering cross-cultural differences and use of statistical tools, and provides brief comments on some notable features of the studies. As indicated, an overwhelming majority of researchers preferred to establish an empirical study based on supply but avoided aspects of demand. More specifically, a well- and fully organized benchmarking study does not appear to have been generally examined in a rigorous way, although gap analysis has attracted much attention in published research and is well established. While this table is not a complete list of the research in the field, it is indicative of the fact that there is diversity with respect to sampling choice, types of benchmarking, use of quantitative or qualitative measures, consideration of cross-cultural differences and use of statistical tools. These are explained in detail below.

1. There is a growing body of research assuming that benchmarking is solely a comparison activity or that every comparison survey is a form of benchmarking (Breiter and Kline, 1995; Boger *et al.*, 1999). Benchmarking is far more than comparative analysis (Watson, 1993). Comparison is only one stage of benchmarking (performance gap analysis); there are other stages, which may be more significant, such as taking action and reviewing outcomes in order to improve performance. The performance is observed

Table 2.1. Overview of past benchmarking research.

Authors	Sampling	Types of industry	Types of bench-marking	Quantitative or qualitative measures	Cultural imp. (supply)	Cultural imp. (demand)	Gap analysis	Objectives	Statistical tools
Gardini and Bernini (2002)	Organizations	Convention centres	External	Qualitative (service) and quantitative (production, selling performance)	No	No	Yes	To seek the best practices	No
Derby City Council (2001)	Destinations	Destination in the UK (1)	External	Quantitative (length of stay, spending) and qualitative (Likert scale)	No	N/A	Yes	To seek the best practices and identify strengths and weaknesses	No
Southern Tourist Board	Destinations	Destination in the UK (1)	External	Quantitative (length of stay, spending) and qualitative (Likert scale)	No	N/A	Yes	To seek the best practices and identify strengths and weaknesses	No
Liverpool City Council (2000)	Destinations	Destination in the UK (1)	External	Quantitative (length of stay) and qualitative (Likert scale)	No	N/A	Yes	To seek the best practices and identify strengths and weaknesses	No
Thomason et al. (1999a)	Customers	Destination in the UK (1) (comparison with previous years)	Internal	Qualitative (Likert scale)	N/A	No	Yes	To identify strengths and weaknesses	No
Thomason et al. (1999b)	Customers	Destinations in the UK (14)	External	Qualitative (Likert scale)	No	No	Yes	To seek the best practices and identify strengths and weaknesses	No
Boger et al. (1999)	Organizations	Hotels in the USA	External	Quantitative (metrics such as room rates)	No	N/A	Yes	To establish the best performance scores	Yes

European Commission (1998)	Destinations	Destinations in Europe	Internal	Case studies	No	No	N/A	To establish the best performance areas	N/A
Phillips and Appiah-Adu (1998)	Organizations	Hotels in the UK	External	Qualitative (Likert scale)	No	N/A	Yes	To establish the best practices	No
Min and Min (1997)	Organizations and customers	Hotels in Korea	External	Qualitative (Likert scale)	No	No	Yes	To establish the best performance scores	Yes
Johns et al. (1996)	Customers	Hotels in the UK	External and internal	Qualitative (free-response survey)	No	No	Yes	To identify strengths and weaknesses	Yes
Department of National Heritage (1996)	Organizations and customers	Hotels in the UK	Generic	Qualitative (scoring)	No	No	N/A	To identify the best practices based on performance scores	No
Seaton (1996)	Destinations	Countries as destinations (6)	External	Quantitative (tourist arrivals, tourism income, etc.)	No	No	Yes	To identify strengths and weaknesses	No
Breiter and Kline (1995)	Organizations	Hotels in the US	External	Qualitative (Likert scale)	No	N/A	Yes	To establish the best performance scores and areas	Yes
Morey and Dittmann (1995)	Organizations	Hotels in the USA	External	Quantitative (costs) and qualitative	No	No	Yes	To establish the best performance scores	No
Bell and Morey (1994)	Organizations	Travel industry in the USA	External	Quantitative (costs and expenses)	No	N/A	Yes	To seek the best practices	Yes

Source: own elaboration from the literature review.
N/A, not applicable.

and a variety of enablers are used to carry out change programmes in the host organization. The lessons learned make the benchmarking approach distinct from comparative analysis. The rule is first to identify performance gaps with respect to production and consumption within the organization and then to develop methods to close them. The gap between internal and external practices reveals what changes, if any, are necessary. This feature differentiates the benchmarking theory from comparison research and competitive analysis. Competitive analysis looks at product or service comparisons, but benchmarking goes beyond just comparison and looks at the assessment of operating and management skills producing these products and services. The other difference is that competitive analysis only looks at characteristics of those in the same geographic area of competition, whilst benchmarking seeks to find the best practices regardless of location (Walleck *et al.*, 1991).

2. Little has been done with regard to the empirical assessment of customer satisfaction as a performance assessment and improvement tool, although benchmarking literature has highlighted its significance in benchmarking (e.g. Johns *et al.*, 1996; Thomason *et al.*, 1999a). The majority of the proposed benchmarking studies have focused on the investigation of the establishment of best performance practices and areas in terms of supply by using qualitative or quantitative measures of one organization and their comparison with another (e.g. Bell and Morey, 1994; Zairi, 1998). It is suggested that feedback received from customers is a suitable way of comparing the performance of an organization with that of another (Kotler, 1994). The availability of alternative service providers (e.g. competitors) appears to be significant in influencing the level of customer satisfaction because customers have a tendency to compare one service encounter with another (Czepiel *et al.*, 1974). The level of customer satisfaction may have a pivotal role not only in identifying the current position but also in designing future performance and highlighting where there is a need for further improvement. According to customers, the performance level of facilities is based on mostly qualitative measures, e.g. the extent to which it provides a satisfactory service or whether it has a favourable image in the market (Um and Crompton, 1990). These measures may then be used to make a comparison between facilities to determine which one performs better than the others.

3. There has been a very limited use of statistical tools to test the significance level of results obtained from the comparison of qualitative measures such as mean scores (e.g. Bell and Morey, 1994; Goh and Richards, 1997). Statistical tests are able to reveal the magnitude of proposed gaps. When needed, performing the relevant statistical procedures confirms the extent to which the survey outcomes are reliable, valid and meaningful for drawing conclusions. The application of external benchmarking, with few exceptions (e.g. New and Szwejczewski, 1995), generally lacks the use of statistical tools such as t-, χ^2 and analysis of variance tests, particularly while measuring the qualitative performance of samples observed and employing structured questionnaires. There may be no need to use statistical tools for the assessment of some quantitative measures, but it is necessary to do so for qualitative measures when a large sample population is involved in the study. Both quantitative (structured) and qualitative (unstructured) research methods are useful in destination benchmarking research in different respects. The former could be used to explore differences between the levels of tourist satisfaction, whereas the latter could support the findings of quantitative research. Structured questionnaire surveys identify the areas where any weaknesses or gaps appear, but are very limited in indicating their root causes (performance benchmarking). To be able to understand this, secondary data collection methods and further empirical research such as observations and interviews with visitors, tourism suppliers and authorities need to be considered in the analysis stage of destination benchmarking (process benchmarking).

4. Benchmarking studies ensure that customers visiting different organizations are homogeneous in terms of their sociodemographic and socioeconomic characteristics as well as in terms of motivations, purchasing behaviour and loyalty. In other words, one customer group shopping at one organization may not be in the same category as another shopping at a different organization. This argument has been underestimated within the benchmarking literature (European Commission, 1998). Giving an example from a destination benchmarking study, it is not reasonable to expect that tourists visiting Italy are as homogeneous as those visiting Greece or that both destinations attract similar markets. In external benchmarking, it is important to identify any difference in the characteristics of the sample population visiting destinations. This type of assessment is helpful for identifying not only the profile of market segments but also partner destinations with whom external benchmarking can be conducted. Such research may be significant for tourism benchmarking research in order to have a better understanding of competitors involved in the same set in terms of a particular market and make a decision about who and what to benchmark. As an example of destination benchmarking, the Mediterranean destinations could select their benchmarking partners from countries in the Mediterranean basin because the majority of tourists in Western European countries tend to take their summer holidays in this region.

5. A considerable amount of research has been carried out dealing with the application of external benchmarking comparing one organization's performance with that of others (e.g. Morey and Dittmann, 1995; Goh and Richards, 1997). Little research has allocated efforts to perform or develop methodologies for internal or generic benchmarking studies. Some of those who studied internal benchmarking compared findings with those of previous years (e.g. Thomason *et al.*, 1999a). Of those who followed generic benchmarking guidelines, some attempted to introduce some international quality systems and tried to explore the extent to which sample organizations conform to these guidelines or standards (e.g. Mann *et al.*, 1999a,b). Some others attempted to establish best practices within the industry based on performance scores marked by both the consultants and customers (Department of National Heritage, 1996). Despite this, both internal and generic types of benchmarking seem worthy of further investigation. The strength of internal benchmarking is that it helps to find the methods that are relevant to a particular culture and practices and to build up local strategies on the basis of the characteristics of the managerial and social culture and specific objectives. The main purpose of internal benchmarking is to improve the performance of tourism businesses or tourist destinations by identifying their own strengths and weaknesses on the basis of the feedback obtained from travellers and the local population. Within the application of generic benchmarking, businesses or destinations in tourism can be advised to look at either others or international standards in order to find effective solutions for their particular problems by having access to best practices recognized nationally or internationally.

6. Previous studies do not seem to have paid much attention to the consideration of cross-cultural differences either between organizations or between customer groups. The possible existence of such differences in organization culture or national culture or in customer groups from different cultural backgrounds could possibly impact upon the transferability of findings and the success of their implementation in the host organization. Marketing literature confirmed the existence of cross-national differences in motivation and perceptions between customers from different countries (e.g. Kozak, 2001, 2002a). In today's developing global management and marketing approach, what is happening in one culture may not be so important, without direct correspondence to other cultures. Additionally, it is well known that, based upon products offered, one particular destination may attract customers of different nationalities. The investigation of potential cross-cultural differences and similarities between various consumer groups representing different cultures in tourism visiting a particular destination is important for destination management to learn the profile of its customers, their values, preferences and behaviour, and to implement effective positioning and market segmentation strategies that are appropriate for each market (Reisinger and Turner, 1998; Pizam, 1999). This requires serious consideration in future benchmarking research.

7. Further differences could be observed among different international destinations with respect to the organizational structure of their governments. For instance, Turkey has a centralized government system where the central government has the power to set goals, make decisions and implement them, while Spain has a decentralized system where local government and city councils are given the power to make decisions and collaborate. As Keller and Smeral (1997) emphasize, keeping bureaucratic barriers to a minimum could improve tourist services and quality, which will lead to enhancing competitiveness in the international arena. The former model may create bureaucratic problems and delays in making efficient decisions since the central government deals with everything in the country. Political unrest may sometimes make it worse. In the latter model, local institutions are given the responsibility of regulating tourism businesses and activities, inspecting and supervising them and developing their own promotion campaigns, locally and abroad, in order to renovate and revitalize the attractiveness of the destination. Briefly, such differences are another piece of evidence indicating that cross-cultural differences in man agerial practices could hinder the successful implementation of benchmarking research findings that a different political system could easily accomplish.

Accordingly, the American Productivity and Quality Center (1999) suggests that there is no single best practice that can bring about performance improvement and help gain competitive advantage. The selection of measures depends on the aims and objectives of each authority. Different businesses or destinations might have different objectives and expectations from the tourism industry. For instance, some destinations offer a variety of tourist facilities and activities and are year-round destinations that attract top-class customer groups, whereas others offer only seasonal facilities and services for middle- or low-income customer groups. As a result, the rationale for measuring performance differs from one to the other. One destination might use it to increase customer satisfaction and subsequently raise the volume of arrivals or tourism receipts. Another may think that it is an effective method of having a sustainable form of tourism development within the area, despite fewer tourists or a lower tourism income. Therefore, the best practice should be accepted to be those practices producing superior results and being judged as good examples.

Summary

This chapter has analysed the development of benchmarking within the tourism industry together with some examples. So far, there has been a very limited use of benchmarking in the tourism industry, and it is still in its infancy and has been restricted to the study of operational units and businesses, rather than measuring the performance of tourist destinations and providing methods to improve it. It is significant that the limited examples of benchmarking carried out within the tourism industry almost all involve the benchmarking process being carried out by third parties external to the organizations being benchmarked. In light of these observations, it is obvious that the benchmarking model needs further development. Thus, the following chapter will attempt to discuss the possible scope of destination management, identify the main reasons for establishing a destination benchmarking study, provide an overall model for those wishing to exploit their performance levels and then analyse its main components.

Towards Destination Benchmarking

3

Introduction

As a first step towards preparing and performing destination benchmarking research and therefore indicating where and how to be competitive, this chapter attempts to identify the main reasons for establishing a destination benchmarking study, discusses the possible scope of destination management, provides an overall model for those wishing to exploit their performance levels and then analyses its main components. Moreover, in line with the theoretical background presented earlier, this part of the book along with the next four chapters will therefore examine the applicability of the benchmarking concept to tourist destinations as a performance measurement, improvement and competitive advantage tool.

Major Characteristics of the Tourism Industry

The tourism product is defined as 'comprising attractions of a destination including images, sites, scenery, events and weather; facilities including accommodation, catering and entertainment; and accessibility with regard to the time and cost it takes to reach the destination' (Lewis and Owtram, 1986, p. 204). As can be seen, attractions, events and accessibility play a pivotal role in the management and marketing of destinations because they attract visitors, and, in turn, gain the competitive advantage. It seems that destinations are accepted to be a key component of the tourism system. Certainly, there are a number of reasons to indicate why the measurement and determination of destination competitiveness has become so important in travel and tourism, e.g. the existence of multiple destinations, the emergence of new destinations, and so on. As a subsector of services, tourism has specific characteristics compared with the manufacturing industry and other elements of the service industry. Such specific characteristics produce differences for the tourism industry in the management and marketing of tourist destinations, managing the host–guest relationship and enhancing the competitive edge. These are listed below (Morrison, 1989; Laws, 1995).

1. Services are composed of intangible rather than tangible attributes. A service is consumed as long as this consumption activity continues. As a result of this, pricing of services is more difficult than pricing of products. The customer needs to use intangible products sought in travel and tourism operations in a shorter period because there are not re-consumable.

2. Production and consumption (enjoyment of services) coincide with time and location. Thus, tourists participate in the creation of the services they purchase. Tourists cannot sample the destination or its subelements before arriving for their holiday. However, they make their holiday decisions either by looking at brochures or by obtaining feedback from their relatives and friends, which is very different from making decisions in the choice of a physical product.

3. Since a much higher level of social interaction always take place between tourists, staff and local residents in buying tourist services than occurs in buying tangible products, emotions and personal feelings, generated by service encounters, influence future purchase intentions. Staff from a variety of tourist establishments and encounters contribute to forming tourists' overall experiences, likes and dislikes with destinations.

4. Distribution channels play an important role in the marketing of tourism products and services. They influence what the customer buys because customers see them as experts and tend to follow their recommendations while taking trips and choosing destinations to visit.

5. Customer experience is shaped by various organizations and even by events to be participated in during the holiday, e.g. advertisements by either governments or tourism establishments, recommendations by friends and travel agents, the quality of food, shopping, the social interaction with other customers and the behaviour of the local people. Any failure of these elements may lead to customer dissatisfaction and repeatedly negative word-of-mouth recommendation.

6. Obtaining objective prior information when purchasing services is more difficult than when purchasing products. Thus, word-of-mouth communication helps potential customers obtain information about the alternative services or tourist destinations they would like to purchase and, in turn, decide which one to purchase.

7. Most tourism services are easy to copy. They may also be impossible to patent. Different hotel establishments may have rooms and restaurants of the same size, and recreation activities with the same features. Production differentiation and changing image perceptions are what make an establishment be perceived as different from others.

It is obvious that the term 'tourist behaviour' is different from the term 'consumer behaviour' in many respects (Gitelson and Crompton, 1983). Expenditure is budgeted and time is planned much earlier because spending time on holidays is an expensive leisure activity. As it is difficult for potential tourists to be familiar with destination services in advance, they need to exist there physically. Potential tourists also have a variety of alternatives due to the expansion in the number of domestic and international destinations. As a result, repeat business or loyalty may be less likely for destinations than it is for individual businesses, even where the destination fulfils tourist expectations, since tourists may look for similar but new experiences with different destinations (McDougall and Munro, 1994) or they may have been dissatisfied with any aspect of their holidays. This means that tourist authorities should always pay attention to keeping their products and services up to date.

Rationale for Destination Benchmarking

As in every industry and business, many tourist destinations are in competition with one another to obtain a greater proportion of international tourism by attracting more foreign tourists (Goodall, 1988). Developments in international tourism and travel have intensified competitiveness between international destinations. New destinations have emerged in the market as tourists and suppliers are now becoming more concerned about environmental and cultural values, e.g. the Caribbean and the eastern Mediterranean. Tour operators and the media are having an increasing impact on the market. Tourists are more experienced and knowledgeable, e.g. in their familiarity with other languages, using a variety of means of transportation, booking their holidays and with having visited the same destination more than once. Competitive analysis is made difficult because of the large number of variables that affect it. The response of customers as to whether these variables are about satisfaction is also important and needs to be included in the analysis.

Competition among destinations might contribute to the development of products and services. Providing better services not only gives an enhanced competitive edge but also raises standards in the industry, which in turn will be reflected on customers as a determinant of greater expectations. As a result, the customer's value chain would become an input of competitive advantage (Porter, 1985). Understanding what satisfies a customer's needs and wants is the basic ingredient of a recipe for arriving at successful marketing and improving competitive advantage (Czepiel et al., 1974). Customers are an important source of identifying external ideas for many products and services; surveys enable them to reflect on their opinions about and experiences at the destination. When tourists are satisfied with the destination, these satisfied customers are likely to come back or recommend the destination to others. In contrast, when customers are dissatisfied, they will have the power to decide neither to come back nor to make favourable word-of-mouth recommendations. As a consequence, customer-centred organizations or destinations are expected to have a greater opportunity to win over the competition (Kotler, 1994).

In order to talk about the competitive advantage of destinations, Crouch and Ritchie (1999) stress that value must be added to the existing economic resources and the tourism industry must concentrate on the term *destination competitiveness* rather than *destination comparison* as service industry is differentiated from manufacturing industry by its more subjective features. The authors further suggest that economic and natural resources can be accepted as the determinants of comparative advantage since similar destinations may have these types of resources, e.g. warm weather, sea and beaches in Mediterranean countries. In other words, destinations with identical products will be alike. A destination positioning strategy could aim to make customers perceive one destination as in some ways unique (Heath and Wall, 1992). If a destination is to be competitive it needs to focus on those factors that can help it to be distinctive. Therefore, the question of how to sell the experience of a vacation at a particular destination rather than the sale of the resource itself might be of great concern in maintaining competitive advantage. This could be accepted as good practice in tourism. Factors such as feelings of safety and security, cleaner beaches and establishments, more hospitable and friendlier local people and better value for money could make one destination more competitive than or distinct from others. This brings about the significance of fulfilling benchmarking studies in order to classify what other destinations provide and how they achieve their objectives.

The literature emphasizes that benchmarking is the method driving organizations towards competitive advantage as it provides an increased awareness of products, costs and markets in a particular industry (Zairi, 1996). It is helpful to look at the competitiveness theory, which points out attempts by organizations to maintain competitiveness among themselves (Porter, 1985). Reflecting on this theory, it is possible to suggest that benchmarking could be an important tool for a destination to enhance its competitiveness. In destination benchmarking research, findings might be interpreted and used to understand how competitive a destination is and in what respects, and identify what methods or strategies it needs to apply to improve itself. This part of the study therefore seeks to set out a rationale for developing a benchmarking approach specifically applicable to international tourist destinations. In line with the discussion of major characteristics of the tourism and travel industry outlined above, key developments supporting the case for tourism destination benchmarking are summarized in Box 3.1 and are considered individually in greater detail below.

1. As a result of increases in the demand for package holidays over the last two decades, destinations have become more important than individual attractions and facilities.

Box 3.1. Reasons for destination benchmarking. Source: own elaboration derived from the related literature review.

Increasing the importance of destinations
Importance of multiple components to overall tourist experiences
Changes in tourists' needs, wants and habits
Tourists' intention of making comparison between destinations
Problem of seasonality
Influence of the destination's performance on its elements

Developments in the tourism and travel industry have created new destinations in addition to previous traditional destinations, e.g. seaside resorts and historical places. New developing destinations threaten mature destinations by offering affordable prices and unspoiled resources, e.g. Turkey, Tunisia and the Caribbean islands as opposed to Spain. Destinations are the focus of attention since they motivate and stimulate visits and are the places where the majority of tourism products are produced and served simultaneously (Ashworth and Voogd, 1994; Goodall, 1990). In other words, much of the tourism industry is located and much of the tourists' time is spent at destinations. Tourist satisfaction with a destination or its overall image rather than a facility may therefore lead to repeat visits and word-of-mouth recommendation (Beeho and Prentice, 1997). A benchmarking programme can be considered as an 'input' that will make a contribution to improving the performance of a facility or a destination (outputs). This, in turn, could bring about increased customer satisfaction, customer retention and revenues.

2. From a tourist's perspective, there is a close relationship between all tourism-related facilities and businesses at the destination.

Tourist motivation has been shown to be multi-dimensional (Pyo *et al.*, 1989). Tourists want to have more than one experience at a destination. When they visit, they stay at a hotel, often eat and drink somewhere outside the hotel, go shopping, communicate with local people and other tourists, and visit natural, cultural or historic places. In terms of supply, the trip is not a single product, rather it is made up of components supplied by a variety of organizations with different objectives. McIntyre (1993, p. 23) describes the destination as 'the location of a cluster of attractions and related tourist facilities and services which a tourist or tour group selects to visit or which providers choose to promote'. Coltman (1989, p. 4) presents a more comprehensive definition as being 'an area with different natural attributes, features, or attractions that appeal to nonlocal visitors – that is, tourists or excursionists'. All these elements make a contribution to tourist experiences in different ways. As a consequence of the 'domino effect', lack of quality experience in even one of these areas may influence the overall satisfaction level detrimentally (Jafari, 1983).

3. Tourists' needs and wants are changing as they are becoming more experienced and knowledgeable about their needs, wants and their future holidays.

Deming (1982) points out that the customer has a significant place in the definition of quality, and suggests that businesses should try to understand what the customer (market) needs and wants both at present and in the future. Tourists are becoming more sophisticated and looking for higher standards in quality, innovation and responsiveness as a consequence of developments in technology, an increase in mobility and an increase in the spread of word-of-mouth communication (Mill and Morrison, 1992). Recent developments in technology and hearing about others' experiences give people access to all the information they need to learn about other places in the world. By increasing the mobility of potential tourists, technology has also provided easy access to the same or other destinations in either the short or the long term. Each holiday taken may update a tourist's expectations for the next holiday and widen their experiences, resulting in a tourist group with higher expectations, needs and wants (Nolan and Swan, 1984; Cadotte *et al.*, 1987). Destination suppliers need to know what their customers look for while holidaying around the world and collect feedback regularly about the level of services they have received.

4. Tourists make comparisons between the facilities, attractions and service standards of alternative destinations as they may have experience of other destinations.

Some researchers argue that different destinations are perceived to have unique advantages and/or disadvantages in the minds of travellers (Haahti, 1986). Since some or most tourists visit several destinations, their personal experiences or word-of-mouth communication could indicate in what respects each destination is good or bad. Therefore, this study proposes that, as with individual businesses, national or international tourist destinations must also be aware of what others are doing, what features of destinations attract tourists and how likely these features are to be satisfactory. A continuous measurement of customer feedback might help to assess one's own and others' competitive positions, target new customers, revise the current marketing plan and develop new products if required (Mentzer *et al.*, 1995). As a consequence, destination managers become open to other practices, e.g. the implementation of guidelines or eco-labels as best practices or looking at other destinations for new ideas or applications. As benchmarking is a continuous learning process, whenever organizations or destinations learn about others or their best practices, they may feel that they need to take steps to improve, too.

5. Seasonality is a key factor making an impact on destination performance.

As tourism is a capital-intensive and high-risk industry, it takes much longer to produce a return on capital investment. Seasonal fluctuations also affect the case in a negative way (Butler and Mao, 1997; Murphy and Pritchard, 1997). Benchmarking could introduce possibilities that may lead to destinations becoming very much aware of their own potential for over-coming seasonal fluctuations. Destination products are more likely than organization products (manufacturing or other service industries) to be sensitive towards seasonal changes in demand. One destination can attract a higher number of visitors in summer or winter time than another, depending on what it offers. For instance, European ski resorts have their high season in winter time and their off-season in summer time, whereas this situation is reversed for summer holiday destinations. A possible problem is to balance seasonality, as it brings negative results for both the destination and the tourist, e.g. keeping a financial balance despite the difficulty of finding qualified personnel the following season, imposing higher prices to offset the losses in the off-season and experiencing other problems such as noise or a dirty atmosphere in the high season.

6.   There is a close relationship between a destination's overall performance level and the performance of all the individual components that make up tourists' experience of a destination.

The literature suggests that an area should have the following characteristics to be considered as a tourist destination: a variety of natural, social and cultural resources and services; other economic activities; a host community; a local council; and an active private *or* public sector (Davidson and Maitland, 1997). As stated earlier, a destination's performance is mainly related to the performance of these elements. When something is wrong with any of these elements, the outcome would be negative, which will be reflected back to these elements. In such a case, tourists want neither to come back nor to encourage others (see Table 3.1). The local community's quality of life would be negatively affected due to poor service standards. They would also earn less from the tourism industry. Employees would fear losing their jobs, resulting in a lower satisfaction with their jobs. Suppliers would earn less. Most importantly, all the cultural, economic and physical resources would be negatively affected if potential consumers withdrew, as there would be less capital for reinvestment. All these elements of a destination highlight the importance of management in order to keep them and the development of the destination

Table 3.1. Customer satisfaction matrix.

If customers are	They will feel	Because they met their	They will be
Very satisfied	Delighted/enthused	Dreams	Your advocate loyal
Satisfied	Excited/contented	Expectations	Retained/interested
Ambivalent	Indifferent	Wants/needs	Attentive
Dissatisfied	Concerned/upset	Minimum requirements/ bare essentials	Questioning/ looking around
Very dissatisfied	Angry/hostile	Worst fears/nightmares	One of your enemies

Source: G.J. Balm.

under control, create and stimulate demand for the destination and sustain a positive vision in the mind of customers, retailers and suppliers. This can be achieved using benchmarking.

What is 'Destination Benchmarking'?

As pointed out at the beginning, this book considers two categories of bench marking in terms of its micro- and macro-applications: organization benchmarking and destination benchmarking. Organization benchmarking deals with the performance evaluation of only a particular organization and its departments. In contrast, destination benchmarking draws a broader picture including all elements of one destination such as transport services, airport services, accommodation services, leisure and sport facilities, hospitality and local attitudes, hygiene and cleanliness, and so on. Since destination benchmarking has been neglected from both the practical and academic perspective, the focus is on developing a specific benchmarking methodology that would be relevant in the context of international tourist destinations. This book also proposes that benchmarking could be used to enhance the performance level of different international destinations by identifying their strengths and weaknesses first in comparison with other similar destinations (external benchmarking) and secondly without such comparison (internal benchmarking). Thus, in light of the context of the usual benchmarking process, the term 'destination benchmarking' can be taken into consideration as:

> the continuous measurement of the performance of tourist destinations (strengths and weaknesses) not only against itself or other destinations in the same or in a different country but also against national/international quality grading systems by assessing both primary and secondary data for the purpose of establishing priorities, setting targets and gaining improvements in order to gain competitive advantage.

The primary objectives of destination benchmarking include assisting the management to set goals to enhance their performance levels in the future, and to establish its own standard values and take action to reach them. This is a method for internal and external benchmarking because feedback can be obtained from both inside and outside. The measurement of one's own performance indicates its current strengths and weaknesses as well as opportunities and threats for the future. Their comparison with other similar destinations may identify how competitive the destination is in various areas and any possible areas needing improvement. These terms could be refined to suit destinations. Strengths refer to things that the destination is good at, or something that makes a significant contribution to delivering tourist satisfaction and repeat business; weaknesses are items the destination lacks or something that causes tourist dissatisfaction and may prevent repeat or potential tourists' visits; opportunities are potential elements at the destination that could lead to tourist satisfaction and repeat business in the future, if developed effectively; threats are potential disruptions that will possibly impact upon tourist satisfaction and demand in the future. Based on these criteria, the application of the proposed destination benchmarking methodology identifies several key issues for drawing a clear picture of destinations under investigation.

Elements of Destination Benchmarking

This study proposes a model for use in practice; this will emphasize the importance of performance measurement and improvement for destinations and the role of benchmarking in it. The development of this model has required the completion of an extensive review of the literature on benchmarking, destination management and related areas (e.g. Camp, 1989; McNair and Leibfried, 1992; Kotler *et al.*, 1993; Laws, 1995). As emphasized earlier, a common benchmarking study, on which the proposed model has been based, is built up of five stages: planning, data collection, analysis, action and review. The planning stage has been replaced by the stage of performance measurement where destination-specific measures of performance are to be identified and the required data are collected to measure one's own performance. The next three stages, data collection, analysis and action, still exist to be used when and where needed.

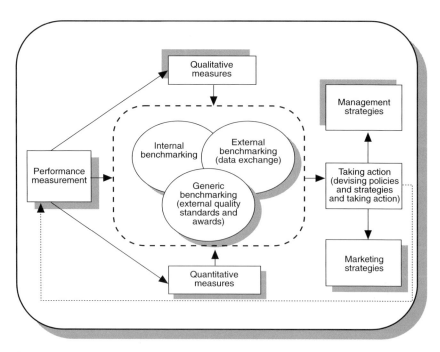

Fig. 3.1. Elements of the destination benchmarking model. Source: Kozak (2004).

Figure 3.1 shows how the model is supposed to work. First comes the measurement of destination performance. The second stage is the involvement in any type of benchmarking activity. The last stage, depending on the outcome of the earlier stages, is to take action, which includes setting goals and implementing the benchmarking findings. Unlike what is shown in Fig. 3.1, the stage of performance measurement is not separated from actual benchmarking. The last stage, taking action, may have different contents for each type of benchmarking.

The relationship between benchmarking and performance measurement and improvement is clear (Walleck *et al.*, 1991; Brignall and Ballantine, 1996). As noted in Chapter 1, benchmarking is a continuous process targeting performance improvement within various aspects of the organization. Identifying the level of each destination's performance based upon feedback about the outcome is vital in order to provide a useful indication of its current tourism position, and demonstrate the extent to which it takes place in the international competitiveness set and needs improvement. Figure 3.2 shows the relationship between benchmarking, performance improvement and competitive edge. A is the point to achieve the place that is close to competitiveness; performance needs to be improved through benchmarking. Point B represents the first stage where performance should be improved to be able to gain a competitive edge. Point C is the location where the enhanced performance will drive the organization/destination through both a competitive edge and a further benchmarking study where the organization/destination is to be selected as the

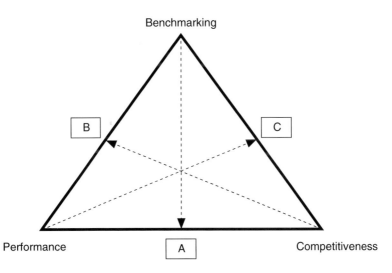

Fig. 3.2. Relationship between benchmarking, performance improvement and competitiveness. Source: own elaboration derived from the related literature review.

partner. As can be seen, it is not wise to think of one separated from the others because all elements of the process are interrelated.

The literature review shows that the idea of benchmarking basically comes from examining the gap between one's own and others' performance levels and (as a result) obtaining new ideas (see Table 1.2 on p. 6). This means that measuring one's own performance and its gaps against that of others is the primary stage in the benchmarking study. Galileo wrote 'count what is countable, measure what is measurable and what is not measurable, make measurable' (Mudie and Cottam, 1993). This could be a valuable point of departure when undertaking a destination performance measurement in terms of either demand or supply to take further action. Highlighting the importance of measurement as a first step in carrying out any type of benchmarking, Karlof and Ostblom (1993) state that 'anything' that can be measured can be benchmarked, e.g. all aspects of an organization's behaviour and performance such as goods, services, processes, staffing, support systems, capital and value for money. To achieve this, the literature suggests two categories of performance measures named 'quantitative' and 'qualitative' measures (Hair *et al.*, 1995). The outcome of these measures could be used in carrying out either internal, external or generic benchmarking. Chapter 4 will concentrate entirely on some specific measures of the destination performance.

The literature suggests that organizations should first begin with internal benchmarking, followed by external benchmarking and generic benchmarking (McNair and Leibfried, 1992; Zairi, 1992). Thus, they attempt to measure their own performance by collecting data on qualitative or quantitative measures. As Fig. 3.1 demonstrates, there is a close relationship between all three types of benchmarking. Internal benchmarking provides an introductory stage to undertaking external and generic benchmarking research. Self-generated data derived at this stage may be supplied either to the partner destination(s) or to international organizations such as the World Tourism Organization (WTO), the World Tourism and Travel Council (WTTC) and the European Economic Community (EEC) to be processed and used for exchange or for producing the best performance measures. The data produced may then be redistributed or circulated to those who are interested. As one objective of benchmarking is to search for the best practices and processes that produce those results, generic benchmarking proposed in this study is supposed to give the destination an objective standard to aim at when internationally recognized best practice awards or classification systems are used as 'good practices' for improvement. This is obviously a part of external benchmarking.

Once data are collected to measure the current performance, a particular type of benchmarking is selected and the other essential stages such as the assessment of benchmarking findings are completed; destination managers need to focus upon the development of action plans where future policies and strategies would be devised. Each stage of the model is explained in the following section. This is an entire model, which can be helpful to find appropriate responses to the questions raised in Box 3.2.

Box 3.2. Questions in benchmarking.

What	What is the objective?
	What to benchmark?
	What are the characteristics of service provided?
	What products and services are provided to customers?
	What do our customers want from us?
	What are we looking for?
	What is/are the most important products/services?
	What can we learn from the partner?
	What information is readily available?
	What data do we need to collect for comparisons?
	What are the partner's objectives?
	What are the similarities and differences between us?
Why	Why benchmark?
	Why choose a particular organization/destination?
How	How is it done or achieved?
	How does the partner do it?
	How do our customers see us?
	How do their customers see them?
	How to implement the benchmarking findings?
Who	Who is the best?
	Who performs the process in question?
	Who are our customers?
	Who are their customers?
How much	How much information is needed?
	How much does it cost to complete the benchmarking process?
How long	How long will it take?
How well	How well do we perform now?
	How well does the partner perform now?
When	When to benchmark?
	When to have a visit?
	When to implement the findings?
Where	Where is customer satisfaction the lowest and highest?
Which	Which functions have the greatest room for improvement?
	Which functions have the greatest potential for differentiating between competitors?

Measuring destination performance

The concepts of competitiveness and performance improvement are interrelated (Zairi, 1996). An improved performance brings advantages for maintaining a competitive edge, as poor performance requires much attention before the destination can compete with others. These two concepts are also dynamic and continuous. Inputs (e.g. changes in customer needs, wants and satisfaction levels) and outputs (e.g. tourist income and tourist numbers) therefore need to be evaluated continuously and changes observed. Based on the related literature (Melcher *et al.*, 1990; Bloom, 1996), it seems that measuring performance, as a key issue in benchmarking, could help destination managers consider the following issues:

- Convert one destination's performance into measures that will then be used to assess if it is comparable and compatible with that of other destinations and how the performance at the same destination changes over time
- Identify areas where destinations are performing well and poorly and particular attention must be given to those areas to bring them up to standard
- Evaluate the magnitude and significance of tourism to the local economy
- Establish cooperation and collaboration with other destinations to share opinions and ideas about both existing applications and possible future developments or trends
- Carry out regular surveys in order to identify customer needs and expectations, and regularly collect feedback from customer groups about the quality of service they have received
- Give customer groups information regularly about the updated performance of the products and services they may receive to help them know what to expect
- Assess if extra infrastructure and superstructure are required and if the existing capacity needs to be improved.

As with an organization's performance (Atkinson *et al.*, 1997), measuring a destination's performance may also help people who live there such as local residents, employees, customers and suppliers to evaluate their contributions and expectations. For example, if beaches are not clean, this means that tourists do not use them or are less likely to leave them clean or the staff are not carrying out their jobs properly. A high level of complaints about local behaviour towards foreign tourists means that it needs to be improved. This may then require establishing cooperation and collaboration with tourism and non-tourism organizations at the destination in order to serve customers better.

Taking customer satisfaction on board as a measure of performance, some slight differences appear between the understanding of methods examining the extent to which customers are satisfied or dissatisfied with the manufacturing and the service industries. In the manufacturing industry, the indicators of customer satisfaction or dissatisfaction are measured by the combination of both quantitative and qualitative measures such as the amount of refunds, claims, recalls, returns, repairs, warranty costs and incomplete orders in addition to the rated customer satisfaction levels, complaints and repeat visits (Camp, 1989). In the service industry, the measurement method could be based on the number of complaints, the rated satisfaction levels, refunds, incomplete orders and repeat visits, which are all common to those in the manufacturing industry (Fornell, 1992). Factors such as reliability, on-time delivery, responsibility, flexibility, awareness of customer problems and handling of complaints are equally important to both industries. On the other hand, in a service industry, it is impossible to review the number of times when services have been unsuccessful or items needed to be repaired once the consumption or purchase process has been completed.

The scope of benchmarking has been expanded to include all key processes and practices as well as products and services (Balm, 1992). A business process requires a series of steps to create an observable or measurable outcome, such as a product or service. Destination attributes can also be regarded as processes since experiences appear as a result of interaction between service providers and customers (see Table 3.2 for an extensive list of attributes that can be considered in any type of destination benchmarking). For instance, facilities such as hotels, restaurants or airports are regarded as a part of the production of tourist operations. As mentioned earlier, the lack of any of those may create barriers in the development of the area as a destination or create problems for delivering services efficiently through customers. Any process within a destination converts input (products, practices and services) to output, which are accepted either as qualitative measures (e.g. customer experiences and perceptions) or as quantitative measures (e.g. tourist expenses and tourist arrivals) used for performance evaluation. The following section provides brief information about the main features of each qualitative and quantitative measure. These will be explained in greater detail in Chapter 4.

Qualitative measures

Qualitative measures are considered as the degree of perceptual values assigned to each numerical value, e.g. number '1' means not satisfied and number '7' very satisfied (Moser and Kalton, 1971; Hair *et al.*, 1995). The level of a customer's satisfaction is regarded as a part of qualitative measures (non-metric or non-quantitative) as it indicates only relative positions and perceptions in an ordered series. In other words, it is not certain how much satisfaction with or image perception of the destination or what percentage of willingness to revisit is acceptable in absolute values to determine whether further stages of benchmarking research need to be employed. For instance, Fournier and Mick (1999) suggest that customers circling the number '4' on a 7-point satisfaction scale may have less equivalent satisfaction levels. As a result, qualitative measures seem to be relatively subjective.

Table 3.2. List of potential attributes for destination benchmarking.

Accommodation	Cleanliness	Hospitality	Facilities in general	Food and drink	Attractions	Airport	Local transport	Tourist information centre	Shopping
Quality of service	Cleanliness of streets	Feeling of welcome	Suitability of nightlife and entertainment	Quality of service	Quality of service	Availability of facilities and services	Frequency of local transport services	Usefulness of information	Quality of service
Cleanliness	Cleanliness of public toilets	Friendliness of local citizens	Availability of facilities/services for children	Range of food and drink facilities	Range of attractions	Speed of check-in/check-out	Comfort of check-in/services	Quality of service environment	Quality of shopping
Speed of check-in/check-out	Cleanliness of beaches	Responsiveness to visitor requests	Availability of health facilities	Range of food and drink	Value for money	Cleanliness	Network of local transport services	Ease of finding its location	Range of shopping facilities
Value for money	Cleanliness of sea	Responsiveness to visitor complaints	Availability of sport facilities/activities	Value for money	Level of language communication	Travelling time between airport and destination	Quality of service	Level of language communication	Value for money
Signposting to bedrooms and public areas		Feeling of safety and security	Availability of facilities for disabled people	Cleanliness					
Adequacy of water supply			Availability of facilities on the beach	Level of language communication					
Adequacy of electricity supply			Signposting to attractions and facilities						
Level of language communication			Availability of parking space						
			Availability of daily tours						

Quantitative measures

In quantitative measures, differences between two or more points are mathematically equal (or at the same distance) and refer to an absolute value (Hair *et al.*, 1995). Both interval and ratio scales are examples of quantitative (metric) measures. As suggested for organizations (Kaplan and Norton, 1992), destinations also consider a variety of quantitative measures dealing with overall performance. Among these are the volume of tourist arrivals, the level of tourism incomes, the level of tourist expenditure and its distribution or the percentage of repeat tourists (financial perspective). Quantitative measures can be extended to include some other measures relating to the level of tourist satisfaction (customer perspective). As far as tourist satisfaction is concerned, for example, satisfaction with time is measured from the time one destination point receives an order to the time it actually delivers the product or the service back to the customer, e.g. the length of time spent at check-in and check-out at the destination airport, at accommodation facilities and waiting for transport at the destination, waiting for food to be served in a restaurant or waiting for a response about a complaint. As such, quantitative measures seem to be more objective.

Types of destination benchmarking

Once the current performance is measured and the area(s) needing improvement is identified, the next stage is to decide which type of benchmarking is to be followed. In Chapter 1, the typology of benchmarking was examined under three categories: internal, external and generic (functional) benchmarking. All these three types of benchmarking could be applied to tourist destinations because they are important for setting appropriate and realistic targets and assessing either internal or external performance of destinations.

Internal benchmarking

Internal benchmarking is an approach that includes the collection of data on one's own performance and its assessment on the basis of several criteria such as objectives or improvements compared with past years (McNair and Leibfried, 1992; Cross and Leonard, 1994). Goals set for taking action come from sharing opinions between departments in the same organization (Breiter and Kline, 1995). The rationale for choosing to apply this approach is the difficulty of activating external benchmarking due to cultural and managerial differences and access to external data. Reflecting on this introduction, internal destination benchmarking refers to a monitoring process of the performance objectives released by authorities prior to commencing the benchmarking study and then taking action. Objectives could be the assessment of percentage changes in quantitative performance variables and changes in mean scores of qualitative variables, e.g. percentage change in economic variables of tourism such as the level of income, the number of tourists, the occupancy rate as well as customer perceptions, satisfaction and complaints in comparison with previous periods. These data may be valuable in enabling destination managers to review their overall performance each year or season and decide whether they need to get involved in external benchmarking. If so, this information could be used as baseline data for external benchmarking with other destinations (Weller, 1996). Chapter 5 is devoted to the formulation of internal destination benchmarking procedures and its possible measures.

External benchmarking

The literature shows that the majority of tourism and hospitality benchmarking procedures have been refined in external benchmarking aiming to identify performance gaps and learn about others' best practices (Breiter and Kline, 1995; Thomason *et al.*, 1999a; Young and Ambrose, 1999). In external destination benchmarking, following the principles of the most common benchmarking model (McNair and Leibfried, 1992), the overall performance of tourist destinations or their specific areas could be benchmarked against other(s) in the same or in a different country, e.g. trends in tourism, capital investment, employment, customer perceptions of satisfaction or image, or structure of tourism demand. It is also feasible to benchmark particular features of service delivery, such as customer care, against practices in service industries other than tourism.

The destination for comparison could be selected from those that are perceived as offering a superior performance in some respects and being in the same competitiveness set (Pearce, 1997). As a part of external benchmarking, in competitive benchmarking, tourist destinations could be compared with their direct competitors operating in different geographic areas or countries. For instance, one purpose of benchmarking might be to compare the performance of Mediterranean destinations as summer vacation and short-haul destinations for European markets. Eventually, benchmarking findings could be useful for destination managers to make a decision about what to do or not to do by looking at the outcome of practices applied within other destinations or choosing good practices that are relevant to them. The operationalization of external destination benchmarking is discussed in Chapter 6.

Generic benchmarking

The existing literature emphasizes that the core idea of benchmarking is to identify the best practices or the best performing businesses in the industry and improve one's own performance by adopting good practices used by others or guidelines established by professional national or international organizations (Evans and Lindsey, 1993; Zairi, 1996). In line with these, within the application of generic (or functional) benchmarking, tourist destinations could look at either other destinations or international standards in order to find effective solutions for their particular problems by having access to best practices recognized nationally or internationally. Therefore, this study suggests that various quality grading and eco-label systems could act as external enablers, as a form of generic benchmarking, that influence the performance of holiday destinations. These systems and benchmarking have the common goal of providing guidelines on how to improve performance, seek best practices and enable continuous improvement (Vaziri, 1992). Generic destination benchmarking and its rationale are addressed in more detail in Chapter 7.

Taking action

The prime purpose of benchmarking is not solely to carry out marketing research identifying what customers most like or dislike. Rather, the main purpose is to develop strategies to provide better services by obtaining feedback from all those involved, e.g. tourists, service providers and local people, and obtaining information about the practices of other destinations. As discussed earlier, benchmarking requires effective collaboration, cooperation and coordination not only between members of the tourism industry but also between members and external organizations. As Jafari (1983) suggests, tourism and other establishments need to be in harmony with the development and promotion of tourism activities in the destination. In this sense, a destination manager could be considered as the authority who will be in charge of directing resources, coordinating not only with local tourism establishments but also with leading national or international tourism and related organizations and directing TQM programmes towards the implementation of the results to achieve goals and objectives. Basically, the potential role of destination managers may be providing local businesses and residents with services such as supervision and inspection.

Each type of benchmarking may require the establishment of separate action plans. The analysis of results derived from internal benchmarking investigation might help to decide which attributes or measures are to be investigated further. The other two approaches (external and generic benchmarking) might assist in identifying gaps, determining strengths and weaknesses of destinations, and deciding which attributes are to be investigated further or which good practices can be adopted from others. The action stage might also help to make future projections and recommendations. An action plan containing future goals and recommendations might consist of how to keep up strengths and minimize weaknesses and threats in order to cope with the new applications and developments. Depending on the outcome, destination managers may wish to change their marketing policies or market segments. It may also be possible to attract similar groups of tourists by preserving the current image and improving the existing performance. To implement the benchmarking results, destination managers might make their recommendations to local authorities (e.g. city councils), local tourist associations and businesses (e.g. tourism offices), local residents and the national tourism policymakers (e.g. the Ministry of Tourism).

Summary

This chapter has attempted to discuss the possible scope of destination management and approaches to it. It has also provided a rationale for destination benchmarking's contribution to achieving and maintaining destination competitiveness. In line with the guidelines provided by the benchmarking literature and the proposed model, a series of proposals have also been suggested to achieve success in destination benchmarking. The performance measurement theory has been briefly reviewed, along with its possible application to tourist destinations and the potential use of internal, external and generic benchmarking. The stage of taking action has been the final subject examined in this chapter. The next chapter will examine the development of quantitative and qualitative measures of destination performance as exemplars and their assessment from the wider perspective of internal and external benchmarking approaches.

Measures of Destination Benchmarking

4

Introduction

This chapter aims to discuss further the development and assessment of qualitative and quantitative measures of destination performance as exemplars, as the primary sources of the proposed model of destination benchmarking. This encompasses a number of measures specifically related to the measurement of overall destination performance and suggests how to evaluate each in the context of internal and external benchmarking procedures. This chapter provides the grounds for what kind of measures can be developed and how they can be applied to tourist destinations from the perspective of internal and external benchmarking.

Rationale for Measuring Destination Performance

In recent years, tourism has become a highly competitive market. For this reason, it is important that destinations are able to measure their competitiveness in order to identify their strengths and weaknesses and thereby develop their future strategies. A Chinese proverb attributed to Sun Tzu, a Chinese General, in 500 BC has gained a respectful response from benchmarking researchers: 'If you know your enemy and know yourself, you need not fear the results of a hundred battles' (Camp, 1989, p. 253). This means that if the destination knows itself and its competitors, it can take steps to ensure its competitive position is maintained. On the other hand, if competitors are believed to be particularly strong, it is important to take action. Battles could be over both internal and external barriers affecting the success of the destination and its competitiveness in the marketplace. When tourist destinations are considered as an element of the marketing mix (place), the importance of their performance levels seems clear.

As the purpose of this book is to show the ways to carry out both internal and external forms of benchmarking, the significant matter is the development of specific measures to evaluate one's own and/or others' performance levels based on various criteria. In so doing, destination managers may be able to monitor their strengths and identify their weaknesses and, if required, compare themselves with their competitors. As mentioned earlier, the benchmarking literature mostly refers to the quantitative measurement of benchmarks due to the ease of measuring and the use of metrics in comparison research, even though it has weaknesses (Phillips and Appiah-Adu, 1998). The criticism of this method is that it does not allow the effects of other conditional (contingent) variables on the business' performance to be considered and, therefore, this appears to focus narrowly on a specific set of performance data. In contrast, this study proposes that both qualitative and quantitative measures could be interpreted simultaneously by carrying out a primary research activity or reviewing secondary research findings. It is proposed that both measures could be interrelated in the investigation of overall performance and benchmarking of tourist destinations.

Indicators of Destination Performance Measures

As discussed in Chapter 3, developing and using destination-specific measures helps to identify the current performance and monitor the direction of changes over a period. Measures identified during the planning stage of benchmarking may also help to determine the magnitude of the performance gaps between destinations and select what is to be benchmarked, as they do in organization benchmarking (Vaziri, 1992; Karlof and Ostblom, 1993). It is also possible to shape future strategies depending upon the measures and their findings obtained in a benchmarking project. For example, it might be necessary to pay more attention to those areas where satisfaction scores indicate lower performance. It is thus crucial to introduce several destination-based performance measures and discuss their rationale in destination benchmarking. This is what this section aims to provide.

Balm (1992) categorized organizational benchmarking measures under four main groups particularly based on manufacturing businesses (see Box 4.1). However, the adaptation of these measures to tourism and hospitality operations seems to be possible since each industry has an 'input', 'process' and 'output' stage in order to serve its customers. The following sections discuss various qualitative and quantitative measures that could be used to measure destination performance and assist in setting up future management and marketing strategies. It also provides possible ways to apply these measures to the practice of destination benchmarking. Qualitative measures include the assessment of tourist motivations, satis-

---

Box 4.1. Examples of benchmarking measures. Source: Balm (1992).

Efficiency versus effectiveness measures: efficiency measures are the amount of revenue per customer or per employee or the weighted occupancy rates, whereas effectiveness measures refer to delivery time per customer, e.g. length of time relating to check-in or check-out procedures per customer. This approach considers that customers care very little about efficiency measures since they are mainly related to business management. Effectiveness measures are more likely to be important to customers since exceeding standards or limitations could influence consumer behaviour and image of the business.

Qualitative versus quantitative measures: qualitative measures refer to textual measures such as customers being satisfied or dissatisfied, whereas quantitative measures refer to numerical measures such as response time at the encounter measured in seconds. The qualitative metrics can easily be converted into quantitative metrics by assigning numeric satisfaction scale such as Likert scales or semantic differential scales. Such scales enable businesses to identify and compare gaps and make action plans. The relationship between these two measures is strong as one's success is linked to the other. Customers pay a lot of attention to all these measures.

Analogue versus discrete measures: analogue measures indicate continuous metrics such as room temperature or the availability of 24 h room service, whereas discrete measures refer to one-time or periodic measurable events such as rooms cleaned per day or the number of customers served at one encounter in a certain time scale.

Confidential versus non-confidential measures: confidential measures are not allowed to share, so that the best or simplest way is to convert confidential measures to a trend, percentage or time trend that is not sensitive and may still convey useful information. Occupancy rates, rate of return on investment and employee turnover can be given as examples of non-confidential metrics and sales revenue, cost and net profit per customer or room for confidential metrics. Even though confidential measures seem to be very significant in evaluating overall performance of a business in a period and understanding how it performed or how it was successful or unsuccessful, confidentiality limits any detailed information being obtained from others' final successes or mistakes. Financial measures are the most important tool in maintaining competitiveness and overtaking competitors.

---

faction, comments, complaints, and the intention of repeat business and recommendation. Quantitative measures comprise the assessment of tourist arrivals and their distribution by nationalities and months, average length of stay, annual tourist incomes, number of repeat visits, and tourist expenditure and its distribution into subcategories.

Qualitative measures

The analysis of demand on the basis of qualitative measures plays a vital role in designing a successful model of destination benchmarking and also for its application in organization benchmarking. As customers are vital in yielding responses to test the effectiveness and efficiency of qualitative measures (Hauser and Katz, 1998), they can be considered as a very important ingredient in designing marketing activities in the tourism and travel industry. Most notably, marketing activities start and end with the analysis and interpretation of outcomes yielded from customer feedback (Quelch and Ash, 1981). The results could be satisfaction, dissatisfaction, complaints, high or low spending, intention to revisit or never come back, and positive or negative word-of-mouth recommendation. In this context, this chapter introduces a number of qualitative criteria that may be used while measuring the performance of destinations in terms of demand.

Tourist motivations

As tourists do not always attach the same importance to product attributes, it is crucial to understand the factors that influence tourist behaviour and which particular elements are seen by them as important (Mayo and Jarvis, 1981). The simplest way of achieving this task is to ask those taking holidays. This task is also a priority in the most common benchmarking (Zairi, 1996). Tourism literature emphasizes the importance of both pull and push factors in shaping tourist motivation and the choice of vacation destinations. Motivations may differ from one person (or group) to another and from one destination to another. Uysal and Hagan (1993) suggest that efforts to understand factors pushing travellers to visit a particular destination, and how these factors are different from or similar to those of others visiting other destinations, may help the destination management in setting effective management and marketing strategies.

Furthermore, some researchers emphasize the importance of motivation in understanding why certain customers choose certain destinations and make certain consumption decisions. Push and pull motivations would be equally effective in eliminating alternative destinations and choosing the actual destination. Push factors are origin-related and refer to the intangible or intrinsic desires of the individual travellers (e.g. the desire for escape, rest and relaxation, adventure, health or prestige), whereas pull factors are mainly related to the attractiveness of a given destination and tangibles such as beaches, accommodation and recreation facilities or historical resources (Uysal and Hagan, 1993).

Tourists' own motivations, such as relaxing, meeting other people and the opportunities for sports or sunbathing, are vital in influencing their decision to go on holiday or in selecting a destination. It is difficult to respond to customer needs and wants and to grasp the extent to which products and services at the destination can match their motivations unless priority is given to examining them. Sandbach (1997) underlines the importance of understanding what customers want, what motives they have and how satisfied they are with various destinations, in order to be competitive in the market. Examination of motivations or the reasons for choosing a particular destination as performance measurement criteria could provide valuable implications for destination benchmarking in order to identify the profile of tourists a destination attracts. Using t- and χ^2 tests, past studies showed significant differences in tourist motivation between two destinations (Kozak, 2002a). These findings could help not only to identify how one destination can differentiate itself from others but also in the choice of a partner destination suitable for external benchmarking.

Motivation is vital in the development of attitudes and yielding satisfaction or dissatisfaction at the end of the holiday (Chon, 1989). The examination of differences of motivation between sample populations representing different cultures is important for managers in understanding customer values, preferences and behaviour. In benchmarking research, examining and understanding motivation is also important. Depending upon the empirical findings, destination management would either promote attributes that best match the tourist motivations or concentrate on a different market where tourist motivations and destination resources match each other. Laws (1995) suggests that the examination of benefits that are important to tourists is crucial for the promotion and planning of destinations.

The examination of tourists' motivation depends on a set of motivations tourists consider while visiting a specific destination or taking a vacation abroad. These can be measured by utilizing a Likert-type scale as it enables the researcher to compare mean values with different markets and other destinations (Hill *et al.*, 1990; Baloglu and McCleary, 1999). Respondents are asked to rate each of the items on a Likert-type scale based on the relative importance of each tourist motivation pushing them into tourism activities. This section of the questionnaire may present statements such as 'I came to XXX to get close to nature' or 'I came to XXX to meet local people', and so on. If respondents think that there is any question that is inapplicable, they are then advised to move on to the next. The 'important–not important' scale is usually used in this type of research (Kozak, 2002a). The reason for using a Likert-type scale and employing a number of multiple push and pull motivation variables was that motivation is multi-dimensional and tourists want to have more than one experience at a destination (Pyo *et al.*, 1989). The higher mean values refer to the level where tourists hold stronger motivations.

Level of tourist satisfaction

In line with the overview of the literature given in Chapter 1, customer satisfaction could be considered as a driver (impacts on word-of-mouth recommendation and repeat visits) and also an output (based on outcomes of actual holiday experiences). Customer satisfaction or dissatisfaction with products and services is regarded as a measure of performance (Bogan and English, 1994). Destination attributes are critical because they influence the choice of destinations (Illum and Schaefer, 1995). The literature review showed that destination attributes had been used in several studies with different research objectives, different samples, different methodologies and different findings. In this study, they have been used for another purpose, specifically to benchmark strengths and weaknesses of two different international tourist destinations by considering actual tourist experiences.

Successful destination management and marketing depend on tourists' perceptions as these may influence the choice of the destination, the consumption of products and services while on vacation and the decision to come back. Some authors therefore draw attention to the importance of customer feedback and customer satisfaction in bench-marking (e.g. Kasul and Motwani, 1995; Zairi, 1996) even though there is very little empirical benchmarking research in the literature conducted by considering customers' opinions. Of these, for example, in an organiza-tion benchmarking study carried out among European businesses with respect to customer satisfaction policy and measuring customer satis-faction, the EFQM indicated that improving business performance and increasing customer loyalty were the two main ways to improve customer satisfaction.

Competitiveness is the key element of management and marketing strategy; therefore, long-range planning and customer satisfaction could be the two major objectives of either tourism businesses or tourist destina-tions. Among the long-term benefits of customer satisfaction are a shift upwards in the demand curve, reduction in marketing costs for existing customers due to increase of repeat business, increase in marketing costs of competitors to attract others' customers, reduction in customer and employee turnover, lower marketing costs for obtaining new customers due to enhancement of positive word-of-mouth communication, and the forma-tion of a positive image of the organization (or destination) in the cus-tomers' minds (Fornell, 1992). Consequently, customer satisfaction could be regarded as a measure of performance (Zairi, 1996) and one of the greatest sources of competitive advantage (Peters, 1994). The concepts of performance and satisfaction are strongly interrelated as the level of prod-uct or service performance brings satisfaction. Bogan and English (1994) emphasize that customer service performance measures should include satisfaction, dissatisfaction, retention and defection benchmarks since the last two represent the customers' intentions for the future. It is claimed that (Cook, 1995, p. 29–30): '... customer satisfaction is a major benefit to be gained from benchmarking. It allows organizations to adopt helicopter vision and helps prevent complacency through developing the discipline of focusing externally.'

It is therefore further suggested that feedback received from customers is a suitable way of comparing the performance of an organization (or destination) with that of another (Kotler, 1994). The availability of alternative service providers (e.g. competitor destinations) appears to be significant in influencing the level of customer satisfaction, since customers have a tendency to compare one service encounter with another (Czepiel *et al.,* 1974). With respect to the methodological procedures of external benchmarking (gap analysis), as suggested in the benchmarking literature, mean values of each variable can be compared with those of another in a different destination (Madigan, 1993). The internal performance of the destination could be measured by employing a set of summary questions in addition to individual satisfaction items. Such questions could refer to the level of overall satisfaction with the destination and the intention to return and to tell others about their positive experiences (e.g. Rust *et al.,* 1996). The examination of the impact of independent satisfaction variables on summary questions is helpful to demonstrate the power of each variable.

Level of tourist complaints

The consumer behaviour literature underlines the significance of paying attention to handling customer complaints, as any unresolved complaint could not only stop repeat visits but also bring negative word-of-mouth communication (e.g. Almanza *et al.,* 1994). Feedback derived from customer complaints could therefore be helpful for marketing management studies in order to monitor the existing problems and the extent to which products and services are found to be satisfactory by customers. Giving an example from practical applications, the Wales Tourist Board (WTB) keeps the records of its visitors' complaints about different categories such as accommodation, cleanliness, service, food, and so on (Laws, 1995). There is less need to take any further action if the number of complaints is below a certain level. The WTB aims to reduce the volume of visitor complaints by establishing accommodation and quality grading systems such as crowns and dragons.

As in all industries, all destinations face the problem of customer dissatisfaction with and complaints about particular products or services at one time or another. It is believed that service providers will improve the product or service as a result of dissatisfaction and complaints, which may prevent other customers from experiencing similar dissatisfaction with those products or services (Richins, 1979). Otherwise, there would be no effective action taken by management to resolve the sources of complaints and improve products and services (Day and Ash, 1978; Krishnan and Valle, 1978). The level of customer complaints has been examined as a measure of benchmarking in earlier studies (e.g. Zairi, 1996; Mann *et al.,* 1999a,b). Destination benchmarking further suggests that the level of complaints at one tourist destination could be a good reason for another to benchmark itself, to avoid making the same mistakes. For instance, tourists' complaints about noise and dirtiness in one destination may be higher than they are in another. This means that the latter needs to consider this situation carefully and examine where the former has gone wrong while it was becoming a popular mass tourism destination. Moreover, the method used by others to resolve customer complaints is the next stage of destination benchmarking. In this manner, not only other destinations or tourism businesses but also practical examples from service and manufacturing industries could be considered (generic or functional benchmarking). Though the content of customer complaints differs from destination to destination and from one industry to another, the basic method of handling them would be similar. This could apply to such examples as the cleanliness of beaches, forgotten wake-up calls or better communication skills with customers.

In order to be able to understand the types of specific complaints, the question could be 'How likely are you to complain about the attribute X in … ?', copying the methodology of customer satisfaction measurement. Findings can be analysed by ranking mean scores. The attributes assigned the highest mean scores will be those that tourists were unhappy with. Those assigned the lowest mean scores will have no major problems. The application of summary questions is also relevant in this example of a destination benchmarking exercise. These can be used to investigate the impact of the level of complaints about each relevant attribute on the level of overall satisfaction or dissatisfaction and on tourists' intention to return and recommend to others or tell others about their negative experiences. Alternatively, tourists could be requested to list the attribute(s) that they would complain about. With this method, findings can be ranked in ascending order on the basis of the number of complaints assigned to each attribute.

As another way of benchmarking customer complaints, the percentage of complaints might be calculated by dividing the total number of complaints into the number of total customers in a certain period of time. The highest and the lowest areas of complaints may be identified by ranking scores. Findings could be helpful to analyse the type of complaints about the destination (internal benchmarking) as well as a comparison with other destinations (external benchmarking).

Level of tourist comments

It is emphasized that asking customers to list any problems they had or any improvement they could suggest might be a method of measuring customer satisfaction and could also provide valuable information about what needs to be changed or improved (Kotler, 1994). In other words, it helps to have a list of dos and don'ts from the perspective of actual customers' comments. As in the analysis of complaints, customers may be asked to list the attributes that they consider to be improved. Alternatively, by adapting the type of questions used to measure customer expectations in the service quality instrument (Parasuraman *et al.*, 1985), customers could be requested to indicate how likely they consider each category of a pre-identified set of attributes to need improvement using Likert scales such as 'strongly agree' to 'strongly disagree'. Those with higher scores will need to be considered for further analysis of benchmarking studies.

Level of attitudes towards destinations

The consumer psychology literature suggests that there is a strong relationship between attitude towards an object and behavioural intention (Woodside and Sherrell, 1977). Likewise, it is suggested further that attitude is a predictor of determining a destination to be selected among alternatives in the awareness set (Goodrich, 1977, 1978). If attitude towards a country or destination is positive, then the intention to visit there will also be positive or higher. Attitudes are believed to be two-directional. Not only do attitudes affect behaviour but also behaviour has an impact on attitudes (Bareham, 1995). Thus, a positive attitude towards a destination can stimulate visits, while actual holiday experiences at a particular destination change the direction of attitudes in a positive or negative way as a result of satisfaction or dissatisfaction with the experience (Mayo and Jarvis, 1981). Both visitors and non-visitors can have attitudes towards a particular destination at different levels (Baloglu, 1998). The destination management may have an opportunity to change actual visitors' negative attitudes into positive ones, but it takes more effort to measure and control non-visitors' attitudes towards the destination. Each destination therefore needs to know its performance levels through considering those strengths and weaknesses that will affect both repeat visits and the nature of word-of-mouth communication to others considering a first visit (Selby and Morgan, 1996).

As in satisfaction measures, mean scores are also widely used in attitude measures (Um and Crompton, 1990). The contribution of the measurement of attitudes to the internal performance of destinations can be similar to that of the tourist satisfaction measurement method discussed earlier. Thus, the relationship between attitudes and the intention to visit or recommend destinations to others is the method that this study suggests for internal performance measurement. To measure external performance with gap analysis, destination management could investigate attitudes of potential markets not only towards itself but also towards other competitor destinations. Either negative or positive attitudes towards competitors provide destination management potential benefits to decide the type of action to be taken.

Level of image perceptions of destinations

Studies of image and attitude are different concepts despite the fact that both are largely used in the field of marketing. Two people may have the same images of a place, but may have different attitudes towards it, e.g. warm weather (Kotler *et al.*, 1996). The place can be perceived to be warm (image), but one may not like warm weather or may not want to travel to a place that is warm (attitude). A number of image studies have been carried out to explore positive and negative perspectives of destinations on several attributes (Richardson and Crompton, 1988). Such research indicates that destination images influence tourist behaviour (Hunt, 1975; Pearce, 1982). Image studies play a key role in the marketing and promotion of destinations, particularly for those who have never been to the destination before (Baloglu and McCleary, 1999). Therefore, benchmarking research could possibly be conducted first to understand the areas where the destination is suffering in terms of its image; and methods can be developed to construct a positive image and to suggest how to use this positive image to make people feel that the destination has its own distinctive quality. Although it is claimed that image perceptions of destinations may not always reflect the reality, unfortunately, they could affect the destination choice of potential tourists (Goodrich, 1978).

As with benchmarking, image studies are an ongoing process of periodically monitoring changes in people's perceptions of destinations. If one wants to use quantitative research methods, an image can be measured with Likert scales (Fakeye and Crompton, 1991). Results can be evaluated either by ranking attributes from the highest (positive) to the lowest (negative) mean scores or, as mentioned in tourist satisfaction and attitude research, by examining the attributes most likely to persuade potential tourists to visit the destination and recommend it to their relatives and friends. If the sample is selected from those who have been to the destination, the impact of the image perception of each item on the level of overall image perception might be considered as a performance indicator. To achieve this, the summary questions adapted from tourist satisfaction research, in addition to the individual image items, are designed as 'overall how would you perceive the image of destination X?' (Baloglu and McCleary, 1999), 'how likely are you to want to visit destination X?' (Kozak and Rimmington, 2000) or 'how likely are you to recommend destination X for a vacation?' (Cho, 1998).

Feedback from repeat tourists

The repeat customers' perceptions of performance changes in relation to several indicators were mentioned in several studies as internal measures of benchmarking (Ferdows and DeMeyer, 1990; Mann *et al.*, 1999a,b). There have been numerous studies linking the concepts of benchmarking and continuous improvement (Ferdows and DeMeyer, 1990; Schroeder and

Robinson, 1991; Elmuti and Kathawala, 1997). The observation of developments in the performance of destinations requires the consideration of customers who have had previous experiences. In terms of evaluating the
repeat tourists' perceptions of changes within destinations compared to
their earlier visits, these instruments provide significant implications for
practitioners. Repeat tourists have a wider and more in-depth experience of
the same destinations than those who are on their first visit (Cohen, 1974;
Crompton and Love, 1985). First-time tourists take time to get to know the
surroundings of the hotel and try to explore other resources at the destination. Repeat tourists not only revisit familiar places but also extend their
knowledge of them and visit other places to gain a broader perspective.
Thus, the observations and comments of repeat tourists could be valuable
for evaluating the overall performance of a given destination and how it is
continuously performing.

In the empirical investigation of feedback obtained from repeat tourists
leading to destination benchmarking, both open-ended and structured
questionnaires may be used. In the former, tourists are requested to reflect
on in which ways the destination has changed for the better and for the
worse since their last visit. Findings are assessed by ranking row scores for
each category. A similar technique can be applied to investigate tourists'
positive and negative experiences at the same time (Pearce and Caltabiano,
1983; Johns and Lee-Ross, 1995). In the structured format of the questionnaire, respondents could be asked to indicate how much each particular
attribute has changed since their last visit. The questionnaire may be
designed to indicate attributes, with those with higher scores being better
than those with lower scores.

Previous benchmarking studies paid insufficient attention to the
assessment of repeat customers' opinions while attempting to measure the
perceived changes in the performance of destinations when compared
with previous visits. As an element of internal benchmarking, destinations
could focus their efforts on gaining feedback from repeat tourists with
respect to changes within the destination itself. This study proposes that
the repeat tourists' opinions about the developments in the facilities and
services of destinations would be worth obtaining for destination benchmarking to maintain continuous progress. As a greater number of tourists
return to Mallorca, it is important to obtain feedback from its repeat customers periodically concerning any potential changes in the destination
overall as well as to get feedback from the first-time tourists.
Improvements to the attractions, facilities and services at the destination
could stimulate further repeat visits as well as future potential tourists, but
any perceived negative trends could prevent the destination from becoming more competitive. However, as previously described (Mansfeld, 1992;
Ross, 1993; Klenosky and Gitelson, 1998), the perspective of first-time
tourists is also important due to the importance of word-of-mouth communication.

Level of future behaviour and intention

The examination of actual tourists' intention of revisiting the same destinations or visiting other destinations in the country and of recommending their holiday experiences to their friends and relatives could be a valuable criterion when assessing the internal performance of one destination. For instance, a high level of intention for word-of-mouth communication could mean that the destination is found to be satisfactory. Its comparison with other destinations could indicate how better one destination performs than others in these respects (external performance). If tourists in other destinations have a higher intention of repeat visits or recommendation, then the reasons for this could be investigated. As for the limitation of this method, it is clear that some tourists tend to visit different destinations for their next holiday despite the fact that they find the previous destination they visited extremely satisfactory. This means that sometimes there could be no association between the perceived performance of one destination and the intention to return, but this may not apply to the intention to recommend.

Potential tourists are expected to have only limited knowledge about the attributes of a particular destination they have not visited before (Um and Crompton, 1990). Therefore, it appears that previous experiences also play a part in tourists' choice of destination (Mayo and Jarvis, 1981; Court and Lupton, 1997). The majority of destination choice sets, posited and empirically tested, considered previous experiences as one of the factors affecting tourists' awareness of a destination (Woodside and Lysonski, 1989). Research findings confirmed that familiarity had a positive impact on the likelihood of revisiting a destination (Gitelson and Crompton, 1983; Pizam and Milman, 1993). In a study of psychometric typology, Plog (1974) presented the behavioural differences of both *psychocentric* and *allocentric* tourists: the former prefer familiar destinations and the latter novel and less-developed destinations. The findings of a research project demonstrated that individuals who had previous experiences with the same destination (or region) were more confident and more likely to go back since they felt more secure.

However, given the fact that tourists are offered a variety of destinations, it may sometimes be impossible to predict which one will actually be selected as the next vacation destination. Repeat visits may not be such prevalent phenomena for tourism as they are for other businesses. Even where the destination fulfils tourist expectations, repeat visits may not be ensured. Some customers will undoubtedly look for similar but new experiences in different destinations, either in the same or in a different country (McDougall and Munro, 1994). With tourism, it is difficult to evaluate a holiday in advance (Zeithaml *et al.*, 1993). For these reasons, positive word-of-mouth recommendation will be considerably more important and easier for a destination to achieve than gaining repeat tourists (Klenosky and Gitelson, 1998). For instance, the results of research by Gitelson and Crompton (1983) reported that 74% of tourists had received travel information from friends and relatives, whereas only 20% had referred to printed media such as newspapers and travel magazines.

Bearing in mind both the benefits and the caveats of measuring future behavioural intention, valuable implications may be provided for destination benchmarking studies as the level of these intentions is closely associated with either the level of satisfaction, attitude or image perceptions, or a combination of all of these. A low level of intention to return or recommend may indicate that the destination has some problems, on the condition that other factors are held constant. The main questions to be asked are how likely tourists are to consider coming back either in the short or the long term and to recommend their holiday experiences with the destination by assigning 'likely' and 'unlikely' Likert scales (Gyte and Phelps, 1989; Danaher and Arweiler, 1996). The level of repurchase intention was presented earlier by the Rover group as a benchmarking measure (Zairi, 1996).

Intermediaries' perceptions of destination performance

Tour operators, as a main supplier in the tourism industry, are considered as another input in destination benchmarking since they can provide an invaluable source of information about different destinations. As a consequence of developments in mass tourism over the last decades, tour operators have gained considerable power in directing tourism demand and marketing tourist destinations. This means that, to a greater or lesser extent, the success of a destination depends on tour operators (Carey *et al.*, 1997). The major tourist-attracting destinations such as Spain, Turkey, Greece and Tunisia are more likely to have a relationship with tour operators in order to bring their tourism supply into the market. The large extent of the tour operators' involvement in the marketing of mass tourism destinations has forced national tourist offices and organizations to enter into a mutual undertaking with them.

Tour operators collect data about different features of destinations, grade accommodation facilities and sell each destination at the same or a different price depending on the quality of tourism supply in the destination and the attractiveness of the destination in the eyes of potential tourist groups. Tour operators have an opportunity to promote one destination and disregard others. This totally depends on the relationship between destinations and tour operators, and the tour operators' perceptions of the destination (Ashworth and Goodall, 1988; Goodall and Bergsma, 1990). When any destination area begins to decline in the eyes of tour operators or any critical problem appears, there is a strong possibility that this destination will be excluded from the market.

Tourist literature is very important when choosing a destination because it is an important factor in the interrelationship between tour operators and potential tourists (Goodall, 1990). Tour operators have an obligation to offer the products and services they promised in the brochure. The major feature of brochures is to create expectations for quality, value for money and image of the destination before a holiday (Goodall and Bergsma, 1990). Brochures are more important for first-time tourists since, without them, tourists may have no prior idea about the destination at all. This grading system in the brochure may additionally influence both the image of accommodation facilities individually and the destination generally (Goodall and Bergsma, 1990). In addition, a few tour operators (e.g. TUI) have recently released a checklist in which every destination is evaluated according to its compliance with the guidelines. Destinations falling below standards are excluded from the list.

In the last few years, tour operators have begun dealing with customer complaints concerning inclusive tours. Many travel agents send a 'welcome home card' inviting their customers to talk about their holiday experiences and to ensure they will remember the agent in the future after their return from holiday. For example, Direct Holidays distributes customer satisfaction questionnaires to every customer at the end of each holiday. Findings are used to assess accommodation, the holiday representative, overall enjoyment and car hire, and to set standards for the quality of their future holiday plans (Seaton and Bennett, 1996). Similarly, with reference to the current author's personal observation, Airtours distributes a similar type of questionnaire to its customers on the way home in order to obtain feedback regarding their experiences with accommodation, the tour operator's services at the destination and satisfaction with the destination overall.

Given these and the fact that tour operators represent a large number of tourists, advice obtained from tour operators could be taken into account as part of the input when deciding how to improve the resorts. They can send feedback compiled with their customers' comments and/or complaints directly to destination management. The context of destination benchmarking could be extended further to include tour operators' own suggestions with regard to improving the performance of resorts or minimizing existing complaints in order to give better service in succeeding years. This can be a good example of how external benchmarking works.

Analysis of qualitative measures

A summary of qualitative measures, discussed above, and their performance indicators are shown in Table 4.1. By using Likert or semantic scales, or percentage values, four different methods can be recommended

Table 4.1. Qualitative measures of destination performance.

Criteria of performance	Tools	Performance indicators
Tourist motivations	Mean scores	Ranking of motivation items
Level of tourist satisfaction	Mean scores	Ranking of satisfaction items
	Summary questions	Impacts of specific individual items on the level of overall satisfaction, intention to revisit and recommend
Level of tourist complaints	List of complaints	Ranking of complaints from highest to lowest
		How likely tourists are to complain about some specific attributes
Level of tourist comments	List of comments	Ranking of comments from highest to lowest
		How likely tourists are to consider some attributes to be improved
Level of tourist attitudes	Mean scores	Ranking of attitude levels
	Summary questions	Impact of specific individual items on the intention to visit or revisit and recommend
Level of image	Mean scores	Ranking of image levels
	Summary questions	Impact of specific individual items on the level of overall image perceptions, intention to visit or revisit and recommend
Repeat tourists' perceptions of changes in the destination	List of positive and negative changes	Ranking of positive and negative perceptions of changes in the destination
Level of future behaviour	Intention to return and recommend to others	How likely tourists are to return and recommend
Intermediaries' perceptions of destination performance	Summary questions	Tourism suppliers' intention to promote the destination
Tourism suppliers' comments and complaints	List of comments and complaints	Ranking of comments and complaints from highest to lowest

Source: own elaboration derived from the related literature.

to monitor changes in the overall performance of the destination (internal benchmarking) and establish gaps (external benchmarking). These are explained in detail below.

Establish gaps between the destination and competitors

The traditional approach to benchmarking is that a standard should be established to close gaps for benchmarking and that customers can be a source of information for establishing performance gaps (Smith *et al.*, 1993; Bogan and English, 1994; Zairi, 1996). The percentage of repeat business or the percentage of tourists expressing a satisfaction level of '3' or '4' on a 5-point scale are examples of customer-driven performance measures that can be used to compare one service encounter with another (Coker, 1996). With reference to the potential use of gap analysis in benchmarking and its subsequent application in benchmarking tourist destinations (Bogan and English, 1994; Min and Min, 1997), mean or ranking scores can be compared with those of other destinations. Negative or positive differences are determined to be the gap between the selected destinations.

However, as emphasized in Chapter 3, the majority of customers may have experience of other destinations, and so are likely to make comparisons between facilities, attractions and service standards of other destinations (Laws, 1995). In general, 'the choice of a particular good or service is the result of a comparison of its perceived attributes with the person's set of preferences' (Fishbein and Ajzen, 1975, in Laws, 1995, p. 113). Accordingly, it is argued that potential tourists select a destination amongst alternatives and evaluate each alternative considering its potential to offer the benefits they look for (Mayo and Jarvis, 1981). As a result, in order to eliminate indecisive indications of customers' characteristics or to ensure that both sample destinations have similar types of homogeneous customers in terms of multiple visits, external benchmarking research could be carried out by developing a direct comparison questionnaire. In so doing, destinations would be able to monitor their performance levels compared with those of others by obtaining feedback from those visiting multiple destinations including the one proposed as the partner. High scores would be potential areas where the destination meets its targets, while low scores would be critical areas where the destination has to consider either raising its standards or leaving this market. The role of these two approaches in activating the proposed qualitative measures is given, to a great extent, in Chapter 8.

Establish gaps between current and past years' performance

This approach was introduced as the first example of benchmarking in the manufacturing industry (Camp, 1989). It refers to the measurement of internal performance and provides two methods to be addressed. First, once qualitative measures are calculated by transforming qualitative data into quantitative data, they should be kept recorded on an annual basis to ease the comparison process and monitor the direction of changes over a period. Findings could also be helpful for creating a database consisting of the analysis of customer feedback and how it changes. Secondly, repeat tourists can be chosen as the sample in order to learn how the destination has changed compared with their last visits, and in what respects.

The examination of the overall performance of a destination compared with previous years potentially may support the success of the destination benchmarking study in a process that aims to make a comparison with other destinations. Meanwhile, a destination might measure its annual or periodic performance level by comparing and contrasting the current results relating to tourist satisfaction and complaints with the latest results in the previous period. Since benchmarking is a continuous measurement and analysis process, the destination could gain much benefit from understanding whether any positive or negative results appear on the sustainability of a destination's performance relating to different qualitative items. This type of qualitative measurement method requires the establishment of a database where findings are accurately recorded and comparisons are made with previous months or years. This method has been put into practice by a few tourist boards in England (Thomason *et al.*, 1999a,b) and by the Department of Tourism in Mallorca (Govern Balear, 1999).

Express standard values

In this approach, authorities may express a desired level of any standard values out of a certain point scale and then benchmark against them (Balm, 1992; Hutton and Zairi, 1995). For example, the desired standard value is assigned as '5' on a 7-point scale. The areas with higher values would be regarded as above the targeted performance or at the desired level and do not need to be improved, but those with lower values would be regarded as failing to reach the target. These areas need to be improved until the desired level (standard value) is reached, e.g. '5' in this example. Alternatively, the highest scale value can be nominated as the best standard value, e.g. '7' on a 7-point scale. The objective could be set to reach that value in the desired areas by monitoring changes in perceptual performance of products and services and administering periodic surveys despite the fact that it is hardly possible to achieve a 100% performance. This approach is also a type of internal benchmarking. In its internal benchmarking programme, for instance, the London Hilton on Park Lane has identified its own standards for each department. Launching its 'Yes, We Never Say No' motto, it encourages employees to achieve these standards by providing them with awards such as the best employee of the month or bronze, silver and gold prizes.

Use of multivariate statistical tests

Multivariate statistical tests are used when there are multiple variables and a relationship between dependent and independent variables needs to be examined. It is the strength of these tests to demonstrate the most powerful factors or attributes in a multiple variance analysis. With their features offering a variety of attributes as a part of the chain to complete the tourist experiences, the overall performance of tourist destinations on the basis of several criteria could be measured with the assistance of multivariate statistical models or tests. As a contribution to the assessment of internal benchmarking of destinations, the impact of each individual destination attribute over the summary questions (overall image, overall satisfaction, overall attitude, intention to recommend or intention to visit a destination) defined as the overall performance measures could be identified by employing a series of statistical tests such as factor and multiple regression analysis. This could demonstrate the method for measuring the internal performance of the destination. The most powerful factors could be accepted as elements of competitive advantage and those that are important to customers, while the rest would be those that need to be developed or reassessed.

Respondents are asked to give an overall evaluation of their satisfaction with the service (or the destination), and also asked to rate the key components of the service process (destination attributes). The level of overall satisfaction is believed to be a function of satisfaction with each service encounter (Bitner and Hubbert, 1994). It is therefore suggested that summary questions be added to the questionnaire involving the level of overall satisfaction, and intention to repurchase (or revisit) and recommend their experiences to others (Rust *et al.*, 1996). This method has already been applied in the marketing literature as well as in the tourist satisfaction literature (Choi and Chu, 2000). The rationale for this type of application is the possibility of avoiding economic, demographic and psychographical differences between those who visit two individual destinations as the performance of each destination is evaluated with its own customers. The operationalization of this approach is explained in Chapter 8.

Quantitative measures

There are a number of criteria to assess the performance of tourist destinations on the table of competitiveness; however, this study attempts to consider only major indicators. These are the volume of tourist arrivals, the volume of repeat tourists, the volume of tourism receipts and the share of tourism receipts in Gross National Product (GNP), tourist expenditure (per person or per group) and its distribution, annual occupancy trends, and average length of overnight stays. These key quantitative indicators are explained in detail below.

Volume of tourist arrivals

As a traditional approach, the number of foreign arrivals has been used to rank all destinations (or countries) on the league table. The idea is that the higher the number of annual tourist arrivals, the higher the destination's place in the competitiveness set. The performance of a particular destination or region is also examined by evaluating the percentage changes over the total number compared with the preceding years. For instance, as a well-established and mature tourist destination, Spain is a country that plays an important role in international tourism. According to the WTO's traditional ranking style of destinations, for the first time, Spain overtook the USA in 1995 as the second most important destination after France, in terms of international tourism receipts. As of 1999, Spain has still been successful in keeping its place as the second most tourist-receiving and tourism income-generating country.

Though this method has been used by leading tourism organizations, primarily by the WTO, over many years, it has several weaknesses including the difficulty of collecting reliable data and of anticipating the future. The number of people taking vacations overall may vary from one year to another. Compared with the previous year's records, numbers tend to increase if the international economic, political and social indicators are positive. They tend to decrease if these factors are negative. Consequently, the number of arrivals at a specific destination has a possible increase if the international trend is upward, but this may not be important in order to draw a strong conclusion about the position of that destination from these figures. The proposed method in this study refers to the calculation of the percentage share of arrivals at the destination out of the actual annual international tourism demand. The findings could show how well the destination contributes to international tourism on the basis of the volume of foreign tourist arrivals. Trends in these percentage values would also indicate how the destination performs in comparison with previous records, as well as with other destinations.

Volume of repeat tourists

The benchmarking literature suggests the consideration of the percentage of repeat customers as performance measures (Kasul and Motwani, 1995; Zairi, 1996). The basic idea of this approach is that the higher the number of tourists returning to the same destination, the higher its status in the market. The way to identify repeat visits as an indicator of performance measurement is twofold: (i) the percentage of those who had made previous visits and their frequency; and (ii) the percentage of those who are likely to come back in the future. The latter has been explained as a part of qualitative measures. These findings might be interpreted overall and by the nationality of tourists compared with the destination's records for previous years as well as those of other similar destinations.

The analysis of the extent of repeat visits can lead to several benefits such as lower marketing costs, a positive image and attitude towards the destination and an intention to tell others (Fornell, 1992). However, according to one approach, a high level of repeat visits is not a panacea since it will not necessarily offer the destination a competitive advantage over similar destinations (Oppermann, 1999). In other words, repeat visits could be a problem as well as a strength. For instance, some mass tourist destinations such as the Spanish islands (the Balearic and Canary Islands) attach themselves to Plog's (1974) pyschocentric tourist typology by attracting a high proportion of repeat tourists, with their low level of income and the tendency to prefer mostly package tours, from European countries.

Volume of tourism receipts

The quality of tourists could be more important than their quantity to the success of any destination. For example, considering the expenditure level of each tourist could be more rational than considering the number of tourists in determining how tourism can provide benefits for the destination. Thus, the notion that the greater the number of tourists, the greater the net income generated by the local economy sometimes cannot be supported due to some destination- or demand-based reasons such as inflation rate, length of stay or low level of income groups (Syriopoulos and Sinclair, 1993). In that case, the volume of total tourism receipts yielded from international tourism could be an indicator of the measurement of destination competitiveness, since the more the amount of tourist spending, the higher the multiplier effect within the local community (Bull, 1995). A variety of local people and organizations benefit from a unit of tourism income due to its high multiplier effect in the economy. The President's Commission on Industrial Competitiveness in the USA defined the term competitiveness as 'the degree to which a nation can, under free and fair market conditions, produce goods and services that meet the test of international markets, while simultaneously maintaining and expanding the real income of its citizens' (cf. Kotler et al., 1993, p. 316).

According to this definition, it is clear that the local economy must gain a net benefit from international tourism activities while asking if the destination is competitive and, if it is, to what extent. Any development in a particular tourism industry is recorded as a direct contribution to the GNP. The comparison analysis on the basis of the proportion of tourism incomes within the GNP between more than two destinations will show which destination is yielding more benefits from international tourism. There are few examples in the benchmarking literature using total revenues or profits as an example of quantitative measures. Of these, Morey and Dittmann (1995) benchmarked total room revenues and gross profit of hotel businesses as an element of quantitative measures.

Level of tourist expenditure and its distribution

The volume of actual tourist expenditure is considered as a part of market segmentation variable in tourism (Pizam and Reichel, 1979). The level of tourist expenditure and its effective analysis could be an indicator of illustrating the profile of tourists visiting one destination, and the extent to which they tend to spend much more while on vacation. For instance, recent research findings show that overseas travellers whose prime travel purposes to the USA are to visit cultural attractions such as museums and national parks are likely to spend more time and money during their trips than other groups. Results of an investigation including the amount of actual tourist expenditure could help destination management decide the type of tourism product they will offer and the type of tourism demand they intend to attract. As a result, a partner could be chosen among destinations that attract both higher spending tourists and lower spending tourists in order to illustrate differences and their sources. If any destination is working with a higher volume of tourist arrivals but with less actual tourist expenditure and tourism receipts, this means that it is rapidly moving towards becoming a mass tourism destination and needs to take precautionary action (Butler, 1980).

The methodology to be chosen to understand the performance of destinations on the basis of the level and the distribution of tourist expenditure while on vacation is to calculate the average volume of spending per tourist or per group or per family (Mak *et al.*, 1977). The other method could be to categorize tourists into several groups such as lower, medium or higher spending (Pizam and Reichel, 1979). The use of these methods can be extended to include the distribution of spending for each tourism product and service, e.g. accommodation, food and beverages, transport, and so on. The distribution of tourist expenditure over the destination products and services illustrates which parts bring more revenue as well as the characteristics of tourists. It is also important to understand the demographic profiles of tourists and explore their impact on how much tourists intend to spend at any destination (Perez and Sampol, 2000).

Annual (seasonal) occupancy trends

The assessment of annual or seasonal occupancy trends as an overall destination benchmark also has a potential benefit to help to design future management strategies. Understanding seasonal fluctuations clearly will help in pricing off-peak and high-peak times in order to try and sustain a certain level of occupancy over the year, e.g. 80%. This may decrease trends for the following year(s), but may stimulate the destination to attract more tourists, as each new tourist will contribute to the accumulation of tourism receipts. The lower level of any occupancy trend, to some extent, signals that there is no need to increase the number of beds at this destination. The comparison of periodical occupancy trends either with previous years or with other destinations may demonstrate how effectively the destination(s) is using its resources and whether it needs to take further action. This type of benchmark was used for individual hotels by Morey and Dittmann (1995) in the tourism literature.

Average length of overnight stays

This type of quantitative measure could provide destinations with some advantages such as giving tourists an opportunity to have more experiences at the destination and positively influence the amount of money they spend on vacation. Findings of previous research confirmed that there was a direct relationship between the average length of overnight stays in a place and the amount of tourist expenditure (Spotts and Mahoney, 1991; Mules, 1998). The latter increases with the former, since the longer the tourists choose to stay, the more likely they are to become aware of facilities and services both where they are staying and in the surrounding area. This will widen the size of the multiplier effect of tourism revenues at the destination. The length of vacations may also reflect the attractiveness of a destination; however, a number of other important factors may also influence length of vacation, such as the availability of free time, the availability of flexible package tour deals and the level of prices.

Analysis of quantitative measures

A list of self-selected quantitative measures introduced above is shown in Table 4.2. As benchmarks for tourist destinations, these measures could be examined in particular ways, e.g. by nationality and season or by comparison with other destinations. This type of assessment helps to measure the real performance of destinations for each category on the basis of, for example, the share of tourist arrivals, the volume of repeat tourists, the level of tourist expenditure and the length of overnight stays.

To interpret the statistical data arising from the quantitative measures, Bloom (1996) proposes the use of internal and external measures. These can be used to analyse the overall performance of the tourism industry in a destination. As noted in earlier chapters, the measurement of external performance is regarded as the comparison of the tourism position of one destination with the position of a similar or competitor destination (external benchmarking). The destination outperforming the other is considered to be superior. The measurement of internal performance is examined as monitoring the tourism position of one destination based on performance targets set by the responsible authorities in their plans (internal benchmarking). This also could cover the analysis of the current position with that of previous years. For example, the consideration of the market share is mentioned as a measure of benchmarking (Mann et al., 1999a,b). Its comparison with other destinations will be an example of external measures, whereas its comparison with previous years' figures of the same destination will be an example of internal measures.

Depending upon the homogeneous or heterogeneous structure of tourism demand through a destination in terms of nationality, potential assessment subjects include the comparison of tourists from different

Table 4.2. Quantitative measures of destination performance.

Criteria of performance	Tools	Performance indicators
Volume of tourist arrivals	Statistical figures	Proportion of tourist arrivals in regional and international tourism
Volume of repeat visits	Statistical figures	Frequency of repeat tourist arrivals Proportion of repeat tourists in total tourist arrivals
Volume of tourism receipts	Statistical figures	Proportion of tourism receipts in regional and international tourism Proportion of tourism receipts in GNP
Level of tourist expenditure	Statistical figures	Amount of tourist expenditure per person or per group Distribution of tourist expenditure by categories
Annual occupancy trends	Statistical figures	Occupancy rates of accommodation establishments by year and months
Average length of overnight stays	Statistical figures	Average length of tourists' overnight stays (in nights)

Source: own elaboration derived from the related literature.

countries. A separate database could be created for each market group to carry out the assessment individually. Findings could then be compared with those of previous months or years or with those of other destinations. This may indicate how well the destination performs with each market group and illustrate differences between current and past figures and between high and low seasons, and provide a background to speculate on the reasons for any differences. This type of analysis has been used by benchmarking literature to monitor changes in operational performance from one year to another (Zairi, 1998). If historical data are included in the database, it can also potentially be used to predict future trends by using a series of statistical tools such as time series or regression models (Hair *et al.*, 1995).

Alternatively, referring to the principles of internal benchmarking, as applied by many national planning organizations, overall standard target values could be designated and all the efforts could be aggregated to reach the desired performance level at the end of the year, e.g. an estimated number of tourist arrivals or a certain amount of tourism revenue expected either in the following year or in the next 5 years as a part of short-term planning and their classification into first-time and repeat tourists. When the estimated target values have reached or exceeded the actual values, these will be credited as improvements. In spite of its benefits for setting objectives and measuring the internal self-assessment performance, this method needs to be assessed cautiously because of the possible tendency to identify the estimated future performance value at a lower or much higher level.

Overall, developments in hardware and software computer systems have facilitated the creation, distribution, analysis and storage of a large amount of data. This brings several benefits for destination benchmarking: the analysis of data by using either basic or advanced statistical tools and storage of data on the database to be used in the long term. The findings might be interpreted separately for each tourism supplier and tourist group from different countries of origin and from different market segments, taking into account age, income, education and number of repeat visits, where possible. Findings could be analysed further and kept on record by creating two categories such as low and high seasons. Comparison between low and high seasons would also be a good benchmark for the destination itself to observe changes and estimate their potential reasons. This research will not attempt to test this approach because it requires carrying out practical and continuous procedures.

An overview of quantitative measures used for a benchmarking study between Mallorca and Turkey is shown in Table 4.3. Based on outputs, these findings are crucial in a destination benchmarking investigation. The comparative assessment of quantitative measures could pinpoint whether the sample destinations have the same structure of tourism development and, if not, where they differ. These types of measures and their assessment, from the perspective of internal or external performance, can be used in destination benchmarking in two ways. The first is the stage before benchmarking. The second is the stage where benchmarking has been completed and improvements are expected.

First, as in individual organizations, destination managers need to gather data to assess the level of their internal or external performance and monitor changes in it periodically. Using either internal or external benchmarking, it is possible for destination managers to evaluate their performance levels and progress recorded compared with the indicators of international tourism and also against other destinations. This process may be helpful in deciding whether the destination needs to be involved in any kind of benchmarking exercise at a broader level. If so, policymakers, destination managers and representatives of tourism businesses may need to collaborate to explore the factors influencing the development of tourism in other countries and what types of problems they are still experiencing or have experienced in the past. The investigation of methods or strategies used to eliminate these problems could also be worth carrying out. For instance, even though Mallorca is a mature mass tourism destination, which particularly attracts tourists in the summer season, it is worthwhile

Table 4.3. Overview of quantitative measures.

Measures	Internal performance		External performance
	Mallorca	Turkey	
Accommodation stock	Largely dominated by small- and medium-scale hotels and apartments. Needs to be upgraded.	As it is a very young destination, there has been a remarkable increase over the last 15 years, especially in large-scale hotels and holiday villages.	There is a greater proportion of small- and medium-scale establishments in Mallorca than in Turkey. Turkey has slightly more rooms than Mallorca.
Tourist arrivals	There has been an increase despite several fluctuations.	Recorded a stable increase.	Mallorca is unable to sustain its proportion in Mediterranean and international tourism. Turkey is progressing well by increasing its proportion in the same figures.
Tourist arrivals by nationality	Heavily dependent on two specific markets, Great Britain and Germany.	Heavily dependent on German and eastern European markets.	As for comparison between Mallorca and Turkey, the former attracts mainly European tourists as the latter focuses on Organisation for Economic Co-operation and Development and eastern European markets.
Length of stay	Average length of stay is 11.8 days. This figure has decreased since 1990.	Average length of stay is 3.56 days. There has been a slight increase since 1990.	Mallorca has a much longer period of stay in general. Tourists from Germany, the UK, France and Italy stay much longer in Mallorca.
Tourist arrivals by months	Tourism demand is highly seasonal, concentrating in peak summer months.	Tourism demand is highly seasonal, concentrating in peak summer months.	As for comparison between Mallorca and Turkey, both have the seasonality problem
Tourism receipts	The contribution of tourism receipts to the national economy is significantly increasing.	The contribution of tourism receipts to the national economy is gradually increasing.	Mallorca has had an unstable record in the proportion of Mediterranean and international tourism. Turkey's proportion in Mediterranean and international tourism is significantly increasing. Compared with those in Turkey, tourism receipts in Mallorca make a massive contribution to the economy.

examining how it is progressing in transforming itself from a summer to a winter destination. This type of data assessment could then be helpful for establishing local or national tourism policies, laws and regulations to bring the tourism industry up to the desired level. However, due to economic and geographical differences, it is only possible to consider the volume of tourist arrivals by nationality, months and length of stay, as quantitative measures for a direct comparison between peer destinations.

Secondly, improvements in qualitative measures are expected to stimulate developments in the success of quantitative measures (see Fig. 4.1). Although the purpose of benchmarking is to sustain quality improvement, the expected result is to enable an increase in outcome or output measures. Quantitative measures seem to be useful in assessing the success of the implementation of earlier benchmarking findings that are based upon qualitative measures, such as tourist satisfaction, if a proper destination benchmarking study is conducted and is given time to obtain the essential feedback in return. These quantitative measures may be influenced by changes in products or markets depending upon destination positioning studies or improvements in the overall performance of the destination as an impact of increase in satisfaction or positive word-of-mouth recommendation. If benchmarking is applied to increase tourist arrivals or revenues and widen its multiplier effect in low season, the recorded progress in input measures must be directly reflected by outcome measures sooner or later. This must be a function of the review stage in benchmarking as sufficient time is needed to implement findings and regularly monitor its impact. When tourists are satisfied, they tend to spend more, recommend their holidays or want to return. This probably increases the number of tourists in the following years and may also increase the total income from tourism. After implementing good practices and taking action for improvement, if there is still no sufficient development in outcomes (e.g. tourist arrivals,

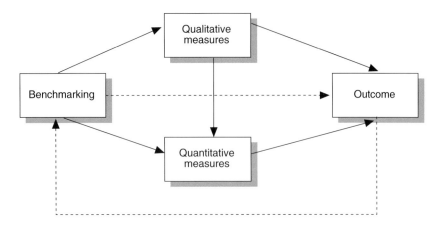

Fig. 4.1. Role of qualitative and quantitative measures.

image or tourism income), this means that the benchmarking project has failed and a new one might be needed.

As far as quantitative measures are concerned, changes in the performance of destinations on the basis of the volume of tourist arrivals and their distribution by nationality and at different times of the year could be observed. This enables seasonality and changes in the distribution of markets to be benchmarked. These historical records provide a good opportunity to evaluate how a specific destination performs over time and to monitor whether improvements in qualitative measures are effective in outcome (quantitative measures) since benchmarking aims at continuous improvement in an operation.

The volume of tourist arrivals is interpreted by various criteria such as years, months, nationality and overnight stays as internal performance measures, and its share in Mediterranean and international tourism as external performance measures. The volume of tourism receipts is analysed as its share in GNP and export earnings as internal performance measures, and as its share of Mediterranean and international tourism as external performance measures. As far as comparison between qualitative and quantitative measures is concerned, quantitative measures such as occupancy rates, number of tourist arrivals, average length of stay, level of repeat visits and the level of tourist expenditure could be easier to measure, to evaluate the performance of the destination and find reliable metrics in relation to comparable destinations. It is known that such measures consist of scales such as interval and ratio, which have a fixed origin or zero point. Assume that one tourist spent £1000 and another only half as much, i.e. £500. Such scores are open to comparison analysis, e.g. comparing the volume of tourism receipts with previous years or with total international tourism figures. Thus, there is no practical difficulty in employing quantitative measures as tools for benchmarking destinations.

Unlike the amount of tourism income and the total number of tourist arrivals, some other proposed quantitative measures such as the examination of the distribution of tourist arrivals by nationalities and by months, and the average length of stay and its distribution by nationalities could be considered as examples of both internal and external benchmarking. Comparison with previous years' figures indicates areas where changes are observed in the market structure (internal benchmarking). For example, a significant increase has been observed in the proportion of those from eastern Europe and the former Soviet states visiting Turkey over recent years. In contrast, there has still been an increase in the proportion of British and German tourists in Spain. In the light of this statement, comparison between peer destinations could reveal in which markets the host and the partner are more attractive and the periods of the year in which tourism is concentrated (external benchmarking).

A number of points need to be considered when creating measures, e.g. making measures easy to control and thinking in a broader perspective

(Hauser and Katz, 1998). When incorporating this idea into the quantitative performance measurement of tourist destinations, limiting the comparison of tourist arrivals only to previous years would be too narrow a choice. Taking the number of tourist arrivals or the value of tourism receipts of a country and comparing them with total international tourism statistics may give a clearer picture of a destination. This type of analysis shows the significance of tourism revenues in the national economy as a measure of internal performance, and in Mediterranean and international tourism as a measure of external performance. It is a weak criterion to consider that the national tourism industry is improving to some extent or that the national economy makes a good profit from the tourism industry once an increase is observed in terms of the number of tourist arrivals or the total income from tourism compared with previous years. It is possible either that international tourism is developing as a whole or that the national economy itself is growing.

Findings of past studies confirmed that as one destination attracts a higher number of repeat tourists, another declines (Kozak, 2000). The consideration of the number of repeat tourists as a criterion could show reasons why repeat tourists are likely to come back or the extent to which the destination is attractive to a particular market group. Is it an attractive destination meeting customers' expectations? Or are there any other reasons reflecting either destinations' or customers' characteristics? The above-referenced study confirmed that familiarity and satisfaction are amongst the primary factors attracting repeat tourists to Mallorca.

In terms of measuring the contribution of tourist expenditure to the local economy in total and its distribution into several subcategories, there are differences between the two destinations. For instance, those in Turkey spent more on clothes than those in Mallorca, while those in Mallorca spent more on daily tours and car hire services than those in Turkey. This part of destination benchmarking research has great potential for further development because the investigation of differences in the amount or the proportion of tourist expenditures on various categories provides answers to a number of questions, e.g. why do those in one destination spend more on one category than those in another destination?

Strengths and Weaknesses of Destination Measures

Based upon the type of measures used and the results obtained in the past study (Kozak, 2000), Fig. 4.1 presents the role of qualitative and quantitative measures in destination benchmarking. Benchmarking is a cumulative assessment of the overall destination performance as one measure is strongly related to another. Along with the findings of past research (Edgett and Snow, 1996; Kozak, 2000), this study suggests that the use of multiple measures is more effective than that of single measures for analysing indepth the performance of destinations. The assessment of performance on the basis of several measures can help to decide whether there is a need to conduct any type of benchmarking. For instance, the assessment of motivations as qualitative measures is vital because further action can be taken by looking into what tourists consider important in visiting a destination, and other destinations can be selected on the basis of the examination of similarities or differences in terms of demand and supply.

The number of tourist arrivals evaluates if there is any difference compared with past years and shows the proportion of tourist arrivals at a destination out of international tourist arrivals. The number of repeat tourists is the indicator of the proportion of repeat tourists and how frequent they are. The amount of tourism receipts refers to the proportion of national tourism revenues gained from international tourism and GNP. Developments are observed on the basis of comparison with the indicators of past years. The level of expenditure helps to illustrate the profile of tourists visiting the destination and the factors affecting their total expenditure. The length of stays helps to examine the profile of tourists in terms of the length of their stay at the destination and if there is any difference in the amount of expenditure between tourists in different categories of length of stay.

The assessment of motivations indicates why a specific destination is chosen for a holiday and whether there are any differences between destinations on the basis of these factors. The level of tourist satisfaction is helpful to indicate the performance of destinations or their specific elements from actual tourists' own experiences and which one destination is likely to perform better than others. The analysis of tourist complaints and comments is useful to identify the type of attributes with which customers expect improvement, with or without comparison with other destinations. Feedback received from repeat tourists is used to evaluate how the destination has performed compared with past years and in what respects. The level of intention to come back or recommend is a measure to indicate how likely tourists are to revisit and recommend the destination in the future, based on the level of their satisfaction with it.

In addition to the measurement of tourist satisfaction, the assessment of tourist complaints and comments also works fairly well in indicating major areas where both destinations need to consider improvements, e.g. level of prices and tourism development in Mallorca; and harassment, poor signposting and poor air-conditioning in Turkey. These are the areas tourists mentioned as important to their holidays but which are lacking or getting worse. These findings were obtained from tourists' own experiences not only in the sample destination but also in other self-selected destinations; therefore, the level of comments or complaints could be effective measures to learn about a destination's performance in the international market and whether it is essential to carry out benchmarking.

As widely emphasized in the literature (Deming, 1982; Peters, 1994; Zairi, 1996), some other criteria such as customer satisfaction or customer feedback may be more difficult to measure and set standard values, but play a pivotal role not only in identifying the current performance but also in designing future performance and highlighting where there is a need for further improvement. According to customers, the performance level of destinations is based on mostly qualitative measures, e.g. the extent to which it provides a satisfactory service or has a favourable image in the market (Morrison, 1989; Um and Crompton, 1990). These measures may then be used to make a comparison between destinations to determine which one performs in any particular area better than others. The outcome of this assessment could have an effect on their future behaviour of returning or recommending. Customers may not be interested in some aspects of the quantitative performance of destinations such as the number of tourists visiting per annum, the amount of tourism income received or the number of hotels or restaurants. These are the areas that destination authorities are responsible for improving in both quantity and quality. Such quantitative performance of destinations is measured using a time frame of several years depending upon the availability of data.

As for the limitations of using such measures in destination benchmarking, the link between qualitative and quantitative measures cannot be established in this study. Moreover, as briefly mentioned in this chapter, there could be several external factors influencing the success of the tourism industry in a destination in either the short or the long term. As they are uncontrollable and unpredictable, this study excludes the possible impacts of factors such as distance and risk and the possibility of emerging alternative destinations. Domestic or international social and political unrest are other issues that need to be considered within the perceived risk of tourist destinations. For instance, the existence of unrest in some countries such as Romania, the former Yugoslavia, Tunisia and Egypt in recent years has negatively affected their trends in the development of tourism activities.

In summary, all these measures are able to demonstrate both similarities and differences not only between the sample tourist groups but also between the sample destinations. It is suggested further that some forms of quantitative measures (e.g. tourist arrivals, tourism revenues and level of prices) and some 'soft' areas relating to qualitative measures (e.g. hospitality or attitude, language communication, visa and passport control services) would not be rational for external benchmarking due to economic, political, geographical and cultural reasons, although they are measurable, comparable and compatible. Perhaps this could provide a piece of evidence to partially support Zairi's (1994) statement suggesting that benchmarking is a method to point out whether the organization (or the destination) is competitive rather than to improve its performance based on the information obtained from others.

Summary

This chapter has provided the basis of what kind of measures can be developed and how they can be applied to tourist destinations from the perspective of internal and external benchmarking. The chapter has also included a short discussion about how tourism authorities can use such data as performance indicators of a destination benchmarking exercise. The proposed measures in this study, referring to the assessment of both internal and external performance of tourist destinations, are believed to foster the overall performance of destinations by identifying their own performance, gaps with others and competitive positions. The list of measures can be increased in terms of both number and methods. Having completed the discussion of measures of destination performance and their potential contribution to the design of an effective destination benchmarking study, the next chapter begins with an introduction to the procedure of internal destination benchmarking.

Internal Destination Benchmarking

5

Introduction

Based upon the model of destination benchmarking presented in Chapter 3, this chapter aims to extend the context of information relating to the practice of internal benchmarking by presenting methods on what and how to benchmark. This part is devoted to discussion of the practical procedures of internal destination benchmarking and the potential methods that can be used to collect and analyse data and present the benchmarking findings, in comparison with earlier studies in the field of benchmarking. This chapter discusses in detail the content of the benchmarking model basically related to the development of destination benchmarking. The chapter ends with an overview of the strengths and weaknesses of internal destination benchmarking.

Practices of Internal Destination Benchmarking

The overview of the literature refers to the existence of two mainstream approaches to benchmarking: internal and external. Those in the first category emphasize the importance of internal benchmarking due to the difficulty of providing access to other organizations, adopting the findings to each specific culture and also differences in objectives, and management and marketing styles between organizations. Furthermore, there appears to be no problem in generating data and implementing the findings in internal benchmarking (e.g. Bendell *et al.*, 1993; Campbell, 1999). Those in the second category address the issue that benchmarking is a valuable method for those who tend to transfer successful models of practice resulting in superior performance elsewhere in the industry. According to this group, the rationale of external benchmarking stems from the idea that it is necessary to discover new methods, products or services in order to be competitive in the international market (e.g. Camp, 1989; Zairi, 1992).

The literature has consensus on the fact that the benchmarking process begins in the host organization in order to specify areas that need to be measured (internal benchmarking), regardless of the application of any kind of benchmarking (Balm, 1992; Karlof and Ostblom, 1993). Internal benchmarking is an approach that includes the collection of data on one's own performance and its assessment on the basis of several criteria such as objectives or improvements compared with past years (McNair and Leibfried, 1992; Cross and Leonard, 1994). Goals set for taking action come out of sharing opinions between departments in the same organization (Breiter and Kline, 1995). The rationale for choosing to apply this approach is the difficulty of activating external benchmarking due to cultural and managerial differences and access to external data. Reflecting on this introduction, internal destination benchmarking refers to a monitoring process of the performance objectives released by authorities prior to commencing the benchmarking study and then taking action. Objectives could be the assessment of percentage changes in quantitative performance variables and changes in mean scores of qualitative variables, e.g. percentage change in economic variables of tourism such as the level of income, the number of tourists and the occupancy rate, as well as customer perceptions, satisfaction and complaints, in comparison with previous periods. These data may be valuable in enabling destination managers to review their overall performance each year or season and to decide whether they need to get involved in external benchmarking. If so, this information could be used as baseline data for external benchmarking with other destinations (Weller, 1996).

Proposed Model of Internal Destination Benchmarking

As it is the key issue in benchmarking, the performance measurement can show the areas that management should focus on as a starting point of internal benchmarking. In particular, if there is any particular area that needs to be improved, then its performance should be measured. It is advised that the planning for performance measurement should begin with setting clear objectives. Organizations generally either have financial, social, or mixed financial and social objectives. In profit-seeking organizations, the primary objective is to yield better financial results. Likewise, tourist destinations also intend to take a greater part in the competitiveness set by increasing their market shares in the number of tourist arrivals and the amount of tourism receipts. Due to cultural diversity among nations, the social objectives remain very weak in the tourism industry. Hauser and Katz (1998) suggest that performance metrics such as market share, sales and customer satisfaction let management learn about where they are at the moment and will (can) be in the future. Some metrics could be easier to measure, but are important to the success of destinations. For example, the number of arrivals at a destination increases as the total number of international tourists also increases. In this case, the most important measurement criteria must include the measurement of percentage changes in the number of tourists visiting the destination out of the total international active tourism demand. Some others such as customer satisfaction or customer feedback may be more difficult to measure and set standard values, but play a pivotal role in designing future performance.

Next, the travel and tourism industry has intangible, heterogeneous and inseparable features and a dynamic structure. It is sensitive to political, social, environmental and technological changes. Tourist destinations are made up of and controlled by a variety of individual organizations and destination stakeholders. Although desired metrics (standards) are to a large extent possible in the application of manufacturing benchmarking, it seems difficult to identify standard metrics in the service industry. It is not even clear to what extent customers should be regarded as being satisfied or dissatisfied with a destination. Therefore, the best method may include measuring the strength of each attribute over some dependent variables such as the level of overall tourist satisfaction, or intention to come back and recommend it to others. The strongest areas would be the strengths and the lowest the weaknesses. The rest would be opportunities and threats for the future. In so doing, it will be the main feature of internal destination benchmarking to measure the overall performance of each destination internally rather than making comparisons with standard measures that have yet to be identified.

Tourism is a dynamic industry making a positive contribution to the development of towns and cities and other tourism destinations and the well-being of their local residents. Destination benchmarking may be vital in providing better quality facilities and services and increasing inputs through tourism activities in terms of supply. The concept of destination benchmarking in terms of supply aims to provide international tourist destinations with an opportunity to increase their economic prosperity, protect environmental resources, preserve cultural values and increase the local residents' quality of life. In terms of demand, it aims to ensure that a high level of tourist satisfaction and loyalty to the destination is maintained by offering a high standard of facilities and services to meet customers' needs and expectations. This is also expected to lead to an increased intention of word-of-mouth recommendation through an improved image in the future. To achieve its aims, a general approach to the proposed benchmarking model, which is specifically applicable to international tourist destinations, was initially provided in Chapter 3. Chapter 4 develops this by focusing on internal and external types of benchmarking. This chapter aims to deliver a more focused structure to the model by providing brief information about methods and tools for use in its operationalization. The model is shown in

Fig. 5.1. The following section provides detailed information about the practical application of the proposed model of internal benchmarking for tourist destinations.

Measuring the internal performance

Reflection on the literature review suggests that any kind of benchmarking begins by measuring one's own performance in order to specify areas that need to be benchmarked (Zairi, 1992; Karlof and Ostblom, 1993), with each destination needing to put into order their own priorities. It is proposed that both internal and external benchmarking help to identify these priorities. A complete internal benchmarking report should include information on what measures have been benchmarked, which methods were used to collect and compare data, where gaps appeared and the potential reasons for them, what has been learnt during the study, how this helps to improve standards, what methods need to be applied in practice and, finally, whether these findings signal the necessity of undertaking an external benchmarking exercise. The reason is that internal benchmarking provides a number of benefits for those who are involved in the process. For example, areas where problems seem to appear could be identified and, if possible, improved without going outside. In doing so, a baseline for comparison with others can be established. The application of internal benchmarking also indicates if the destination authorities need to go outside in order to observe what and how others are doing.

Collecting the data

In the data collection stage, several primary and secondary research methods are identified and the most appropriate method is selected. Included in

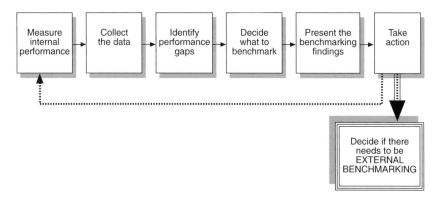

Fig. 5.1. The proposed model of internal destination benchmarking.

these methods are telephone surveys, questionnaire surveys, site visits and sources of statistical records (Watson, 1993; Bogan and English, 1994). The literature refers to the collection of two types of data in a benchmarking project, namely internal and external data (e.g. McNair and Leibfried, 1992). Using these as the background information in destination benchmarking, the former refers to the allocation of primary data concerning the performance of the sample destination. The internal data are kept to use for internal benchmarking. They can be distributed to other destinations when external or generic benchmarking is applied. The latter deals with the allocation of both primary and secondary sources of data relating to the factors affecting other destinations' overall performance in particular and the tourism industry in general to carry out the comparison procedure (gap analysis). When using any of these methods, destination managers need to identify the critical processes or activities to achieve a successful result. It is possible to extend the context of the data collection stage to include not only customers but also tourism suppliers and retailers, such as tour operators and travel agents, which promote destinations by organizing and selling tours.

Identifying performance gaps

The gap analysis not only includes a comparison of research between two destinations but also illustrates gaps between what a particular destination was expecting and what it is really achieving and between levels of its current and past performance. Thus, this approach requires the benchmarking of each destination on an individual basis. Various methods can be used to evaluate the potential changes in a destination's current performance. First, the highest and the lowest scores for each qualitative measure are identified. Attributes with the lowest scores need improvement. Secondly, repeat tourists might be chosen as the sample in order to learn how the destination has changed compared with their previous visits and in what respects (as an example for this approach, Box 5.1 summarizes the potential benchmark elements to which customers give priority and which therefore should be taken into account). Next, data on quantitative measures are assessed to examine changes over the years. Annual reports may help to understand how the destination performs compared with its previous performance. The findings should indicate where the destination has problems and whether these can be eliminated using internal resources rather than external ones.

The findings of the proposed model, as a type of internal benchmarking, could make a contribution to exploring and understanding a destination's performance without comparing it with other destinations (Kozak, 2000). In comparison with the earlier benchmarking studies, although there is no difference for measuring the internal performance of destinations when using quantitative measures, it differs when using qualitative

---

Box 5.1. Good practices of internal benchmarking for airport management.

Provide sufficient dining facilities for passengers
Provide sufficient facilities for parents with children
Provide sufficient facilities for disabled people
Provide sufficient WC facilities
Train check-in and check-out staff
Train police and immigration officers
Use several languages for signposting and announcements
Provide enough screens displaying arrival and departure of flights and their details
Locate information desks in places where they easily can be seen and reached

---

measures. As quantitative measures are metric values, they can be compared with the indicators of previous years (Zairi, 1998). This indicates whether there has been any improvement. However, the most common benchmarking approach is relatively simple when analysing qualitative measures. It reports only mean scores for each item on both perceptions of two organizations or destinations (Breiter and Kline, 1995; Edgett and Snow, 1996). Conclusions are drawn by simply comparing the two sets of mean scores and their rankings (gap analysis).

The model in this book differs from those proposed by earlier research projects, which claimed just to establish gaps in numeric values between the two organizations, but not to indicate if customers would be likely to return (Thomason *et al.*, 1999a). The analysis of intention to recommend and revisit is likely to show the strongest as well as the weakest attributes in a destination; in other words, the attributes to which attention should be paid as a part of an internal benchmarking study. This study therefore proposes that internal qualitative measurement of tourist destinations needs to consider how outcomes would influence the overall satisfaction and future intention of such destinations' own customers. This implication also applies to building a theoretical structure for organization benchmarking. One major criticism of benchmarking is that it avoids the creative thinking of decision makers (McNair and Leibfried, 1992). This limitation could be overcome by focusing on the internal performance of destinations based on the findings of qualitative measures and their assessment with advanced research tools or content analysis identified in this study.

Deciding what to benchmark

The main purpose of internal destination benchmarking is to improve the performance of tourist destinations by identifying their own strengths and weaknesses on the basis of the feedback obtained from travellers and the local population. From the research findings, it appears that internal benchmarking may be used as an alternative method to external benchmarking. In today's multi-functional and multi-cultural world, some destinations may have their own cultural, economical and political characteristics, which have limited application to transfer to others or cannot easily be revised by looking at others, e.g. hospitality, hassle, low currency exchange values, and tourist and visa regulations in Turkey. As the findings of past research on destination benchmarking suggest, these indicators may be measurable and compatible, but not comparable for use in external benchmarking (Kozak, 2000). In deciding which elements to benchmark, internal benchmarking suggests three methods.

First, the performance levels of each benchmark based upon the selected measure can be ranked from the highest to the lowest values. Those with the lowest scores or lower than the expected score can be chosen as the potential areas for improvement. This also applies to the assessment of the relationship between individual measures and the level of overall satisfaction and the intention of repeat business and word-of-mouth recommendation by performing regression analysis for qualitative measures. As this study demonstrates, statistical methods such as factor and regression analysis can be efficient tools in identifying the strongest and the weakest destination attributes influencing the level of overall satisfaction and respondents' future intentions. For instance, hospitality and prices (in Turkey) and hygiene and cleanliness (in Mallorca) came out as the strengths of the sample destinations, and 'hassle' as the main problem (in Turkey).

Secondly, the comparison of the current performance with that of past years on tourist satisfaction and expenses may be another dimension for internal benchmarking. The examination of the overall performance of a destination compared with previous years may potentially support the success of the destination benchmarking study in a process that aims to make a comparison with other destinations. Meanwhile, a destination might measure its annual or periodic performance level by comparing and contrasting the current results relating to tourist satisfaction and complaints with the results in the previous period. The areas with lower scores will indicate where an internal benchmarking study is needed. As benchmarking is a continuous measurement and analysis process, it could be of benefit to understand any positive or negative results on the sustainability of a destination's performance relating to different qualitative items. This type of qualitative measurement requires the establishment of a database where findings are accurately recorded and comparisons are made with previous months or years. In addition to comparison with previous years, repeat customers' perceptions of changes in the performance of organizations could be regarded as an important internal benchmark.

Next, some of the comments made by customers are valuable for undertaking internal benchmarking, such as what and how to improve, e.g.

level of prices and tourism development in Mallorca, and harassment, poor signposting and poor air-conditioning in Turkey. As a response to the hassle problem in general and the long queues at the destination airport, visitors in Turkey state that they want to make their own decisions about where to shop and they should be allowed to pay for their visas before arrival. Those in Mallorca are more concerned about overdevelopment and segmentation. They want the local culture and environment to be protected and different resorts to be provided for different market segments. These are the areas tourists mentioned as important to their holidays but which are lacking or getting worse. These findings are obtained from tourists' own experiences not only in the sample destination but also in other self-selected destinations; therefore, the level of comments or complaints could be effective measures to learn about a destination's performance in the international market and whether it is essential to carry out benchmarking studies.

Presenting the benchmarking findings

Once the assessment of changes in one's own performance levels is completed, there is a need to assess how big the problem is and how ambitious the goals are. It will not be necessary to take an external benchmarking approach if the destination itself can provide solutions for overcoming the problem and is able to reach its goals. However, it is surely necessary and must be encouraging to review other holiday destinations if the destination management is interested in being open to external ideas and practices and wants to take further steps in international tourism.

Taking action

In taking action following the completion of the main stage of internal benchmarking, implementation of results is limited to feedback obtained through internal data (e.g. customers' opinions and comments) and internal communication (e.g. comments and opinions of the local people involved in tourism). Once the strategies are proposed and are given support, implementation is turned into practice. By using internal benchmarking, environmental sources, human resources management, collaboration management and market segmentation may be improved.

Previous benchmarking studies had paid insufficient attention to the assessment of repeat customers' opinions while attempting to measure the perceived changes in the performance of destinations when compared with previous visits. As an element of internal benchmarking, destinations could focus their efforts on gaining feedback from repeat tourists with respect to changes within the destination itself. This study proposes that the repeat tourists' opinions about the developments in the facilities and services of destinations would be worth obtaining for destination benchmarking to maintain continuous progress (see Box 5.2). Improvements to the attractions, facilities and services at the destination could stimulate further repeat visits as well as future potential tourists, but any perceived negative trends could prevent the destination from becoming more competitive. However, as previously described, the perspective of first-time tourists is also important due to the importance of word-of-mouth communication.

Giving an example from the findings of an internal benchmarking study, the level of facilities and services at the destination airport and language communication in German were found to be the attributes needing improvement in Turkey. As both benchmarking studies are consistent,

---

Box 5.2. Repeat tourists' perceptions of Turkey and Mallorca. Source: Kozak (2000).

Data were collected by administering an open-ended questionnaire in order to consider the repeat tourists' perceptions of changes with respect to the performance of sample destinations by examining under two categories such as positive (or better) and negative (worse). Respondents were asked to indicate in which respects they had noticed any significant differences in comparison with their previous holidays. The attributes that were found to be better and worse than previous years were then ranked on the basis of percentage scores. No statistical test was applied because data were evaluated within a single destination (internal benchmarking). About two-thirds of the sample population of British tourists had at least one previous experience in Mallorca (67%), whereas one-third of those travelling to Turkey had at least one previous experience in Turkey (36.7%).

According to their perceptions, airport facilities and services, road and traffic conditions and cleanliness were the three most important attributes that were believed to have been improved in both Mallorca and Turkey, but with a higher percentage in favour of Mallorca. Such destination attributes as people, accommodation facilities, shopping and other facilities, language communication, service, catering for families, exchange rates, food, value for money, beaches, facilities on beaches, air-conditioning, water supply quality, safety and nightlife/entertainment were amongst others mentioned. Albeit a very small sample, these are potential benchmark elements to which customers give priority and therefore should be taken into account. As far as tourist perceptions of negative changes in Turkey are concerned, overcommercialization and its subsequent results such as busy atmosphere, overdevelopment and an increase in the number of buildings were the most significant problems that need to be taken into consideration. It is clear that these are the direct consequences of attempts to become a mass tourist destination. Those with smaller observation values do not seem to be creating any problem at the moment, but attention should be paid to improve them before the number rises.

it is clear that these attributes need to be improved through benchmarking. Taking the destination airport in Turkey on board for further examination, observations show that it does not meet the customers' needs as it is a small airport and check-in and check-out services can sometimes be very slow. If internal benchmarking research is conducted, the airport management could take the necessary action by obtaining feedback through its staff members and passengers. There might be no need to visit another destination airport to monitor what they have achieved in this matter. One possible method could be softening the formal regulations to ease the arrival and departure of those foreign tourists visiting the destination (see Box 5.1 for further examples). Alternatively, if the feedback from tourists is alarm that the destination is becoming overcommercialized or losing its cultural charm, then it might need to return to its normal life. One may see some examples of the stated problems in Table 5.1 and possible solutions to eliminate them by undertaking an internal benchmarking study.

The analysis of results derived from internal benchmarking investigation might help to identify gaps, determine strengths and weaknesses of destinations, and decide which attributes are to be investigated further. The action stage might also help to make future projections and recommendations. An action plan containing future goals and recommendations might consist of how to keep up strengths and minimize weaknesses and threats in order to cope with the new applications and developments. Depending on the outcome, destination managers may wish to change their marketing policies or market segments. To implement the benchmarking results, destination managers might make their recommendations to local authorities,

Table 5.1. Examples of destination-based complaints and solutions.

Complaint	Solutions
Overcrowding	Limit visitor access
	Expand carrying capacity
	Increase availability of public transport
Overdevelopment	Apply land use planning
	Upgrade existing facilities
	Disperse visitors to other resorts and attractions
Litter	Conduct awareness campaign
	Establish regulations
	Provide litter containers
	Introduce awards/rewards
Airport noise	Consider changing take-off and landing patterns
	Establish land use controls near airports
Noise pollution	Conduct awareness campaign
	Establish regulations
	Limit visitor access

local tourist associations and businesses, local residents, and the national tourism policy makers, e.g. the Ministry of Tourism.

Strengths and Weaknesses of Internal Destination Benchmarking

With regard to the strengths of internal benchmarking, it provides the ability to deal with partners who share a common language, culture and systems, having easy access to data, obtaining internal feedback, making people aware of the benchmarking study and giving a baseline for future comparisons (Breiter and Kline, 1995). As a result, the outcomes of an internal benchmarking can be presented quickly, and an in-depth analysis of one's own destination makes it easier to collect data about the potential partner and understand its performance in a short time. Moreover, internal benchmarking helps to find the methods relevant to a particular culture and practices and build up local strategies on the basis of the characteristics of the managerial and social culture and specific objectives. There is no need to spend time in collecting data from others and observing their performance levels.

In a similar way, conducting an internal benchmarking could bring the following benefits for destination authorities: identifying the factor most crucial to the success of a destination, the type of products or services provided to customers, attributes leading to customer satisfaction, attributes causing problems and those with an opportunity for improvement. A possible way of evaluating a destination's current performance could be to look at previous years' records. Previous annual reports such as number or contents of customer complaints, rate of repeat business, occupancy rates and the amount of tourist expenses may help destination management understand if the destination performs better or worse than its preceding years or its standards. Data on both qualitative and quantitative measures need to be gathered and kept as annual records in order to achieve successful results in this kind of self-assessment performance measurement.

On the other hand, as to its limitations and weaknesses, internal benchmarking seems to be contrary to the purpose of benchmarking, which basically requires looking at others and obtaining information about new practices. There are no external data for comparison and no comparable practices to use as examples when carrying out an internal benchmarking process. In the increasingly competitive world of tourism, it may be a mistake to exclude outside observation. If so, it might be unreasonable to expect a destination to reach the level it aims to achieve in international competition. It is claimed that this type of benchmarking study is time-consuming because competitors could be busy with increasing their market share while the sample organization/destination is busy with measuring its internal performance (Cook, 1995). A summary is provided in Table 5.2.

Table 5.2. Strengths and weaknesses of internal destination benchmarking.

No.	Strengths	Weaknesses	When appropriate to use
1	Share common language, culture and system	There are no external data for comparison and comparable practices to use as examples	Several units in the same destination exemplify good practice
2	Having easy access to the data	Competitors could be busy increasing their market share while the sample destination is busy measuring its internal performance	Time and resources are limited
3	Easy to implement the findings		The tourist authority has no experience in applying benchmarking
4	Making people aware of the benchmarking study		Information and data exchange with external organizations may be undesirable
5	Giving a baseline for future comparisons		

Summary

This chapter has addressed the application of internal benchmarking in destinations. The main purpose of internal benchmarking is to improve the performance of tourism businesses or tourist destinations by identifying their own strengths and weaknesses on the basis of the feedback obtained from visitors and the local residents. The literature has consensus on the fact that the benchmarking process begins in the host organization in order to specify areas that need to be measured (internal benchmarking), regardless of the application of any kind of benchmarking. The reason is that internal benchmarking provides a number of benefits for those who are involved in the process. For example, areas where problems seem to appear could be identified and, if possible, improved without going outside. In doing so, a baseline for comparison with others can be established. The application of internal benchmarking also indicates if the destination management needs to go outside in order to observe what and how others are doing. In line with this, the following chapter presents the concept of external destination benchmarking and examines how to expand it by presenting methods on what, how and who to benchmark.

External Destination Benchmarking

6

Introduction

The necessity of developing an external destination benchmarking approach emerges from the fierce competition among international tourist destinations and rapid changes in customer needs, wants and expectations. It seems obvious that destinations need to benchmark their facilities and service levels against those of their counterparts. In conducting external benchmarking, current performance levels in terms of the competition are measured. Benchmarking can enable a destination to learn from others' successes as well as to evaluate mistakes. Therefore, based upon the model of destination benchmarking presented in Chapter 3, this chapter aims to extend the context of information relating to the practice of external benchmarking by presenting methods on what, how and who to benchmark. The chapter also presents brief information on the strengths and weaknesses of this form of benchmarking.

Practices of External Destination Benchmarking

External benchmarking is a management technique that initially identifies performance gaps with respect to any production or consumption part of the organization and then presents methods to close the gap. The main objective is to seek answers to such questions as 'what we and others are doing', 'how' and 'why'. The gap between internal and external practices displays where to change and if there is any need to change. Benchmarking research is designed simply to learn from an organization's own experiences as well as from other organizations that have experienced similar situations. It may therefore enable a destination to learn from others' successes and mistakes as long as benchmarking is regarded as an experience-based research activity. It can be possible to investigate the reasons for the result obtained by other destinations and develop methods to avoid it if it is likely to appear in the destination under investigation. By learning what other destinations are doing, destination management can build a stronger case for allocating resources in ways similar to those of successful destinations. Without external benchmarking, no comparison can be made and therefore the performance gap cannot be established.

When external benchmarking is used, it is impossible to speculate on which attributes need to be taken into consideration for improvement until the comparison activity is completed and its results are fully presented. The reason is that the host and partner might both be performing well on attribute X. A negative gap on the part of the host will help to identify what to investigate further. In line with this, a model of external destination benchmarking with its main stages is suggested. This includes defining the mission statement of benchmarking, choosing a partner destination, collecting the data, examining gaps, deciding what to benchmark, presenting the benchmarking findings and taking action, and each is explained below.

Proposed Model of External Destination Benchmarking

Figure 6.1 shows a general approach to the proposed benchmarking model that is specifically applicable to international tourist destinations. This model focuses on the external type of benchmarking and aims to deliver a more focused structure of the model by providing brief information about methods and tools for use in its operationalization. Reflection on the literature review suggests that any kind of benchmarking begins by measuring one's own performance in order to specify areas that need to be bench-

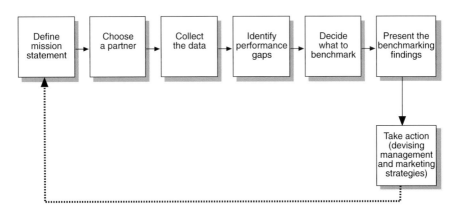

Fig. 6.1. The proposed model of external destination benchmarking.

marked (Zairi, 1992; Karlof and Ostblom, 1993); each destination needs to put their own priorities in order. It is proposed that both internal and external benchmarking help to identify these priorities. Therefore, this approach aims to measure one's own and others' performance on the basis of various criteria, compare it and identify if there is any room for improvement in the host destination by looking for good practice and successful strategies used by other destinations. As a result, based upon the methodology used and the findings assessed, this book suggests carrying out an external benchmarking exercise in the following order.

Defining the mission statement of benchmarking

It is recommended that a mission statement be developed in advance of commencing the benchmarking process (Bendell *et al.*, 1993). The mission statement refers to the objectives of the desired exchange. The clear statement of objectives helps to clarify goals and to define the types of data that are needed to obtain the desired outcomes and why they are necessary (McNair and Leibfried, 1992). In a competitive environment, each destination management has to check the positions of its products and services on a regular basis. If necessary, older strategies may be replaced by newer ones. Thus, the objective of external benchmarking for tourist destinations can be defined as 'to benchmark our performance levels against those of other competitive destinations in order to seek better practices and to gain high performance levels with a higher level of service quality, image and positive word-of-mouth recommendation'. The benchmarking process would be a waste of time if the mission is not clearly identified or what is to be expected from this is not sufficiently clear.

Choosing a partner

In the form of external benchmarking, the term 'host destination' refers to the destination whose performance level will be benchmarked against others. The term 'partner destination' refers to the one with which the host is being benchmarked. Comparison of features of destinations considering their similarities and differences may help in the choice of the right partner. In organization benchmarking, there exist various approaches as to how to choose a partner. While some benchmarkers select partners themselves, some others use databases such as those formed by the International Benchmarking Clearinghouse and the UK DTI (use of quantitative, i.e. hard, data). In destination benchmarking, there is limited material on international tourist destinations, but publications such as international tourism statistics, industry reports, government sources and academic papers can be helpful in choosing a partner.

Additionally, one can talk about two methods for this purpose (use of qualitative, i.e. soft, data): site visits (observations) and tourists' observations about other destinations. As widely emphasized in the literature (Watson, 1993; Cook, 1995), visits to other destinations can provide an opportunity to make observations regarding what and how they are doing. When these observations have been completed, a decision can be made. Generally, it is expected that destinations that are performing better on a number of criteria and thought to be worth sharing ideas with can be approached as potential partners. Another method is to obtain feedback from customers visiting other destinations. All these methods would be helpful in evaluating the main features of other specific destinations and their performance levels. To give several examples, mass tourism destinations such as Cyprus, Greece, Tunisia, Portugal, Spain and Turkey seem to offer similar types of products with similar marketing campaigns, facilities and attractions.

Destination managers need initially to pay attention to the characteristics of destinations, to their similarities and differences, when choosing the right partner (McNair and Leibfried, 1992). As the choice of partner varies with the objective, a categorization of destinations is required. These are capital cities, developed traditional centres, touring centres, purpose-built resorts and mega holiday villages (Laws, 1995). This kind of categorization can be helpful in choosing a partner destination against which benchmarking is to be conducted. International tourist destinations differ depending upon the types of tourism activities and tourism demand they have. When choosing a partner, customers' satisfaction levels, and their sociodemographic, socioeconomic and holiday-taking characteristics and motivations should be investigated. This book also considers the number and types of tourism businesses and activities, their current position, and performance indicators such as customer satisfaction and occupancy rate. This could help destination authorities obtain a broader picture of their own and their partner's visitors. This type of approach is helpful in making a decision about who and what to benchmark.

The destination for comparison could be selected from those that are perceived as offering a superior performance in some respects and being in the same competitiveness set (Pearce, 1997). As a part of external benchmarking, in competitive benchmarking, tourist destinations could be compared with their direct competitors operating in different geographic areas or countries. For instance, one purpose of benchmarking might be to compare the performance of Mediterranean destinations as summer vacation and short-haul destinations for European markets. Eventually, benchmarking findings could be useful for destination managers to make a decision about what to do or not to do by looking at the outcome of practices applied within other destinations or choosing good practices that are relevant to them. For consideration in external benchmarking, an example set of standards applied in various Mediterranean destinations is shown in Table 6.1.

In Butler's (1980) theory of destination life cycle, a destination sooner or later will reach the saturation point where it will begin losing its attractiveness to a particular market, and destination managers may have to set new management and marketing policies and goals to remain in the market. This could be a reason to look at other destinations and examine their policies and practices. Next, the availability of supply-based factors distinguishes one destination from another and is regarded as a significant factor in maintaining competitive advantage. Competitors could therefore be

Table 6.1. Sample standards applied in various destinations.

Variable	Standard
Standards applied in Vis (Croatia)	
The bathing season starts when the sea temperature is	$\geq 20°C$
The average surface area of sandy, pebble and rocky beaches	10 m^2 per user
Each available dwelling unit can provide accommodation for	Four tourists
Labour force needed per accommodation unit	0.7 persons per hotel room
	0.8 persons per room in a marina hotel
	0.2 persons per berth in the marina
	0.1 person per room in private residences
	0.1 person per house in rural tourism
Ratio of residents to tourists	1:1.4
Standards applied in Brijuni (Croatia)	
Length of beach coastline	2.0 m per person
Length of coastline used as a nudist beach	5.0 m per person
Length of riding area allocated per horse rider	100 m
Length of road for horse-drawn carriage	200 m per carriage
Length of bicycle path	50 m per cyclist
Length of jogging path	20 m per jogger
Seaside promenade	10 m per person
Sea area for rowing use	1 ha per boat
Sea area for sailing use	0.5 ha per boat
Standards applied in Rhodes (Greece)	
Tourist density	50 guests per ha in high-category hotels and similar establishments
	90 guests per ha in medium-category hotels and similar establishments
Density of users on sandy beaches	6 m^2 per bather for medium-category hotels and similar establishments
	8 m^2 per bather for high-category hotels and similar establishments

Source: UNEP (1997).

monitored on a regular basis using various criteria such as analysis of customers' characteristics, the structure of marketing channels, destination
image, tourist satisfaction and the availability of tourist resources.
Destinations could also compare their performance levels *vis-à-vis* other
similar destinations and competitors' strategies. This might enable destinations to reinforce the analysis of their markets and identify their own as
well as others' strengths and weaknesses. The findings of benchmarking
analysis may help destinations develop the correct positioning strategy and
identify areas needing improvement.

Collecting the data

In developing a case study, Yin (1994) suggests six sources of evidence for
data collection. These are documents, archival records, interviews, direct
observation, participant observation and physical artefacts. The first five of
these seem relevant to building a case study of destination benchmarking.
Documents include the review of articles, books, brochures and newspaper cuttings. Archival records contain the analysis of the historical data on
the number of tourist arrivals, tourism income, accommodation capacity,
occupancy rates, and so on. Interviews refer to the design of the structured
and open-ended surveys and brief interviews. Direct observation is used as
a way of observing facilities, services and products offered and backed up
by photographs taken in both destinations. Finally, participant observation
is the activity of visiting the partner destination as a customer and taking
package holidays on several occasions. Further information about each
method is provided in the following chapters (see Chapter 8).

Use of multiple sources of data collection methods provides sufficient
evidence to carry out a full destination benchmarking study. Both quantitative and qualitative research methods are suitable to use in destination
benchmarking research in different respects. The former is used to explore
differences between the levels of tourist satisfaction, motivations and tourist
expenditures. The latter gives an overview of secondary sources of data, the
administration of open-ended questionnaires and personal observations.
This could support the findings of quantitative research. Structured questionnaire surveys only show where any weaknesses or gaps appear, but are
limited in indicating their root causes (performance benchmarking). To be
able to understand this, secondary data collection methods and further
empirical research such as observations and interviews with customers,
tourism suppliers and authorities need to be considered in the analysis
stage of destination benchmarking (process benchmarking). As each destination is different, it is necessary to take a more qualitative approach, and
the focus should be on process/practice benchmarking as it attempts to
identify why one is better than another.

Identifying performance gaps between destinations

The analysis of the findings and determining the gap between the host and
the partner destination is the context of the next stage in external benchmarking. This step determines the consequence of the performance gaps, if
any, on the basis of strengths and weaknesses of destinations.
Benchmarking metrics identified during the planning stage should be used.
The results of the analysis stage are important for discovering similarities
and differences between the destinations under investigation and making
decisions as to whether there is any necessity to move on to further stages
of benchmarking. Therefore, the formulation of a basic framework for
external destination benchmarking requires answers to the following questions:

- What are the socioeconomic and sociodemographic profiles of customers visiting similar destinations?
- Which push and pull motivations are important to sample populations
  visiting each destination?
- How likely are sample populations visiting both destinations to be satisfied with the same attributes?
- How do customers see the perceived performance of an attribute at
  one destination in comparison with its performance at other destinations they have visited before?
- How much do they contribute to the local economy in total and in
  what categories?
- Do all these elements differ from one customer group to another visiting a different destination or between those visiting the same destination?
- How do customers see the perceived performance of one attribute at
  one destination in comparison with its perceived performance at other
  destinations they have visited previously?

Once data have been collected and analysed, the strengths, weaknesses, opportunities and threats of each destination can be clearly understood and recommendations for improvement formulated. In order to be
able to make an effective analysis of performance gaps between destinations, two methods are recommended. First, there has been a very limited
use and variety of statistical tools to test the significance level of results
yielded from the comparison of qualitative measures such as mean scores.
There may be no need to use statistical tools for the assessment of some
quantitative measures, but it is necessary to do so for qualitative measures
when a large sample population is involved. There may be gaps, but it is
difficult to perceive how significant and how large they are. Unlike the traditional gap analysis model, this study suggests using statistical methods to
reveal the magnitude of the proposed gaps. The result will either be positive, negative or neutral. Attributes with larger statistical values result in

larger gaps than those with smaller mean values in terms of mean scores. This type of analysis also helps to concentrate on those attributes with larger or smaller statistical values, depending upon the future objectives (see Chapter 8).

This method has one major drawback, namely if two destinations have different types of customers and different types of products and services. In such a case, a questionnaire to be designed for direct comparison can be recommended as it gives customers an opportunity to make a direct comparison between their holiday experiences at the destinations they have visited. There is no need to carry out a similar type of statistical analysis for this type of survey. Following this form of analysis, the current competitive gap is a measure of the difference between the destination's internal performance and that of the partner. A negative gap means that external operations are the benchmark and their best practices are clearly superior. A positive gap is indicative of internal operations showing a clear superiority over external operations (Camp, 1989). It is also possible to see that a benchmarking gap might be neutral where no identifiable difference in performance between compared attributes or overall is found. A large negative gap will be a warning signal, which means that a radical change is required, e.g. Mallorca with its larger negative gaps on the level of prices and hospitality compared with Turkey (see Chapter 8).

Focusing on the right issues (deciding what to benchmark)

The gap analysis model is used to identify which attributes need to be put on the list for external benchmarking. Those with negative gaps are accepted as the areas that need attention. This stage also considers whether there are any factors influencing the possible application of one practice to another due to the possible differences between two destinations. The findings of external benchmarking identify performance gaps between destinations and opportunities for improvement (McNair and Leibfried, 1992). Depending on the gaps, attributes to be involved in the main benchmarking study should be selected. Prioritizing what to benchmark should incorporate the following questions (Balm, 1992):

● Is the attribute the cause of customer dissatisfaction?
● Is the current performance on this attribute far from where we would like to be?
● Is the attribute a vital one for both customers and destination management?
● Is the attribute making businesses and destinations non-competitive?

Although it seems easy to learn how people perceive destinations by employing a set of attributes, destination benchmarking has a problem in finding the most appropriate attributes to measure. Here, attention must be paid to both controllable (e.g. facilities and services) and uncontrollable attributes (e.g. weather and culture). The measurement of controllable attributes in destination benchmarking offers more potential for bringing about improvement. For instance, people can perceive climate, culture or natural attractions at one destination as being worse or better than at another. This does not necessarily mean that these attributes should be considered as benchmark elements. They are unique to different destinations and it is hardly possible to change them in the short term or even in the long term.

In benchmarking, variables are classified as being changeable in either the short or long term. Depending on the destinations' policies, either of these variables can be taken into a benchmarking study. Watson (1993) emphasizes that the importance of benchmarking emerges from the reality of what measure or measures gives the best results in terms of what needs to be known and can potentially be changed. To accomplish this, there should be a prioritization process according to whether the element is important to customer dis/satisfaction, whether results are unexpected and whether there is a possibility of improvement (Balm, 1992). Prices, hospitality (culture) and accommodation services are some of the areas providing opportunities for Turkey to focus on for improvement as these are potential core competencies in the future.

The main benchmark elements to be measured can be divided into the two broad categories of supply and demand. The former can be related to the contribution to the local economy, marketing and promotion of the destination, and availability of infrastructure and superstructure. The latter can be related mainly to tourist perceptions and experiences, their profiles, expenditure levels, repeat visits, and so forth. Therefore, sometimes one type of research method, e.g. customer surveys, may be inadequate to understand the relevant aspects of any destination such as analysis of tourism development, product development or effective factors in the past and in the present. This may require other methods such as statistics, observations, case studies and documents.

Personal observations can make it possible to present the likely reasons for the performance gaps between the two destinations, e.g. level of prices, the destination airport, local transport services and facilities for children (see Box 6.1 as a particular reference to how two different airports are viewed). Personal observations preclude the need for lengthy reports. To extend their use, reverse engineering could be applied as in past studies of organization benchmarking. A group of representatives from holiday destinations would travel as customers to unfamiliar destinations to analyse how they are doing and concentrate on particular aspects of the destinations. Thus, personal observations or site visits, as a significant tool of external benchmarking, might be helpful to identify good practice exemplars in other destinations and apply them to the host destination subject to revision if required. Findings of an empirical study purely on destination

Box 6.1. Observations on what two airports offer their passengers. Source: Kozak (2000).

The findings of questionnaire surveys confirmed that those visiting Mallorca were more likely to be satisfied with the availability of facilities and services at the destination airport than those in Turkey. Observations appear to give strong support to the validity of this finding. Palma has had a brand new airport since the summer of 1997, which is much better than the old one. Dalaman airport in Turkey was opened for military purposes in 1976 and became an international airport in 1988. Dalaman airport serves ~4 million passengers, whereas 15 million/year pass through Palma airport. Mallorca provides a larger airport with 150 check-in desks, seven X-ray check points and 52 departure gates. In comparison, Dalaman has ten check-in desks, two X-ray check points and six departure gates.

   There is sometimes a long queue at the airport in Turkey since it is obligatory to have passports checked and get them stamped by the police. One customer complained that ' ... Dalaman airport on arrival ... Passport control is far too slow ... ' while another came up with a solution by highlighting that ' ... Longer queues at the airport ... Takes a long time passing through ... We should be able to pay our visa to a travel agent in the UK instead of having to queue here ... '. In Mallorca, even though British but not German citizens are obliged to show the police officers their passports, it takes only a few seconds. That is why check-in and check-out services in Mallorca take a much shorter time than those in Turkey. Check-in and boarding services in Mallorca are more organized. Passengers are taken to the gate 45 min before departure, but this sometimes varies due to flight delays. In terminals C and D, each gate is separate. In Dalaman, passengers may be called any time between 15 min and 1 h before departure.

   Another main feature of Palma airport is that it provides many more facilities. There are many restaurants and cafes in which to eat and drink and many places to have a rest before departure, as one customer agreed: 'I think that the airport has greatly improved; there seems to be more space for passengers, more shops and a better customer service for passengers ... '. The airport in Turkey is so much smaller that there are only two cafes and a couple of hundred seats. Palma airport has a better air-conditioning and lighting system, more toilets (almost one for each gate) and more public telephone kiosks throughout the airport. It has a better transport service with small vehicles available within the building for wheelchair users and elderly passengers. It also has separate service desks at both departure and arrival lounges for each flight company and tour operator. Except on Fridays, Saturdays and Mondays, there seem to be enough trolleys at Palma airport, but at Dalaman the airport building is so small that there are no trolleys for departing passengers. Observations further revealed that Palma airport was much cleaner than its counterpart in Turkey. Each dining room at the departure gates in Mallorca is cleaned immediately all the passengers have boarded. Palma airport has many litter bins, one for each gate and others located in corridors, while Dalaman airport lacks litter bins due to security concerns.

continued

Box 6.1. *Continued.*

Finally, unfavourable observations about the airport in Mallorca are as follows. As the airport is so large, some tourists may feel confused or tired. A quotation from one tourist demonstrates the importance of this problem: ' ... The new airport is much too large ... Have heard some visitors will now find an alternative holiday destination because of the long walks within the airport complex ... '. Permission for smoking at the airport seems to be the next problem. Flight delays in Mallorca ranging between 1 and 12 h sometimes upset passengers. This is a very common situation particularly between Thursdays and Mondays. Passengers have to wait for boarding without being given any further information. As a consequence, in order to better serve air passengers visiting Palma airport, a collaboration project between tour operators and airport management has been released. TUI and Neckerman und Reisen (NUR) are involved in this pilot project, which is looking for ways to minimize the disadvantages of heavy traffic in the summer season and to promote staggered arrivals and departures.

benchmarking indicated the existence of several good practices in the Mallorcan resorts, which could be copied by their Turkish counterparts without any major modification, e.g. the picture of a dish with its price, kids' clubs and playgrounds in individual restaurants, menus with half-price for children under 12 years old and Blue Flags, and their effective application in practice such as good and frequent signposting on beaches, facilities specifically designed for disabled people, and leaflets about a variety of attractions and events written in various languages (Kozak, 2000).

Presenting the benchmarking findings

This stage summarizes the exercise of external benchmarking. It presents all the findings and their potential use. Following the benchmarking process, it is possible to learn about the present and future performance of destinations. Presenting the findings helps to elicit what strengths and weaknesses have emerged and what opportunities and threats exist to maintain continuous improvement. Moreover, this stage aims to seek answers to such questions as: how to collect data from other destinations, whether there are any performance gaps, where and why, what are the other similarities and differences, whether the results are applicable, and whether there is any need to apply the results in practice. Depending on these findings, further recommendations on what needs to be done and how to do it can be made before taking action.

Upon deciding which attributes should be benchmarked, site visits to the partner destination could be arranged in order to conduct more detailed investigations into how their partner is performing and how it has achieved success on particular results or subjects. During this stage, local private businesses and public authorities may be interviewed, formal policies and legislation could be examined and the overall position of the destination could be monitored. All these activities can be carried out in the host destination. The outcome will produce a table similar to Table 6.2, but in an extended form. This type of summary table is useful in helping to decide which areas to focus on. The complete benchmarking report will include information on what measures have been benchmarked, which methods were used to collect and compare data, where gaps appeared and what the potential reasons are, whether the partner is a suitable one in relation to applying its practices or strategies, what has been learnt during the study and what methods need to be applied in practice.

The measurement of one's own performance indicates its current strengths and weaknesses as well as opportunities and threats for the future. Their comparison with other similar destinations may identify how competitive the destination is in various areas and any possible areas needing improvement. Based on these criteria, the application of the proposed destination benchmarking methodology identified several key issues for drawing a clear picture of Mallorca and Turkey as summer holiday destinations, of which some details are given in Table 6.3. This table is the summary of what a benchmarking study aims at or is expected to provide. By producing a similar kind of table after completion of the main part of benchmarking (preparation and analysis), destination managers could continue to proceed with the next stage, which is taking action.

Taking action

Having learnt from the data and knowledge during the benchmarking process, this is the next stage in order to set goals for improvement and develop action plans. In this stage, the results of the benchmarking study can be reported to the people it affects or to whom it concerns, e.g. local authorities, airport management, tourism and travel businesses and associations, and local residents. Although the objective of benchmarking is to change either the structure of the organization or some of its operations in a way that increases its performance, it is not reasonable to expect destination managers to suggest their members change all their products or the style of services or practices they offer where any customer dissatisfaction may result or where destination benchmarking research gives negative scores; but they could show ways (as discussed in the section on practical implications below) in which to improve those areas that bring higher tourist satisfaction and competitive advantage.

The analysis of results derived from external benchmarking investigation might assist in identifying gaps, determining strengths and weaknesses

Table 6.2. Main differences between Mallorca and Turkey.

Factors	Mallorca	Turkey
I. Political factors		
EU membership	A member of the EU	Not a member of the EU
Government system	Decentralized system	Centralized system
II. Cultural factors		
Hospitality	Local people see foreigners as tourists and do not pay much attention. Harassment is very rare.	Local people regard foreigners as guests and attempt to treat them in a hospitable and friendly way. Local shopkeepers see tourists as customers from whom they can earn money
Bargaining while shopping	Not a cultural tradition	A cultural tradition
Cultural attractions	Has limited cultural attractions	Has diverse cultural attractions
Language communication	Welcomes all people from the UK and Germany either as tourists or as residents or entrepreneurs	Used to be a closed country to Europe. Learning another language is becoming more important among individuals
III. Economic factors		
National economy	A homogeneous economy	A diversified economy
Accommodation stock	Small- and medium-sized establishments. Self-catering apartments	Medium- and large-scale establishments. 4- and 5-star hotels, clubs.
Strength of currency	Much stronger	Much weaker
IV. Geographical factors		
Size of land	Smaller	Much larger
Natural attractions	Has limited natural attractions	Has diverse natural attractions
V. Demand-based factors		
Number of previous visits	Higher number of repeat visits (British tourists)	
Type of holiday	Greater intention to choose half-board and self-catering (British tourists)	More likely to book all-inclusive and stay in holiday villages (German tourists)
Length of holiday	Less than 2 weeks (British tourists)	Less than 2 weeks (German tourists)
Income levels	Higher income levels (British tourists)	Lower income levels (German tourists)
Number of people in the party	Higher proportion of companions (British tourists)	
Booking holidays	Much earlier, e.g. at least 7 months in advance (British tourists)	Earlier, e.g. at least 4 months in advance (German tourists)
Age		Younger age (German tourists)

Table 6.3. SWOT analysis for Mallorca and Turkey.

continued

	Mallorca		Turkey	
	British	German	British	German
Strengths	Sea, sun and sand	Sea, sun and sand	Sea, sun and sand	Sea, sun and sand
	Nature	Nature	Culture, nature and history	Culture, nature and history
	Frequent loyalty	Language communication	Hospitality	Accommodation services
	Hospitality	Frequent loyalty	Level of prices	Local transport services
	Language communication	High level of trip satisfaction	Good value for money	Level of prices
	Cater for families	High level of intention to come back and recommend	Language communication	Cleanliness and hygiene
	High level of trip satisfaction	Attractive in winter season	Local transport services	High level of trip satisfaction
	High level of intention to come back and recommend	Good airport facilities	New accommodation	High level of intention to come back and recommend
	Attractive in winter season	Cater for families	High level of trip satisfaction	Frequent loyalty
	Good airport facilities		High level of intention to come back and recommend	
Weaknesses	Old accommodation	Poor sports facilities and activities	Harassment	Harassment
	High level of prices	Poor quality of accommodation	Lack of cleanliness	Poor language communication
	Poor cleanliness	Poor food	Poor signposting	Lack of cleanliness
	Negative attitude of shopkeepers	High level of prices	Poor airport facilities and services	Poor signposting
		Lack of cleanliness	Poor air-conditioning	Poor air-conditioning
Opportunities	Level of prices	Repositioning and improvement of resorts	Young destination	Young destination
	Repositioning and improvement of resorts	Attractive in winter season		
	A brand-new airport			

Table 6.3. Continued.

Mallorca		Turkey	
British	German	British	German
Attractive in winter season Shorter flight Special programmes for people who return	A brand-new airport Shorter flight Special programmes for people who return		
Threats			
Overcommercialization and overdevelopment Noise Mixture of family and young individual tourists Heavily dependent on British market	Level of prices Quality of accommodation Overcommercialization and overdevelopment Heavily dependent on German market	Harassment Overcommercialization and overdevelopment Poor cleanliness of sea and beaches Poor hygiene and sanitation Poor road and traffic conditions	Harassment Overcommercialization and overdevelopment Dependent on German market
Competitive level			
Easy access to the market (shorter flight time) Caters for families Variety of leisure facilities and activities Relaxed atmosphere (no hassle) A brand-new airport Mature (experienced) destination Attractive for winter tourism	Easy access to the market (shorter flight time) Caters for families A brand-new airport Relaxed atmosphere (no hassle) Mature (experienced) destination Attractive for winter tourism	Culture and history Hospitality Level of prices (good value for money) Local transport services Young destination Good shopping opportunities	Culture and history Hospitality Level of prices (good value for money) Accommodation services Variety of watersport activities Young destination

of destinations, and deciding which attributes are to be investigated further or which good practices can be adopted from others. Thus, depending on the existence and the size of the gap examined in the preceding stage, destination management might have an opportunity to make a decision as to whether it needs to take further action and make improvements in particular elements of the destination. The review stage helps the destination understand whether the process has achieved its objectives (revisiting mission statement). It is thus crucial to introduce several destination-based performance measures and discuss their rationale in the form of external destination benchmarking.

While taking action as a result of external benchmarking, opinions can be received through both internal and external data. Further sources are also available through internal and external communication with the representatives of the local and other destinations and through personal observations (reverse engineering). The completion of this stage could then be followed by encouraging internal communication among the related bodies of the destination such as professional organizations, government offices, local residents and travel agents. Through internal communication, the management can discuss the outcomes of the external benchmarking activity and its implications for the performance improvement of their own holiday destination, inform members about good practice applied by other destinations, encourage them to get feedback on what to do and how to do it in the future, and ask for support in the implementation of the required changes or strategies.

While setting goals and establishing action plans, destination management can benefit from the findings of either internal or external benchmarking exercises depending upon which one has been followed. In the case of external benchmarking, methods used by other destinations and thought to be rational and applicable to one's own purposes can be considered. Attention needs to be paid to the factors that affect the success of practices and the overall performance of benchmarking studies, e.g. cultural differences between tourist-receiving and tourist-generating countries, and between different tourist-receiving countries. Types of customers visiting different destinations, the power of marketing channels and their restructuring, and differences in laws and legislation between tourist-receiving countries are also the subject of benchmarking research between destinations.

Destination benchmarking studies confirmed that there are different dimensions related to both tangible and intangible aspects of destinations (Kozak, 2000). For instance, intangible aspects include the quality of facilities, the attitude of local people towards tourists and a sense of personal safety. As success will depend on delivering the right mix of components to meet customer demand, a programme of destination benchmarking needs to involve consideration of all facilities and services that affect the tourist experience. Referring to the findings of benchmarking research on tourist destinations, some items are not related to only one specific resort in Turkey or Mallorca, but could have been a reflection of tourists' multiple experiences in the country. For instance, Mallorca has only one international airport where nearly 15 million passengers are served annually. Any tourist who would like to visit another resort on their next trip to Mallorca would have to use the same airport. Similarly, resorts are connected to each other by local transport services. A good network of public transport services will enable both tourists and local people to have access to other resorts and main tourist attractions. In terms of hospitality, local people in Turkey usually welcome foreign tourists in a friendly and warm manner.

This points to the importance of the implementation of a destination-based TQM programme providing a means of cooperative decision making, collaboration and communication between a set of organizations such as local and central government, private industry and the related international organizations (Goodall and Bergsma, 1990; Inskeep, 1991). This is one of the major roles given to the destination management, which could be led by a 'destination manager'. The benefits of such cooperation would be avoiding wasting financial resources, providing better communication channels to set plans, making decisions and putting them into practice. For instance, being aware of its advantages, the government of the Balearic Islands has recently begun to pay attention to the protection of natural resources and to upgrade and enhance the national heritage by developing an integrated approach involving collaboration between public and private sector representatives.

As far as marketing strategies are concerned (marketing management), it might be possible to keep the attention of repeat tourists or obtain new tourists, promote holidays with self-catering and bed and breakfast, and attract those travelling alone or with fewer companions and those taking shorter holidays. Using Porter's (1996) variety-based positioning strategy, specific products and services differentiating one destination from others could be focused on. The level of prices can be reduced to attract tourists in the off-season period. In line with Porter's (1996) 'needs-based positioning strategy', a particular segment of customers might be targeted, e.g. family groups in Alcudia and young independent tourists in Arenal in Mallorca (or the use of homogeneous market segmentation strategy; Fornell, 1992). Alternatively new products can be developed, as Mallorca and Turkey currently do, e.g. improvement of sports and recreation activities.

In terms of improving the quality of products or services (performance management), several strategies can be set up. For instance, in increasing the standard of hygiene, sanitation and cleanliness, an effective code of practice may be established to encourage both customers and service providers to become environmentally friendly and sensitive towards the health of others. Eco-label systems or their variants, as part of a generic destination benchmarking exercise, can be helpful in this matter. Training programmes can be instigated among staff and shopkeepers to encourage them to behave towards tourists in a friendly manner and to be keen to listen to their complaints. This may require revising the existing laws, regulations and practices and upgrading the tourist infrastructure, as enablers of performance improvement through destination benchmarking.

The action stage might also help to make future projections and recommendations. An action plan containing future goals and recommendations might consist of how to keep up strengths and minimize weaknesses and threats in order to cope with the new applications and developments. Depending on the projected future performance, destination managers may wish to change their marketing policies or market segments. It may also be possible to attract similar groups of tourists by preserving the current image and improving the existing performance. To implement the benchmarking results, destination managers might make their recommendations to local authorities, local tourist associations and businesses, local residents and the national tourism policymakers. To give a good example of organization benchmarking, the Confederation of British Industry published a report of benchmarking results in relation to the performance of 3- and 4-star hotel businesses in the UK (CBI News, 1997). This suggests that both businesses and local authorities cooperate to produce new ideas in order to benefit from developments in tourism, e.g. setting targets for growth and developing practical and realistic strategies.

In summary, the stage of taking action is one of the most difficult parts of the benchmarking process, as local authorities, tourism organizations and businesses may not intend to implement findings or to take long-term decisions. This may be due to lack of human or financial resources and the sensitivity of the tourism industry to economic, political and social changes. The establishment of action plans may also be influenced by cross-cultural differences in managerial practices, beliefs and values between peer destinations in the case of external benchmarking although they take place in the same competitiveness set in terms of the market structure and tourism products on offer (see Box 6.2). This issue also applies to the consideration of cross-cultural differences between tourist groups in the case of either internal or external benchmarking.

Strengths and Weaknesses of External Destination Benchmarking

It seems obvious that destinations need to benchmark their facilities and service levels against those of their counterparts. In conducting external benchmarking, current performance levels in terms of the competition are measured. Benchmarking can enable a destination to learn from others' successes as well as to evaluate mistakes. By learning what other destinations are doing, destination management can build a stronger case for allocating resources in ways similar to those of successful destinations.

Box. 6.2. Cross-cultural differences in beliefs and values. Source: Kozak (2000).

According to the results of questionnaire surveys, hospitality and customer care were the most significant attributes contributing to the level of tourist satisfaction in Turkey. As part of the term of 'interactive quality' described as an outcome resulting from interaction between the customer and personnel or other people, this attribute was also one of the most critical elements of those destinations in Turkey that gave one of the largest positive gaps in comparison with that in Mallorca. This means that both British and German tourists were mostly satisfied with the helpfulness and friendliness of local people and staff in Turkey. This could be because the tradition in the country views travelling at home or abroad as a sign of prestige and sees the function of host to tourists as one commanding respect, regardless of tourists' culture or nationality. Since the Turkish culture is sensitive to nature and beauty, service providers are highly recommended to wear elegant work uniforms, to be stylish and to keep every place in the business as clean and tidy as possible. There is also a motto established by the Ministry of Tourism, which is highlighted every April during 'tourism week': 'Tourists want hospitality and friendliness'.

Despite the strength of Turkey's tradition of hospitality, a major complaint from tourists has always been harassment by shopkeepers and restaurateurs. This finding corresponds to the proposition of the dual-factor theory in customer satisfaction measurement. This theory suggests that a person may be both very satisfied and very dissatisfied with a product or a service. The difference between cultures in western and eastern countries is emphasized in this case. While local shopkeepers see inviting tourists into their shops to buy something as a way to encourage business, tourists from the West perceive this as being harassed, because in their culture the customer is expected to make the first move. The absence of this type of complaint in Mallorca may signal that cultural differences between these communities (between German and Mallorcan and between British and Mallorcan) would be minimal.

Without benchmarking, no comparison can be made and therefore the performance gap cannot be established. Reviewing both the proposed model and the findings discussed earlier, it seems possible to suggest that an external benchmarking approach offers destination managers three benefits: (i) measuring one's own performance and comparing it with others; (ii) identifying the strengths of the destination; and (iii) searching for best practice in other destinations to apply to their own cultures, and how to do this (Table 6.4).

First, this study suggests that the examination of quantitative measures is not enough to evaluate the performance of destinations. There are other specific measures of success that will lead to the destination raising its sights and achieving higher performance levels. The success of these

Table 6.4. Strengths and weaknesses of external destination benchmarking.

No.	Strengths	Weaknesses	When appropriate to use
1.	Helps to measure one's own performance and compare it with others	Takes more time to carry out the procedures	Innovation is sought
2.	Helps to identify the strengths of the destination	Takes more resources to carry out the procedures	It is the time to seek good practices in other organizations
3.	Helps to search for best practice in other destinations to apply to their own cultures and how to do this	Implementation is slower because of the 'not invented here' syndrome Cross-cultural differences in managerial practices, laws and legislations	

measures, called qualitative measures, may also make a contribution to the success of quantitative measures – more tourists returning, more word-of-mouth recommendation, more customers and increased tourism revenues, and, as a result, possibly a higher share of international tourism. The essence of performance measurement in destination benchmarking research could be the identification of the profile of tourists, their motivations, their satisfaction levels, their comments for improving destinations with poor scores (or images), and comparison with competitive areas. All these suggestions may also apply to the competitor destinations in an external benchmarking study. Such an analysis may be helpful in identifying where one destination differs from another and areas where further improvement is needed. The identified measures could also make possible a continuous review of destination performance.

Secondly, this type of benchmarking exercise is helpful in determining how one destination differentiates its products and services from another, e.g. variances in customer service, quality and image (strategic benchmarking). Attributes making one destination distinctive or more competitive than its rivals are described as 'determinant' attributes in the marketing literature (Swan and Combs, 1976). Destination satisfaction may be vitally important for maintaining a regional competitive advantage. As noted earlier, the concepts of benchmarking and competitiveness are strongly related. It is extremely important in maintaining competitive advantage in international tourism to know how to sell the experience of a holiday in a particular place (Crouch and Ritchie, 1999). Factors such as cleaner beaches and establishments, more hospitable and friendlier local people, and cheaper prices could make one destination more competitive than others. For instance, as shown in Fig. 6.2, Turkey is perceived as superior to Mallorca on prices, hospitality, accommodation services, local transport services and clean environment, the potential elements making it a direct competitor of Mallorca. Mallorca out-performs Turkey on the availability of facilities and

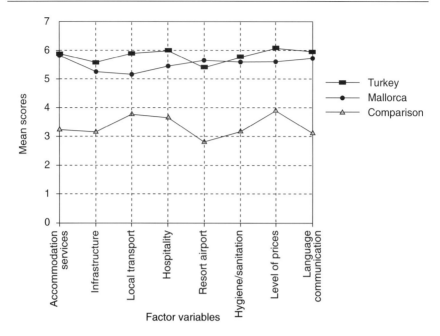

Fig. 6.2. Comparison between satisfaction levels of British tourists. Source: Kozak (2002b).

services at the destination airport, in offering family-oriented products and offering a relaxed atmosphere without hassle (Kozak, 2000). Destination managers should set action plans to keep the current strength of their desti-nation's performance on these attributes. Porter (1996) views this type of analysis as a 'variety-based positioning strategy', which is based on the choice of a specific set of product or service varieties rather than looking at market segments.

As emphasized earlier, some attributes are not related to only one spe-cific destination, but could have been a reflection of tourists' multiple experiences in the country or in the region. For instance, Mallorca has only one international airport. Similarly, local transport is important as it pro-vides connections to other neighbouring resorts. Hospitality and welcom-ing in a friendly manner is a general characteristic of the Turkish community, not limited to only one destination. All these statements also apply to the assessment of quantitative measures such as the number of tourist arrivals and the amount of tourism income. These measures are more appropriate for showing a general structure and picture of tourism in a country rather than in a particular destination. Given these reasons, it is possible to suggest that the outcomes of a benchmarking project make a direct contribution to enhancing 'regional or national competitiveness'.

The findings of external benchmarking are also capable of indicating similarities between destinations. Taking the level of tourist expenditure on board, no significant difference is observed between the amount of total tourist spending in Mallorca and Turkey, although Grabler (1997) expected that there would be differences between destinations for different age groups based on average incomes. The survey further indicated that the majority of German tourists (70% in Turkey and 53% in Mallorca) mentioned that they had spent nothing on visiting attractions. Similarly, some categories such as local transport, car hire and day trips attracted a high proportion of low spenders in both places. It is important to analyse these findings to explore how likely the respondents are to be active and interested in seeing other places. It is unreasonable to expect that people spend more on local transport than on day trips and car hire services if they want to travel more widely. These findings require further investigation in both places if a benchmarking study is to be carried out on this subject.

Finally, this study suggests that external destination benchmarking might be helpful in identifying several examples of good practice in other destinations. To achieve this, feedback can be obtained from customers through their comments and perceptions of holiday experiences in the host and partner destinations and through applying 'process benchmarking', which requires personal observations to register how others are doing. Following this type of approach, several examples of good practice are observed in Mallorca, e.g. a bigger airport with a relaxed atmosphere and air-conditioning, frequent signposting on beaches, facilities for disabled people, and half-price special menus for children under 12 years old. Two items identified in Turkey as examples of good practice are the hospitality and the local transport services.

However, there are several limitations in external benchmarking (see Table 6.4). It may not be possible to succeed in improving pure service-based attributes (some dimensions of service quality) such as hospitality or the attitude of local people or language communication by copying service practices elsewhere because of cultural differences. It is more likely that success can be achieved in improving the tangible elements of tourism products and services such as facilities and services for children, accommodation, airport facilities and services, local transport services and sports activities (service quality and technical quality); and improving hygiene and cleanliness, economical use of energy and water, disposal of waste, and so on (standards of environmental quality). Thus, the external part of benchmarking has different limitations in different countries. Attention must be paid to the distinctive features of each destination on the basis of economics, cultural practices, beliefs, laws and regulations, which may lead to ethical dilemmas. This could be a barrier influencing the development and implementation of action plans, and whether they are successful or require revision.

These arguments provide grounds to suggest that some qualitative measures may be evaluated as a good example of internal benchmarking rather than of external benchmarking considering a comparison activity between peer destinations. As a consequence of the differences mentioned above, one could suggest that some variables relating to social, economic or political issues could be measurable and compatible but might not be used for benchmarking against other destinations, e.g. level of prices, hospitality or harassment, language communication or formal regulations such as visa or passport control. The concept of destination benchmarking seems to be closer to the involvement of facilities relating to sport, beaches, airport, transport, accommodation, food and drink, child care, signposting and tourist information centres (physical aspects of quality). In other words, the performance of such facilities could be measurable, compatible and also comparable for benchmarking against those of other destinations.

As a result, rather than copying what others are doing, external benchmarking could be considered as 'a learning process for drawing lessons from one organisation and translating them into the unique culture and mission orientation of a different organisation', as Watson (1993, p. 6) suggests. This statement, along with the research findings (Kozak, 2000), convincingly supports what the benchmarking literature suggests as being 'apple to apple comparison', which means choosing similar items, practices or activities and focusing upon them (McNair and Leibfried, 1992). The success in the preparation, analysis and action stages of benchmarking is likely to influence success in the later stages. It is worth noting that external benchmarking should be perceived as a tool not only for performance management and improvement but also for revising marketing strategies.

Summary

This chapter has set out a general discussion of the application of external benchmarking in tourist destinations and its implications for benchmarking theory and practice. It was based on the findings emerging from the case studies on specific destinations in Mallorca and Turkey. The relevance of benchmarking to tourist destinations was examined through measuring comparative destination performance and taking action. As to the benefits of external benchmarking, it assists in measuring one's own performance and comparing it with others, and in identifying the strengths of the destination and searching for best practices in other destinations. However, in response to this, some practitioners argue that differences in culture and language to set up the objectives between the two destinations can be influential while implementing new policies or the benchmarking findings. As a subelement of external benchmarking, the following chapter looks at the practice of generic destination benchmarking.

Generic Destination Benchmarking

7

Introduction

Demands for better service and environmental quality at tourist destinations are rapidly increasing. Destination authorities need to achieve a better overall level of performance in order to be competitive. Both quality grading and eco-label systems can act as external enablers that indirectly influence the performance level of tourist establishments in particular and destinations in general because these systems and benchmarking have common features such as providing guidelines on how to improve performance, seeking best practices and requiring a continuous process to ensure continuous improvement and a better image. The main objective of this chapter is therefore to introduce existing or proposed quality grading and eco-label systems as a form of generic benchmarking. How benchmarking, linked to external awards and grades, can offer advantages and bring about improvements in competitiveness for destinations is also discussed. The chapter ends with an overview of the strengths and weaknesses.

Practices of Generic Destination Benchmarking

The existing literature emphasizes that the core idea of benchmarking is to identify the best practices or the best performing businesses in the industry and improve one's own performance by adopting good practices used by others or guidelines established by professional national or international organizations (Evans and Lindsey, 1993). In line with these, within the application of generic benchmarking, tourist destinations could look either at other destinations or at international guidelines or standards in order to find effective solutions to their particular problems by having access to best practices recognized nationally or internationally. For example, complaints about service quality and environmental deregulation might not be limited to particular destinations. Methods of improving these attributes could be modified to be used internationally, e.g. use of quality grading and environmental labelling (eco-label) systems. Therefore, this chapter suggests that various quality grading and eco-label systems could act as external enablers, as a form of generic benchmarking, that influence the performance of holiday destinations. These systems and benchmarking have the common goal of providing guidelines on how to improve performance, seek best practices and enable continuous improvement (Vaziri, 1992). As these various systems also have valuable roles to play in bringing about improvements in tourist destinations, they could be accepted as benchmarks indicating how the relevant organizations are performing against various standards.

Eco-labelling in tourism considers all the tourism products, hotels, restaurants, tour operators, travel agents, leisure parks, and so on, and refers to a wide variety of awards. Among those that are relevant to destinations are British Airways for Tomorrow, Green Globe 21, Blue Flag and TUI's Guidelines for Environmental Management. Others are relevant to individual organizations, e.g. Green Leaf and Tourfor Award, and guidelines developed by local tourist boards such as the Scottish Tourist Board, the Costa Rican Tourist Board, the Tourism Council of the South Pacific and the Caribbean Tourist Board (World Tourism Organization, 1993; Stephens, 1997). Mihalic (1998) draws attention to the importance of eco-labelling in tourism for improving the ecological quality of products and maintaining competitive advantage. She provides some indicators of eco-label systems in tourist destinations: hotels that pay attention to minimizing the harmful effects of tourism on the environment, travel agencies that offer special discounts for tourists who are likely to use public transport or those who print their catalogues on recycled paper. Some of the destination criteria used by eco-labels are sea water and beach quality; access to beaches; water supply and water-saving measures; waste water disposal and utilization; solid waste disposal, recycling and prevention; energy supply and energy-saving measures; traffic, air, noise and climate; landscape and built environment; nature conservation; animal welfare; environmental information; and environmental policy and activities.

As Table 7.1 shows, there is a distinction between quality grading and eco-label systems in terms of the type of sample to be aimed for. Quality grading systems seem to address solutions for performance improvement mostly in individual organizations, whereas eco-label systems are partly destination-based. Another instance is that the former often refers to the use of qualitative measures such as the appearance and behaviour of staff, quality of facilities, atmosphere and customer satisfaction. Conversely, the latter systems focus mostly on quantitative measures such as water and electricity supply and consumption, recycling, waste water generation per

Table 7.1. Standards and awards in tourism.

Systems	Area	Applied for
Quality standards and awards		
ISO9000 Series	International	Individual organizations
Baldridge Awards	USA	Individual organizations
The EFQM Quality Award	European	Individual organizations
Hospitality Systems (AA, RAC, ETD, STD)	National	Individual organizations
Eco-labelling standards and awards		
TUI's Guidelines	International	Individual organizations/tourist destinations
European Blue Flag	European	Tourist destinations
EU Eco-label Scheme	European	Individual organizations
Tourfor Award	European	Individual organizations
Green Globe 21	International	Individual organizations/tourist destinations
Local guidelines and awards	National	Individual organizations/tourist destinations

Source: own elaboration.

room, provision of equipment, level of water and air pollution, and so on. Therefore, although it still seems to be feasible, an alternative option might include the development of a more comprehensive quality system, which will address tourist destinations overall by combining these two systems.

A broad application of generic benchmarking at tourist destinations could possibly be composed of overall standards pointing out their physical, service and environmental quality levels produced in accordance with the guidelines of the existing national or international systems of which some characteristics are summarized in this chapter. These could be made up of both qualitative (e.g. how to carry out processes and how to behave towards tourists or serve them) and quantitative measures (responses to questions such as how much, how long, how many, and so on, e.g. time and productivity). The required data could be collected from actual experience and outcomes to form broader performance standards and measures. This responsibility could be taken by the WTO, WTTC or a similar organization in collaboration with national or regional tourist boards to keep records, establish outputs and monitor changes.

The common relationship between eco-label systems and benchmarking is that the former is used as an example of the best practice benchmarking towards achieving continuous improvement of environmental quality. As noted in Chapter 1, benchmarking is a way of learning good practices from higher achievers in the same market. Although the benchmarking approach requires a partner to carry out the study, it is also evident that some guidelines and standards identified by public and voluntary organizations could be regarded as input in an external benchmarking exercise. Camp (1989) emphasizes the importance of such associations in gathering data about the practical applications in a particular industry. Guidelines, eco-labels and quality grading systems could therefore be useful for enhancing standards in the tourism industry. As benchmarking is a continuous process, destinations and their elements such as hotels, restaurants, recreation facilities and beaches might identify ways of improving the environmental and service quality of their facilities. Some of the benefits derived from such a benchmarking application might be the following.

- Assists in exploring what needs visitors might have and suggests ways to meet them.
- Assists in how to achieve best practices and discover innovative practices by using best-in-class examples.
- Assists in establishing effective goals and objectives.
- Assists in gaining continuous improvement in the performance of the destination by obtaining support from well-motivated human resources.
- Assists in identifying critical success factors indicating where the destination has strengths and weaknesses.
- Assists visitors in what to expect in their subsequent visits to accommodation establishments or destinations.
- Assists in establishing networks with other members of quality grading and eco-label systems and sharing experiences.

In short, the benefits of using quality grading systems and eco-labels as benchmarks for tourist destinations could be an improved image, improved tourist satisfaction, decreased operational costs, use for promotion and advertising, taking further advice from outside and, as a result, enhanced competitive advantage. If these systems are sufficiently understood, they could help tourists to structure their expectations in line with the facilities and services likely to be offered. Individual organizations need to aim for such systems, which will support their desired market position and which can be used to help them promote it. Consequently, any action to encourage appropriate benchmarking participation by tourism organizations and destination management is likely to have a positive effect on the performance of the overall destination and its competitiveness.

As a result of all these benefits, the destination can be provided with an opportunity to enhance its competitive position in the international market. There is a close relationship between benchmarking and competitiveness, with the former being expected to bring about the latter (Camp, 1989; Zairi, 1994, 1996). In this sense, quality grading and eco-labelling systems, as elements of generic benchmarking applications, might be able to improve competitiveness in different ways. Each way is explained in detail in the following paragraphs. Improved productivity and efficiency through quality or eco-label systems may result in reduced production and marketing costs and increased customer satisfaction. Less money spent at production leaves more to be spent on service standards and marketing activities. Money can be saved on research and development projects as a result of guidelines provided by such systems. With specific reference to the use of eco-labels, the implementation of environmental programmes and eco-labelling systems to minimize waste and save energy not only creates a better and cleaner environment, but may also enhance competitiveness with similar destinations, due to the underlying significance of cost minimization in marketing services.

Proposed Model of Generic Destination Benchmarking

In the benchmarking literature, organizations always need a partner with which to exchange ideas or get feedback about better or new practices. This partner can sometimes be another organization within the same or a different industry. In the case of common guidelines launched as the best practices and believed to be valuable for organizations to reach objectives, all these classification and grading schemes and awards mentioned within this chapter can also be worthwhile partners. All these grading systems could be taken into account as a benchmark element to understand better how the owners or holders performed to obtain those standards. By taking their existing procedures on board, further actions can be taken within the organization. Winning organizations are or should always be open to external outcomes, which may account for the high investment in research and development. Winning organizations feel themselves to be a step further ahead than others, enabling them to search for better applications for meeting customers' requirements and for changes in their wants and desires. Mediocre organizations will lag behind others or may leave the market.

A number of tour operators and destination management authorities have attempted to transform the image of some destinations by either developing their own eco-labels or adopting others (see Box 7.1 for an example of tour operators). This is the result of an interaction between suppliers of tourism products and services, intermediaries (tour operators or travel agents or destination marketing organizations) and customers. A newly emerging type of tourist wants to spend vacations in a place that is 'not spoiled', and expects intermediaries to recommend the most appropriate places to go. In the next stage, intermediaries require tourism suppliers to pay attention to the preservation of the natural and cultural resources they supply and benefit from. When destinations become less likely to perform at the same level, then customers can be directed towards other destinations. In the final stage, tourism suppliers and destination management release policies and guidelines about how they expect customers (users) to behave and how to use resources without damaging the environment. Eco-labels would be a symbol of auto-control appearing among these three groups.

Box 7.1. TUI's guidelines for environmental management.

As the first tour operator in the world to establish policies for environmental management, the TUI has developed its own environmental standards. Environmentally responsible tourism has become its main policy: it aims to be aware of the environment and sustain it in order to sustain the tourism industry. The TUI gathers information from >100 overseas destinations, which is entered into an environmental database to be used for planning and designing brochures. This information is used to keep customers informed of the environmental quality of the destination they are likely to go to on holiday. The destination criteria used by the TUI are as follows:

Bathing water and beach quality
Water supply and water-saving measures
Waste water disposal and utilization
Solid waste disposal, recycling and prevention
Energy supply and energy-saving measures
Traffic, air, noise and climate
Landscape and built environment
Nature conservation, spices preservation and animal welfare
Environmental information
Environmental policy and activities.

These are examples of a destination benchmarking study. The tour operator, to be regarded as a third party, establishes criteria that have to be met by the destination. The findings will indicate the performance of the destination from the environmental quality or environmental management effectiveness viewpoint and will affect its success in the market. Where the destination does not meet its criteria, the tour operator offers financial and technical aids. In other words, the destination (benchmarker) is given a chance to increase its awareness and improve its environmental performance.

The TUI has also established checklists to monitor the environmental policies and practices used in hotels, clubs and apartments in its membership. The waste water treatment, solid waste disposal and recycling, water supply and water-saving measures, energy supply and energy-saving measures, noise protection, cleanliness and hygiene and quality of beaches are some of the criteria that the TUI requires such accommodation facilities to take into consideration. Along with the guidelines of the TUI, the German Travel Agents Association, DRV, released a comprehensive programme for environmental management. The DRV guidelines advise hotel management on how to be efficient and environmentally friendly in water management, waste management, energy consumption, interior decoration, production and services of food, leisure facilities, staff training and communication skills with customers.

In addition, the EFQM model is committed to promoting quality as a fundamental process for continuous improvement within organizations. As in all other quality awards, organizations have a great opportunity to gain benefits from this model and its indicators launched in the public domain. This opportunity can be extended to include an organization's efforts to gain the award. The model has two main parts with a total of nine criteria. The enablers consist of leadership, people management, policy and strategy, resources and processes. The results include people satisfaction, customer satisfaction, impact on society and business results. The level of customer satisfaction has the highest percentage (20%) within the whole model. The percentage weightings are used to compare a company's scoring profile with the best in Europe. The award is given to the organization making a significant contribution with its approach to the philosophy of TQM by satisfying the expectations of customers, employees and others who are interested in the organization.

The criteria of the EFQM model are used to benchmark organizations. Within the time period of preparing to apply for the award, the organization will have to review its overall performance, attempt to develop new techniques, look at others and, most notably, follow guidelines and consider what the organization requires itself to do to reach the standards of the award. For instance, Tang and Zairi (1998) used the enabler criteria of the model to benchmark education and financial sectors on the basis of leadership, policy and strategy, people management, resource management and process management. In its present form, the EFQM model is suitable to be extended to include quality measurement of tourist destinations and its improvement (see Table 7.2 and Fig. 7.1).

The standards set by quality and eco-labelling systems, as noted, can be viewed as defining how a synthetic partner performs and thus form a basis for destination benchmarking when other information is lacking. Guidelines for best practice are, of course, available to members of the tourist industry. Such guidelines provide direction, implicitly or explicitly, on ways of improving or on what to do to reach these standards. Therefore, such guidelines help destination management to access external ideas and

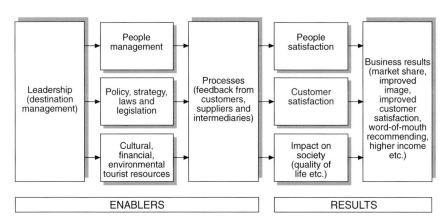

Fig. 7.1. Generic destination benchmarking model. Adapted from the EFQM model.

Table 7.2. An expanded version of EFQM-based destination benchmarking.

Criteria	Details
Enablers	
Leadership	Refers to the behaviour of the destination management team in accomplishing its objectives
Policy and strategy	Focuses on finding the most appropriate answers as to how the destination management team formulates, reviews and implements their unique policies and strategies in tourism
People management	Focuses on finding the most appropriate answers as to how the employees and the local residents are managed to become productive and effective
Resources	Focuses on finding the most appropriate answers as to how the destination management team is able to manage their existing economic and human resources in an effective and efficient way
Processes	Focuses on finding the most appropriate answers as to how the destination management team identifies, manages and improves its processes
Customer satisfaction	Focuses on discovering the most appropriate solutions as to what method is used to make customers satisfied with their present vacations and loyal to the destination in the future
Results	
People satisfaction	Focuses on discovering the most appropriate solutions as to what method is used to make both the employees and local residents satisfied with their visitors as well as with what they are doing and being hospitable towards visitors
Impact on society	Focuses on investigating the direct or indirect positive/negative impacts of what the destination management team tries to achieve in their tourism-based policies and strategies (impacts on society in terms of economic and social structure and natural environment)
Business results	Focuses on looking at what the local tourism industry has gained as a result of the practical application of policies and strategies through the use of the benchmarking process (changes in the number of visitors, in the amount of tourism incomes, in the level of multiplier effect and in the proportion of income over GNP)

practical methods. As with individual organizations gaining the Baldrige Awards, the managers of international tourist destinations can get some insight into their own performance levels by relating their operation to guidelines. Building on such insights is one way to make destinations better and more competitive. Figure 7.2 indicates the practical application of

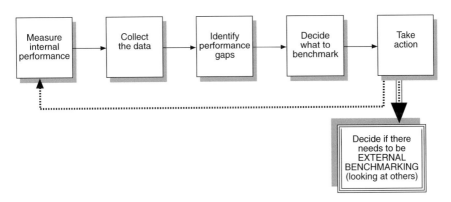

Fig. 7.2. The proposed model of generic destination benchmarking.

generic benchmarking and its extension to include tourist destinations. Detailed information about each stage is provided below.

Measuring the internal performance

Reflecting on the fact that the benchmarking process begins in the host organization, attempting initially to measure the internal performance of destinations provides opportunities to understand what measures need to be benchmarked, and identify areas where problems seem to appear. The results may help to indicate if the destination authorities need to go outside or look at external awards or standards established nationally or internationally. As is known, finding a proper partner is one of the main difficulties in benchmarking. Thus, when an organization or destination has problems with any environmental and service quality issue, it can get further information to resolve it either by contacting the organization supplying quality grading or eco-labels, by applying its guidelines in practice or by arranging partnerships with other organizations experiencing similar problems. By becoming members of the Green Globe 21 or Blue Flag, for example, destination authorities have an opportunity to obtain advice and to exchange ideas and experiences with other colleagues. These connections are accepted as a 'benchmarking network'. Green Globe 21, for example, firstly examines existing policies and practices, and then provides guidelines and targets to be followed. The list of guidelines, called the 'Green Globe Annual Review', includes case studies from other members. These may stimulate destination managers to develop new policies and reset its targets. They can simply adapt case studies to suit their own structure.

The author's personal observations in Santa Ponsa and Alcudia showed that Mallorca has a good and efficient system for delivering a cleaner environment. Mallorca has a well-designed Blue Flag signposting system at

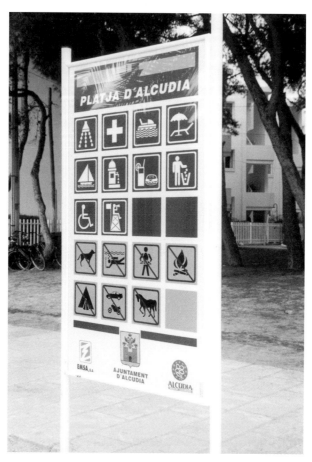

Fig. 7.3. A good example of a Blue Flag signpost, Alcudia, Mallorca.

regular distances, informing users about the availability of facilities and activities on beaches and about any restrictions (Fig. 7.3). There are six signposts in Alcudia. There are many litter bins close to both sides of pedestrian walkways. For example, in Alcudia, there are small and large litter bins on beaches about every 20–25 m (Fig. 7.4). There are toilets for both men and women, and buffets (cafeterias) every 100 m on the beach. The sand is clean as it is cleaned regularly, but the seashore and sea seemed to be dirty. Perhaps that is why one tourist observed that '... Streets seem dirtier and lots of cigarette ends on beaches ...'. Similarly, keeping streets and beaches clean seems to be harder in Marmaris and Fethiye, the Turkish resorts in the south-west part of the country, because all litter bins were removed due to security concerns or in some places were replaced by small ones (Fig. 7.5). There does not seem to be a major

Fig. 7.4. Beach-located litter bins, Alcudia, Mallorca.

problem with the cleanliness of the sea yet as Turkey is a very new destination in international tourism; but action should be taken to make it better if
any lesson needs to be learnt from Mallorca in this respect.

Collecting the data

Grading schemes are perishable and time-sensitive, as is benchmarking.
Thus, the organization will be monitored and inspected regularly in order
to identify whether it has improved or worsened or remained at the same
level. Kozak and Rimmington (1998) therefore suggest the use of external
awards (e.g. Welcome Host, Merit and Investors in People) and hospitality
grading systems (e.g. AA, RAC, ETB, STB) as examples of benchmarks that
use good practices as criteria for assessment to offer advantages and bring
about improvements in competitiveness for both small hospitality businesses and tourist destinations. As quality grading and eco-label systems
are accepted as the best practices that organizations or destinations must
consider as examples within their field, they could be taken as sources of
information. Grading systems clearly identify the best areas in which organizations should perform. For example, the minimum bed sizes, the availability of equipment in bedrooms, such as table, electric sockets, TV, radio
and smoke alarms, might be regarded as some of the best tangible benchmark elements for a hotel organization. Clean bed linen, access to double
beds from both sides, attending to customer complaints, offering breakfast,

Fig. 7.5. A small litter bin; these are located throughout the beach in Marmaris, Turkey.

dinner or room service, and general cleanliness will be the intangible benchmarks that help hotel management learn how to improve its services.

Identifying performance gaps

Benchmarking requires continuous attention to fulfil the targeted performance improvement (Camp, 1989). The aim of quality grading and eco-label systems is to sustain continuous improvement, which is also the aim of destination benchmarking. The practical procedure of quality grading and eco-label systems could therefore be accepted as a kind of continuous benchmarking measurement as they are given annually and renewed or revised periodically, provided that the criteria in the pre-identified guidelines are still being met. The awards or labels may be lost if the organization or the destination fails to fulfil the criteria at any time during the year.

The external systems such as quality systems, eco-labels and guidelines could play a greater role in raising awareness of the importance of benchmarking in continuously improving the quality of services and environmental resources. When such generic measures are taken into account as a sample case for maintaining performance measurement and improvement, destinations or their individual organizations may be able to understand how closely they are following guidelines identified as the best practices. The size of the gap may be revealed by the review scores.

Deciding what to benchmark

The significance of quality grading and eco-label systems is that they ensure the minimum standards of services and facilities offered by businesses and local authorities at the destination. Such systems could therefore be taken as critical success factors, which are important in determining the strengths and weaknesses of the destination in general and its facilities in particular. Candidates are provided with checklists from which they can identify the extent to which their operations comply with the code of practice and pinpoint which practices are in need of improvement. Findings of empirical research reflecting critical success factors with regard to different departments within the organization are important when considering which attributes are given priority by both customers and organizations (Brotherton and Shaw, 1996). Authorities may be interested in learning about new ideas outside, and benchmarking can help them identify not only which areas of performance need most attention but also how much improvement can be recorded (Coker, 1996). Critical success factors are mostly available to determine measurements to be focused on improvement. Here, critical performance indicators such as guest comments, consumer feedback and repeat business will enable authorities to evaluate their performance levels and take further actions for improving their service levels. Some of the critical success factors to be regarded as benchmark elements as a main part of classification and grading standards and awards are welcome, friendliness and attitude, customer care and attention, atmosphere and environment, quality of food and drink, hygiene and sanitation, safety and security, level of service, tourist information, and furnishings/furniture.

Furthermore, it is necessary to learn about customers' expectations from the organization. If they need further improvements in the organization, then a benchmarking study can be arranged. All classifications are designed to convey information to the customer about the type of property. If customers have initial information about the items of each classification scheme or have a prior experience with the other facility holding the same level of classification, then they may expect the hotel to have facilities and services to meet their expectations and needs. If this is not the case, it may give rise to negative experience and dissatisfaction. The benchmarking of hotels in accordance with elements in classification schemes will enhance their importance in that critical situation. For example, accommodation classification standards are compulsory in many European countries, e.g. Italy, Portugal, Spain and Greece (Callan, 1994), as they provide the balance between what hospitality organizations require and what customers expect. Such classification and grading standards offer small and medium hospitality organizations a variety of benefits such as improving quality, building a different image among customers, use for promotion and advertising and taking further advice from outside. For example, some national standard organizations in the UK such as the AA and RAC carry out frequent market research with hotel customers to reflect changes in customers' expectations, the range of services on offer and the potential markets in the industry. Whenever classification and grading schemes are improved, organizations will have to go further by maintaining continuous improvement and not lagging behind the requirements they need to offer. According to industry practitioners, 'a national classification system is necessary because it leads to the improvement and upgrading of the product itself and of the services offered' (Spachis, 1997, p. 93).

Taking action

Quality grading and particularly eco-label systems could be a symbol of self-monitoring appearing among tourists, intermediaries and suppliers. A new breed of tourists wants to spend vacations in an unspoiled place, and expects intermediaries to recommend the most appropriate destinations. As a result, intermediaries require tourism suppliers to pay attention to the preservation of the natural and cultural resources they supply and benefit from. Since most tours are booked through travel agents, destinations have to meet the criteria demanded for inclusion in travel brochures. If destinations do not meet expected standards, customers may be advised to avoid them. As a final stage, tourism suppliers and destination authorities provide several guidelines about how they expect customers (users) to behave and how to use resources without damaging the environment, e.g. keeping beaches and streets clean, keeping equipment at hotels safely and saving energy and water.

Both industry and non-industry organizations recently have focused their attempts on the practical application and implementation of a variety of guidelines, checklists and policies to safeguard and promote the cultural and natural resources of tourist destinations. The three leading international organizations, the WTTC, the WTO and the Earth Council, established a consortium in 1996 and released an action plan entitled 'Agenda 21 for the tourism and travel industry: towards environmentally sustainable development'. The project aims towards sectoral sustainable development, identifying priority areas and providing further steps on how these are to be achieved. It requires partnership between government, industry and non-government organizations. The major priority areas are:

- planning for sustainable tourism development
- training and enhancing public awareness
- providing exchange of information between developed and developing countries
- designing new products by considering their sustainability implications
- providing effective partnerships for sustainable development.

There are a number of examples from the practice. The European Union encourages the use of the 'Blue Flag' strategy within coastal destinations. As a part of its policy for responsible tourism, the Africa Travel Association has released a set of guidelines to minimize visitor impacts on wildlife, local culture and community. The European Tour Operators Association delivers guidelines to its members requesting them to be sensitive towards the natural and cultural environment in the local community and recommending their customers to behave in the same way. The International Hotel and Restaurant Association aims to assist its member companies in delivering services with best practices. Moreover, at the International Conference on Biodiversity and Tourism held in Berlin in 1997, the ministries of tourism declared their agreement on taking all necessary measures to deliver sustainable tourism development in their native countries. Surely, the main objective of all these tasks is to deliver better services and ensure that customers are satisfied, while at the same time minimizing the impact on environmental resources.

The application of generic benchmarking and the implementation of its results require a close coordination between private and public organizations. For example, the implementation of the eco-label for the hospitality industry in Vienna was established by the city administration in coordination with the municipality, the Vienna Business Agency, the Chamber of Commerce, the Chamber of Employees, the Austrian Trade Union and the ministry for environment. These partners constitute the advisory board of the partnership and are responsible for strategic decisions and internal support. The city administration is primarily responsible for the administration and development of the programme that aims to encourage organizations to apply for the label and help them to fulfil all requested criteria (Martinuzzi, 2000).

Consistent with the two earlier benchmarking types (i.e. internal and external benchmarking), the analysis of results derived from generic benchmarking investigation might assist in identifying gaps, determining strengths and weaknesses of destinations, and deciding which attributes are to be investigated further or which good practices can be adopted from others. Thus, depending upon the existence and the size of the gap examined in the preceding stage, destination management might have an opportunity to make a decision as to whether it needs to take further action and make improvements in particular elements of the destination. However, attention needs to be paid to the factors that affect the success of practices and the overall performance of benchmarking studies, e.g. cultural differences between different tourist-receiving countries. In terms of improving the quality of products or services (performance management), several strategies can be set up. Training programmes can be instigated among staff and shopkeepers to encourage them to behave towards tourists in a friendly manner, be keen to listen to their complaints, and respect the natural environment. These may then require a revision of the existing laws, regulations and practices and upgrading of the tourist infrastructure, as enablers of performance improvement through destination benchmarking.

Strengths and Weaknesses of Generic Destination Benchmarking

Table 7.3 summarizes the information on the strengths and weaknesses of generic destination benchmarking from the practical point of view. As emphasized earlier, the prime purpose of carrying out benchmarking studies is to learn about best practices from other counterparts/partners and the

Table 7.3. Strengths and weaknesses of generic destination benchmarking.

No.	Strengths	Weaknesses	When appropriate to use
1	The standards set by quality and eco-label systems offer simple examples to explain how such initiatives could form a basis for destination benchmarking	Customers may not consider some specific attributes as important while choosing the destination. For example, they may not want the hotel to have leisure facilities or activities for children or the beach to have showers	When radical change is needed
2	Helps to convince customers that the quality of products and services provided by a supplier will meet their requirements	There is a need for concern as to whether such best practices are suitable for the structure and culture of every destination	When improving activities or services for which partners do not exist
3	It might become possible to develop professional networks with international organizations and tour operators		When pressures prevent benchmarking within the same industry and in the same destination

way to achieve them (e.g. Camp, 1989; Geber, 1990). The standards set by quality and eco-label systems offer simple examples that can be used to explain how such initiatives could form a basis for destination benchmarking. Guidelines towards best practice are, of course, available to members of the tourist industry. Such guidelines provide feedback on ways of improving or what to do to reach these standards. These could help destination management to access external ideas and practical methods. Like individual organizations gaining the Baldrige Awards, international tourist destinations could also get some feedback about their performance levels. This could be one aspect of applications that makes destinations better and more competitive.

Moving from the role of expectations in the theory of customer satisfaction measurement (Parasuraman *et al.*, 1985), it is necessary to learn about customers' expectations from a particular element of a destination. All quality grading and eco-label systems are designed to convey information to the customer about the type of facility a destination has and provide the balance between what tourism establishments require and what customers expect. Such standards offer a variety of benefits such as improving quality and building a different image to use for promotion and advertising. One of the objectives of these systems is to convince customers that the quality of products and services provided by a supplier will meet their requirements. When guests arrive at a destination, they might want to see varied menus, clean rooms, streets and beaches, and helpful and informative staff. If customers have initial information about the items of each system or have previously been to a similarly graded destination, then they may expect it to have facilities and services to meet their expectations and needs. For instance, if tourists observe one destination with a clean environment and beaches, then they would expect other destinations to have a similar performance. Where this is not the case, it may give rise to negative experience and dissatisfaction. This might then influence the overall performance of destinations.

In spite of its potential benefits, the consideration of generic benchmarking solely on the basis of the existing quality grading and eco-label systems has several limitations. First, in terms of the importance of quality grading and eco-label systems in selecting tourism establishments or tourist destinations, it is not reasonable to say that these are the only issues on customer choice because of the difficulty of taking location and price into account as assessment measures. Although Callan (1994, 1996) states that quality grading systems play a general role in the selection of hotels by UK customers, customers may not consider some specific attributes as important while choosing the hotel or the destination. For example, they may not want the hotel to have leisure facilities or activities for children or the beach to have showers. This means that grading or eco-label systems may sometimes fail to guess what a customer wants and needs. Next, it is normally expected that any highly graded hotel organization should have a high quality of service and facilities. The hotel, even a lower grade facility, should consider the importance of that issue in delivering better services to the customer. In a similar way, beaches with Blue Flags may be considered as better or cleaner than those without, although this is not necessarily so. A lower grade does not necessarily mean that the hotel or the destination delivers a lower level of service quality. Such a destination may have fewer facilities, but not necessarily poor quality services and facilities. However, in practice, this does sometimes happen. Finally, there is a need for concern as to whether such best practices are suitable for the structure and culture of every destination.

Although generic benchmarking suggests that individual organizations or destinations should look not only at others in the same industry but also at best practice recognized in the national or international arena (Breiter and Kline, 1995; Cook, 1995), the problem with such applications is that there are a variety of national and international quality award and eco-label systems. It is difficult to know which one to follow. The solution could be to establish an individual quality award and eco-label system by utilizing the existing applications and considering each country's or destination's own features. The literature review revealed that there is no particular quality grading system devoted to identifying the broad picture of tourist destinations, although the evidence given by some tour operator guidelines such as TUI has the potential to be developed further. The existing hospitality classification and grading systems are limited to guidelines for increasing physical and service quality within accommodation establishments and dining services as the eco-labels comply with specific guidelines for maintaining environmental quality standards.

Summary

This chapter has introduced quality grading and eco-label systems as a form of generic benchmarking studies and reviewed several benefits of this application to destinations, tourists and individual organizations. Beyond the level of customer services on the demand side and infrastructure on the supply side, the existence of quality grading and environmental management is viewed as a part of national or international generic benchmarking enablers that are supposed to make a contribution to the host destination internally or externally. By applying these enablers, individual organizations and destination management could improve their existing products and services and, if necessary, identify ways of developing new ones, which could also lead to a better demand–supply relationship with customers and destinations. Having completed introducing the three types of destination benchmarking, the next chapter provides a discussion of the methodology, research design and procedures to be employed in its empirical investigation.

Data Collection and Analysis

8

Introduction

This chapter provides a discussion of the methodology, research design and procedures to be employed in the investigation of destination benchmarking research in accordance with the proposed qualitative and quantitative measures. The chapter begins with a brief overview of the literature on designing research methods. Then, it moves on to the operationalization of the destination benchmarking methodology by discussing the design of both quantitative and qualitative research methods. The chapter concludes by examining how data derived from such methods can be used to produce an overall picture from the destination benchmarking perspective, and to observe and document changes in the market structure.

Research Methods

The positivist approach consists of inductive and deductive research methods (Bryman, 1988). In the former method, theory reflects the accumulated findings of empirically established facts (moving from empirical findings towards theoretical implications). In the latter method, empirical research is based on the existing theories. Hypotheses are derived from theories and are then empirically tested. Research findings are analysed to determine if they make a contribution to the existing theories (moving from existing theories towards theoretical implications). The following stages are suggested in designing a systematic line of methodology research (Bryman, 1988; Dann et al., 1988; Bryman and Cramer, 1990). The first stage is 'conceptualization', where research problems are identified. The next is 'operationalization', which aims to undertake the task of setting and testing hypotheses.

In order to establish more accurate and original research problems, the first two stages require an extended review of previous relevant literature contributions. The third stage, 'measurement', employs any of the nominal, ordinal, interval or ratio methods. This is followed by the stage of data collection by identifying the sample population and utilizing quantitative and/or qualitative research methods. The final stage, 'data analysis', presents the findings. The objective of the last three stages is to seek a causal connection between hypotheses and empirical data and draw conclusions.

As each method has its own strengths and weaknesses (see Table 8.1), the literature in the field suggests that both qualitative (unstructured) and quantitative (structured) methods could be used for various purposes (Bryman, 1988). Some questions can be answered by carrying out quantitative research and others can be examined by following the guidelines of qualitative research. Moreover, quantitative research aims to test existing theories as qualitative research is associated with the generation or the development of theories. The latter is also used to assess the relevance of existing theories. This book considers the use of quantitative and qualitative research methods in tandem (combined approach). In other words, this is an amalgam of quantitative data, observational data and documentary evidence elaborated to contribute to the existing benchmarking literature (deductive research approach).

Formulation of Data Collection Procedures

There is an ongoing argument with respect to choosing either quantitative or qualitative research methods for benchmarking although a great deal of

Table 8.1. Advantages and disadvantages of research methodologies.

Methodology	Advantages	Disadvantages
Quantitative (structured)	Easy to administer Simple to code	Forces respondents to reply Limits respondents to given dimensions
	Easy to employ statistical methods Facilitates comparison of several products	Measures are not the unique features of the product
Qualitative (unstructured)	Allows respondents to describe their impressions freely Direct contact with respondents (via focus groups, open-ended surveys, etc.) Content analysis is used	Data are highly variable Statistical procedures are limited

Source: Echtner and Ritchie (1991).

research has been conducted using both methods (McNair and Leibfried, 1992; Karlof and Ostblom, 1993; Watson, 1993). Moreover, based on the assessment of past empirical benchmarking studies, Dorsch and Yasin (1998) made the criticism that most benchmarking publications have been produced by researchers from the industry and several differences have been observed with respect to the methodology chosen. While academic researchers used both quantitative and qualitative methods, researchers from the industry avoided quantitative approaches. Despite this ongoing debate in benchmarking, the application of destination benchmarking research suggests the assessment of primary and secondary sources of data gathered using both quantitative and qualitative research methods. Qualitative research methods present the collection and the analysis of verbal data such as open-ended questionnaires, observations, case studies, interviews and documents, whereas quantitative research methods refer to the collection and the analysis of either primary or secondary numerical or statistical (non-verbal) data.

Bryman (1988) comments that both research methods can be used as a complementary ingredient of empirical surveys. The review of the literature indicates that telephone surveys, mail surveys and personal interviews (including questionnaire surveys in the presence of the researcher or project coordinator) are the predominant methodologies used by organizations to obtain customer feedback (Mentzer *et al.*, 1995). As already emphasized earlier in Chapter 2, the application of benchmarking in the fields of tourism and hospitality has been limited to the use of customer surveys (CBI News, 1995; Department of National Heritage, 1996; Cheshire, 1997), with the exception of secondary sources of data and observations. Destination benchmarking needs to fill this gap. Therefore, this chapter is based primarily on designing a questionnaire survey along with observations and secondary sources of data. When either one or another method is used, the important issue is that questions must be right, unambiguous, clear, well defined and be presented in a language relevant to the respondent (Lewis, 1984). The suggested essential activities for generating a potentially effective questionnaire and identifying elements of good practice in quantitative and qualitative research are listed in Table 8.2.

Application of quantitative research methods

This stage includes an in-depth analysis of methods used to collect both primary and secondary sources of data as a contribution to the relationship between the application of quantitative research methods and carrying out a destination benchmarking investigation. The type of questions to be asked in a survey is related to the type of research problems and objectives. In identifying target markets, two conceptual approaches are presented (Kotler *et al.*, 1993). One is to collect data about the current tourists' country of

Table 8.2. Elements of good practice in quantitative and qualitative research.

Research activities	Details
1. Quantitative research methods	Refer to the collection and the analysis of either primary or secondary numerical or statistical (non-verbal) data.
1.1. Primary data collection	Used to obtain first-hand information from the sample population or about the object or subject under investigation.
Generating items	Primary stage in a questionnaire design. An essential stage to identify attributes that will be used in a benchmarking study. Items can be generated through both primary and secondary sources.
Identifying the construct	The construct is the structured form of questions and consists of various types of scales such as Likert and semantic differential. Easier to manage and assess the findings.
Pilot survey and revision of the instruments	Carried out to ensure that respondents are able to understand the wording and content of the questionnaire and willing to provide the information requested. Also useful to develop the final draft of questionnaires.
Data collection (main survey)	This stage encompasses the choice of sample destinations and sample populations, the calculation of the sample size and the delivery of questionnaires.
Reliability assessment	Performed to test the reliability and internal consistency of items in a structured questionnaire. The higher the value, the better the instrument.
Validity assessment	Performed to examine whether the scale measures what it purports to measure. The higher value between the scale and the related item indicates that the instrument is valid. In other words, it is capable of measuring what it has been designed for.
Employing statistical tests	χ^2, analysis of variance and *t*-test are used to test whether any difference exists between sample groups. Factor analysis is performed to demonstrate the extent to which questions seem to be measuring the same variables and the degree to which they could be reduced to a more general and smaller set of factor attributes. Regression analysis is performed to determine the aggregate impact of certain independent variables on dependent variables (e.g. performance measures and total tourist expenditure). All these tests could be helpful in destination benchmarking.

Table 8.2. *Continued.*

Research activities	Details
1.2. Secondary data collection	A type of data collection entirely from secondary sources such as reports, books, articles, newspapers, and so on.
2. Qualitative research methods	Present the collection and the analysis of verbal data such as open-ended questionnaires, observations, case studies, interviews and documents.
Open-ended questionnaires	Helps the researcher obtain detailed information in tourists' own words about their positive or negative holiday experiences in the destination. Also a useful method to obtain comments from tourists for improvement. Content analysis is a method for use in analysing open-ended questionnaire data as well as documents.
Observations (inspections)	A research technique to observe objects and subjects in their natural surroundings (different aspects of destinations) and find out if there are any differences between them. The researcher has the ability to obtain first-hand knowledge by watching, rather than receiving reports prepared by others.
3. Analysis of data	The next stage where data are assessed to test hypotheses and draw conclusions. Data are usually processed and analysed using either computer-based statistical tests or content analysis.
4. Overall analysis	Findings could illustrate the areas where gaps appear and identify the root causes of problems in one destination and examples of good practice in another.

origin, their demographic profiles, their reasons for coming, their satisfaction levels, the level of their repeat visits and their total spending while on vacation. Such information may be helpful in analysing the market to determine which group is easiest to attract and so to bring more benefits. The other approach is to reach those potential markets that are interested in the destination. However, this type of research has some limitations such as accessibility, time and cost. Based on Kotler *et al.*'s approach together with other contributions reviewed in earlier chapters, the purpose of conducting primary research is to obtain first-hand information in terms of both supply (e.g. tourism establishments, local residents) and demand (e.g. customers).

Quantitative data are gathered by delivering different types of survey instruments designed in the format of a structured questionnaire. A questionnaire includes a set of questions for obtaining a statistically useful process or personal information. A questionnaire survey, either open-ended or structured, provides various advantages (Pizam, 1994a). First, it provides flexibility in choosing the desired data collection method (postal survey, personal interviews, and so on). Secondly, results can be generalized either to the whole population or to other similar populations. Thirdly, it is a cost-effective type of research design; and finally, it gives an opportunity to collect a large amount of information, which improves the accuracy of results. Thus, questionnaire surveys are also regarded as essential benchmarking tools when properly employed during the research (Bogan and English, 1994).

A number of relevant attributes or items need to be identified to be able to examine the performance of one destination from the customers' point of view and consider them while benchmarking. Item generation is a process that requires three steps (McDougall and Munro, 1994). The review of relevant literature could be a starting point. Next, open-ended interviews with experienced individuals and questionnaires could lead to further items. The last step could be to ask a team of specialists to review the proposed instrument and its clarity. Analysis of the literature displayed substantial variations in the number and nature of attributes considered relevant to tourist motivation and satisfaction with destinations (e.g. Goodrich, 1977; Pizam *et al.*, 1978; Dorfman, 1979; Pearce, 1982). It is also debatable whether attributes relevant to different customer groups and different international destinations are transferable between different contexts. It is known that the list of items in a survey has been generated by the researcher, not by the respondents (Dann, 1996). Thus, a pool of destination attributes should be generated through both primary and secondary sources (Robson, 1993). This process is briefly explained in the following paragraphs.

Design of an individual survey instrument

As already emphasized earlier, the most common criterion in benchmarking is that it should start with understanding the performance of a specified organization or destination (McNair and Leibfield, 1992; Karlof and Ostblom, 1993). The findings of questionnaire surveys are expected to be useful for carrying out internal and external benchmarking procedures. An independent and simple questionnaire is needed to measure a destination's performance before comparisons can be made and also to prepare the ground for external benchmarking research. Concerning the application of the gap analysis model, the findings will be compared with those of another similar questionnaire distributed in the partner destination. This part of the research presents detailed information about the development of an individual survey instrument.

The literature suggests that Likert-type scales can be used to evaluate tourist experiences at the destination, since they are effective in measuring customer attitudes, easy to construct and manage, require little time to administer and avoid the risk of verbal bias (Bonifield *et al.*, 1996). Results can be analysed by using statistical techniques (Osgood *et al.*, 1971). Empirical research findings demonstrate that the Likert scales are also more reliable and valid (Fishbein and Ajzen, 1975) and are suitable for a large data set (McDougall and Munro, 1994). These type of scales have been widely used in tourism and travel research in order to identify the tourists' perceptions of attributes, attitudes, satisfaction levels and motivations. These scales may also be used in the benchmarking measurement processes as they enable the researcher to identify and compare gaps and make action plans (Madigan, 1993). Some examples of such scales in various versions are provided in Table 8.3. As shown, all odd-numbered scales have a middle value that is often labelled 'neutral' or 'undecided'. It is also possible to use a forced-choice response scale with an even number of responses where the respondent is forced to make a decision (see Table 8.4).

Design of comparison survey instrument

As noted earlier, there has been insufficient attention paid in the literature relating to the consideration of those visiting the peer destination as the sample population and the investigation of their comparative satisfaction levels. As demonstrated, few studies measuring customer perceptions of destinations have investigated perceptions of different destinations within the same questionnaire. One disadvantage of this is that attribute scales do not necessarily reflect perceived superiority or inferiority. Despite this, it is believed that the comparison of a destination with others offering similar types of holidays enables the destination not only to evaluate the nature of the competition but also to identify new market opportunities by reflecting how others are performing (Goodall, 1990).

The literature suggests that, like Likert-type scales, semantic differential scales also can be used to evaluate tourist experiences at the destination. Semantic differential scales include a set of bipolar adjectives, e.g. good–bad, cheap–expensive. Empirical research findings demonstrate that, like the Likert scales, semantic differential scales are more reliable and valid (Fishbein and Ajzen, 1975) and are suitable for a large amount of data (McDougall and Munro, 1994). These scales may also be used in the benchmarking measurement processes as they enable the researcher to identify and compare gaps and make action plans (Madigan, 1993). Thus, this questionnaire aims to measure the performance of one destination over another on several attributes by employing a revised form of semantic differential scales and asking respondents who have recently been to both destinations to compare them directly on the same questionnaire.

There are two different opinions about the measurement of customer satisfaction (Singh, 1991). The first accepts the idea that customers must have their own experiences with the product or service in order to make a

Table 8.3. Examples of various constructs with odd numbers.

To investigate the primary reasons influencing tourists' destination choice process (motivations)

Extremely important	Very important	Slightly important	Neither important nor unimportant	Slightly unimportant	Very unimportant	Not important at all

To measure the level of tourist satisfaction with destination attributes

Delighted	Pleased	Mostly satisfied	Neither satisfied nor dissatisfied	Mostly dissatisfied	Unhappy	Terrible

To measure the level of tourist satisfaction with destination attributes

Definitely satisfied	Most likely satisfied	Satisfied	Neither satisfied nor dissatisfied	Dissatisfied	Most likely dissatisfied	Completely dissatisfied

To measure attitudes of tourists towards local residents and destinations

Strongly agree	Agree	Somewhat agree	Neither agree nor disagree	Somewhat disagree	Disagree	Strongly disagree

To measure performance of destination attributes

Extremely good	Good	Partly good	Neither good nor poor	Partly poor	Poor	Extremely poor

To measure future intentions of tourists

Definitely	Most likely	Likely	Maybe	Unlikely	Most unlikely	Not likely at all

Table 8.4. Examples of various constructs with even numbers.

To investigate the primary reasons influencing tourists' destination choice process					
Extremely important	Very important	Slightly important	Slightly unimportant	Very unimportant	Not important at all
To measure the level of tourist satisfaction with destination attributes					
Delighted	Pleased	Mostly satisfied	Mostly dissatisfied	Unhappy	Terrible
To measure the level of tourist satisfaction with destination attributes					
Definitely satisfied	Most likely satisfied	Satisfied	Dissatisfied	Most likely dissatisfied	Completely dissatisfied
To measure attitudes of tourists towards local residents and destinations					
Strongly agree	Agree	Somewhat agree	Somewhat disagree	Disagree	Strongly disagree
To measure performance of destination attributes					
Extremely good	Good	Partly good	Partly poor	Poor	Extremely poor
To measure future intentions of tourists					
Definitely	Most likely	Likely	Unlikely	Most unlikely	Not likely at all

judgement about the level of satisfaction (direct measure of satisfaction). The second primarily focuses on the indirect measures of satisfaction by considering customers' general opinions about a particular product or service. Despite this classification, marketing literature has paid most attention to direct customer experiences while investigating the level of satisfaction. Klaus (1985, p. 21), for example, defines satisfaction as 'the consumer's subjective evaluation of a consumption experience based on some relationship between the consumer's perceptions and objective attributes of the product'. Previous benchmarking research demonstrated that organizations also ask their customers to compare their performance with their competitors while carrying out competitive benchmarking analysis (Mentzer *et al.*, 1995).

For the reasons given above, this chapter not only suggests using a modified scale but also proposes a different scale developed for the purpose of gathering data by asking tourists who had already visited the partner destination in order to make a direct comparison with their perceptions of the host destination. In other words, this proposed method asks respondents to compare only two destinations directly. When the survey is conducted in the host destination, respondents are requested not only to state their satisfaction perceptions of that destination but also to compare them with those of the partner destination if they have been there recently. This is intended to give tourists an opportunity to match the performance of both destinations with respect to facilities, activities, levels of tourist services, and so on. The intention is to generate reliable results for determining which one performs better from the customers' point of view.

This technique stems from the assumption that people are more likely to compare something reliably by considering their own experiences. This is done on the basis of 'something here is better than another in X' or 'X is more expensive than Y'. Respondents are asked to rate an attitude object on a series of 5- or 7-point scales anchored at each end by bipolar phrases. To give an example, it ranges from an extreme of 'much more expensive' (1) to 'much cheaper' (5) for a statement aiming to measure the perceived level of food and beverage prices at the given destination compared with that of another. The same set of destination attributes in the individual questionnaire can be asked in this questionnaire, but with a revised label and scale. Unlike previous comparison research, this book suggests using verbal rather than numerical labels as there were variations in the format of labels, e.g. much better–much worse in one question and much cheaper–much more expensive in another (see Table 8.5. for a list of examples).

This method could be criticized on the basis that it cannot easily be extended to more than two destinations since this would make the evaluation process more complex and lengthy. It is, however, a useful tool for two-directional benchmarking studies. Similar types of scales previously have been applied within the marketing literature to measure how a customer perceives any service or product compared with the expectation (disconfirmation method). Incorporating this view into research studies, the respondent was asked to make a comparison of experiences in one destination compared with those in another (Kozak, 2002b).

Administration of pilot surveys and revision of instruments

The main purpose of pilot surveys is to be sure that respondents are able to understand the wording and content of questions and are willing to provide the information requested (Chisnall, 1992). Depending on the observations during the pilot survey, the main statements or items to be used in the actual questionnaire survey can be reduced or increased. Among other major benefits of the pilot survey are gaining familiarity with respondents and their views, which may lead to some modification of questionnaire content, trying out field-work management arrangements and gaining a preliminary estimate of the likely response rate (Veal, 1992). Furthermore, conducting a pilot survey helps to test the reliability and validity of the scale (Moser and Kalton, 1971) and perform an item analysis to eliminate items with the weakest item-to-total correlation values from the further stage of the survey (McDougall and Munro, 1994).

Application of qualitative research methods

This part of the data collection stage is related to the design of open-ended questionnaires to compare one destination with self-reported multiple destinations and the administration of observations. Although the application of such qualitative methods in benchmarking provides much detail, findings require an objective assessment. Employing qualitative research methods has several advantages indicating the value of gaining a clear understanding of tourists' judgements in their own words and interpretation while examining comparative performance of tourist destinations. Some significant feedback was obtained from the results of open-ended questionnaires on the benefit of using open-ended questions in destination benchmarking projects and from the information that the researcher was given by tourists in short face-to-face interviews at the destination airports while carrying out the surveys (Kozak, 2000). Complaints about the noise of young people after midnight reported by family groups in Mallorca and an extensive problem of harassment and the lack of air-conditioning systems reported by those in Turkish destinations were among missing attributes in the main questionnaire survey, but need attention for improvement.

Design of open-ended questionnaires

As an ingredient of qualitative (unstructured) research methods, open-ended questions can be used to collect data regarding both negative and

Table 8.5. Some examples for direct comparison surveys.

1. In comparison with Destination X, quality of service at my accommodation in Destination Y was

Much better	Better	About the same	Worse	Much worse	No opinion

2. In comparison with Destination X, my accommodation in Destination Y was

Much cleaner	Cleaner	About the same	Dirtier	Much dirtier	No opinion

3. In comparison with Destination X, the local transport service in Destination Y was

Much more frequent	More frequent	About the same	More infrequent	Much more infrequent	No opinion

4. In comparison with Destination X, the beaches and sea in Destination Y were

Much cleaner	Cleaner	About the same	Dirtier	Much dirtier	No opinion

5. In comparison with Destination X, food and beverage prices in Destination Y were

Much cheaper	Cheaper	About the same	More expensive	Much more expensive	No opinion

6. In comparison with Destination X, quality of food in Destination Y was

Much better	Better	About the same	Worse	Much worse	No opinion

7. In comparison with Destination X, local people in Destination Y were

Much more friendly	More friendly	About the same	More unfriendly	Much more unfriendly	No opinion

8. In comparison with Destination X, local people in Destination Y were

Much more helpful	More helpful	About the same	Less helpful	Much less helpful	No opinion

9. In comparison with Destination X, nightlife and entertainment in Destination Y was

Much better	Better	About the same	Worse	Much worse	No opinion

10. In comparison with Destination X, availability of facilities and services for children in Destination Y was

Much better   Better   About the same   Worse   Much worse   No opinion

11. In comparison with Destination X, the airport in Destination Y was

Much cleaner   Cleaner   About the same   Dirtier   Much dirtier   No opinion

12. In comparison with Destination X, overall value for money in Destination Y was

Much better   Better   About the same   Worse   Much worse   No opinion

13. In comparison with Destination X, the standard of spoken language in English in Destination Y was

Much better   Better   About the same   Worse   Much worse   No opinion

14. In comparison with Destination X, tourist information in the English language in Destination Y was

Much more adequate   More adequate   About the same   More inadequate   Much more inadequate   No opinion

15. In comparison with Destination X, signposting to attractions and facilities in Destination Y was

Much more organized   More organized   About the same   More unorganized   Much more unorganized   No opinion

16. If an opportunity was given, would you prefer a holiday in X or in Y?

In X   In Y   Not sure

positive comments of customers (Danaher and Haddrell, 1996). These could then be compared with the customers' overall evaluation of the service or the destination. Some previous research has been undertaken to investigate tourists' positive and negative experiences (Pearce and Caltabiano, 1983; Johns and Lee-Ross, 1995; Jackson *et al.*, 1996) and their image perceptions of destinations (Reilly, 1990) by distributing open-ended questionnaires to allow the respondent to reply in their own words, but not in an attempt at a direct comparison with other establishments or destinations. Open-ended questions may also be devoted to obtaining detailed feedback about repeat tourists' perceptions of attractions, facilities, services and hospitality at the destination, compared with their previous visits, and any further comments. In other ways, it is essential to identify the ways the host changed for the better and/or for the worse since the tourists' last visits. An example of this type of questionnaire is presented in Box 8.1.

   The use of this sort of questionnaire also has valuable implications for research on the competitive measurement of destination performance. This instrument was designed to measure one's performance against not only a specific destination but also its major competitors. It could be regarded as a valuable instrument in comparing a destination's performance with that of some other self-selected destinations probably in the same competitiveness set and dealing with similar issues. The destination authority is able to understand its own perceived performance not only against one destination but also against its main competitors. In addition, this instrument helps to view both positive and negative aspects of the tourism product one particular destination delivers. For instance, harassment was found to be the most serious problem in Turkey compared with other European destinations, though outside Europe, e.g. in Gambia, the problem is perceived to be worse. Similarly, Turkey is perceived to have a better tradition of hospitality than several of its European counterparts.

Observations (site visits)

As these are recommended for benchmarking individual organizations (Karlof and Ostblom, 1993), site visits provide first-hand information about destinations and offer an opportunity to observe different aspects of destinations, find out the situation in each area or whether there is any difference between these areas (e.g. the availability of facilities and activities, environmental legislation and tourism laws) when benchmarking is carried out between two organizations or destinations operating in different countries. Camp (1989) states that direct site visits are the most credible method in benchmarking, as an opportunity is created to prepare a checklist indicating what has and has not been done. Site visits organized in the 1950s between US and Japanese businesses led them to gain new ideas and successful results in their operations. Pizam (1994b) further states that observations, both participant and non-participant, are a part of research

Box 8.1. An example of an open-ended questionnaire.

Dear Guest,

The following questions are provided for you to compare the destination X with ***another destination Y which you have visited since the beginning of 2002.*** If you have visited X before, you are then asked to say how it has changed. Thank you for your assistance.

1. The overseas destinations I have visited since the beginning of 2002 are:

....
....
....

2. The destination I have compared with X is: ....

3. The destination in which I stayed in X was: ....

4. In what respects is X better than the other destination?

....
....
....

5. In what respects is X worse than the other destination?

....
....
....

6. Overall which destination was best and why?

....
....
....

If you have visited X previously, please answer the following three questions.

7. When have you been to X before (the latest visit)? ....

8. In what ways has X changed for the better since your last visit?

....
....
....

9. In what ways has X changed for the worse since your last visit?

....
....
....

Thank you for taking part in this questionnaire survey.

techniques to observe objects and subjects in their natural surroundings. The researcher has the ability to obtain first-hand knowledge by watching, rather than receiving reports prepared by others. From the participant observation point of view, Jorgensen (1989, p.12) notes that:

Through participant observation it is possible to describe what goes on, who or what is involved, when and where things happen, how they occur, and why – at least from the standpoint of the participants – things happen as they do in particular situations. The methodology of participant observations is exceptional for studying processes, relationships among people and events, continuities over time and patterns, as well as the immediate socio-cultural contexts in which human existence unfolds.

Benchmarking could concentrate not only on measuring outcomes (identifying standards of performance measurement) but also on examining processes as to how the product is produced (practices). Measuring the level of performance seems to be an inadequate way to investigate in depth the reasons for any anticipated gap. Practice or process benchmarking may help to present the answer(s) to this. Camp (1989) therefore suggests that both are essential criteria in benchmarking, but the former (performance benchmarking) should be followed by the latter (process/practice bench-marking). Although it is difficult to quantify the results of observations, they could still be used as ingredients when interpreting the findings of both pri-mary and secondary sources of data. Observations are sometimes regarded as an alternative method of data collection and sometimes as a supplemen-tary method depending on the type of research (Moser and Kalton, 1971; Robson, 1993). Personal observations preclude the need for lengthy reports. To extend their use, reverse engineering could be applied as in past studies of organization benchmarking. A group of representatives from hol-iday resorts would travel as customers to unfamiliar destinations to analyse how they are doing and concentrate on particular aspects of the destina-tions. Thus, personal observations or site visits, as a significant tool of external benchmarking, might be helpful to identify good practice exem-plars in other destinations and apply them to the host destination subject to revision if required (see Box 8.2).

Face-to-face interviews

Benchmarking research requires further methodological research such as interviews with tourists, authorities and tourism stakeholders at destinations in order to be able to present guidelines on how to achieve performance improvement on the basis of practice/process studies. There is a need to conduct face-to-face interviews not only with customers but also with ser-vice providers or those involved in the decision-making process about the development of the tourism and travel industry in the region. This type of method may help to discover customer likes and dislikes and, as a result, to come up with effective solutions in a short time. Three types of interview exist in the literature of research methodology. The choice and their use are determined by the purpose of the benchmarking study to be carried out. The first is **the structured interview**, which takes the form of a question-naire. Respondents are asked the same questions and in the same

> **Box 8.2.** Using observations in destination benchmarking. Source: Kozak (2000).
>
> The method of observations was used in a destination benchmarking project to: (i) partially illustrate the root causes of differences between two destinations; and (ii) to monitor whether there are examples of good practice for use in destination benchmarking. Harassment is a serious problem in Turkey. Mallorca makes a more attractive destination particularly for family groups by providing a variety of facilities and activities. Mallorca has a richer and much better airport in terms of the variety of facilities, cleanliness and efficiency. Although it is progressing well in delivering a cleaner service, there are still customer complaints about dirtiness. Mallorca has the advantage of better language communication with its customers. Finally, reaching the saturation point of the destination life cycle model, Mallorca is a more mature, overdeveloped and commercialized destination. Thus, there could be some lessons that Turkey will learn from experiences of tourism development in Mallorca. This study indicated the existence of several good practices in the Mallorcan resorts, which could be copied by their Turkish counterparts without any major modification, e.g. kids' clubs and a playground in individual restaurants, menus with half-price for children under 12 years old, Blue Flags and their effective application in practice such as good and frequent signposting on beaches, facilities specifically designed for disabled people, and leaflets about a variety of attractions and events written in various languages.

sequence. The purpose is to minimize any bias. The next is **the semi-structured interview**. The interviewer has a list of general areas to cover, but some questions might be omitted depending upon the circumstances. The last one is **the unstructured interview** referred to as informal. This type of method is an effective way of collecting in-depth data. There is no predetermined list of questions, so the respondent is allowed to talk freely as long as the content is related to the topic.

Selection of Sample Populations

It is often practically impossible to include the entire population in a questionnaire survey. In such cases, a sampling frame must be chosen (Bryman and Cramer, 1990). The sampling frame must be defined within the parameters of the population. For example, if the target is package tourists, the questionnaire must only cover these groups (Lewis, 1984). It is believed that tourists usually need quite a long time to be able to assess the various amenities on offer (Saleh and Ryan, 1992). In conducting tourism benchmarking research, both stratified and systematic sampling methods should be applied to collect data, as the target population is overwhelmingly large. In the stratified sampling method, a specific category of population is selected. Following the guidelines of the disproportionate stratified sampling method, only those from a particular country or countries can take part in the questionnaire surveys depending upon the extent to which they represent the majority of the sample destination's outbound tourism demand. The sample from this population is then selected by a systematic sampling method. Findings of each survey derived from the respondents are analysed separately as each attribute of the destination could have different importance and satisfaction measures for different customer groups and the two groups might tend to complain at a different level of dissatisfaction (Pizam and Milman, 1993). It is also highly possible that motivations and the level of tourist expenditure may differ from one group to the other.

Collecting Primary Data

There are different approaches to investigate how, where and when to measure the level of customer experiences in the tourism industry. Some researchers have asked tourists to fill out a questionnaire in order to find their pre-holiday and post-holiday opinions about a specific destination (Duke and Persia, 1996). Others preferred to conduct a survey just after the holiday (Vogt and Fesenmaier, 1995). Haahti (1986) delivered questionnaires while the tourists were still at the destination, whilst other researchers suggest that the customer experience is best measured after the tourist has completed the tour or service experience (Danaher and Mattsson, 1994). Though there is no consensus on how to measure the level of customer experiences, the literature suggests that satisfaction is an overall post-purchase evaluation (Fornell, 1992). The literature further emphasizes the measurement of customer satisfaction immediately after purchase (Peterson and Wilson, 1992). This study therefore proposes that the randomly selected tourists can be approached just before the end of their holiday and questionnaires collected before they board the aircraft in order to obtain fresh feedback about their perceptions of each destination. In so doing, tourists may have available time and the benefit of the entire holiday to assess their perceptions of destination facilities, attractions and customer services, estimate roughly how much they spent in total and keep their complaints, if any, in mind (Stronge, 1992). In line with experiences gained from previous empirical investigation (Hurst, 1994), it is believed that 'en route surveys' are a cost-effective and popular tool used in tourism and travel research.

Collecting Secondary Data

One of the methods of benchmarking investigation is to search for the secondary sources of data in order to have a cost-effective study and to investigate in depth the periodical developments in the performance of an organization or a destination and indicate the possible reasons as to why any destination performs better or worse in any respect. In developing a case study, Yin (1994) suggests two sources of evidence for collecting secondary data. These are documents and archival records. Documents include the review of articles, books, brochures and newspaper cuttings. Archival records contain the analysis of the historical data on the number of tourist arrivals, tourism income, accommodation capacity, occupancy rates, and so on. The importance of collecting and interpreting statistical data stems from measuring internal and external performance levels, setting targets, recording developments and comparing results periodically (Bloom, 1996).

Analysis of Quantitative Data

Once the data are collected, they need to be categorized and analysed. Data collected through structured questionnaires are analysed by employing the Statistical Package for the Social Sciences (SPSS) computer program because this is a comprehensive and flexible statistical analysis and data management system. Moreover, it can generate tabulated reports, charts and complex statistical analyses. In order to achieve this, each response to a structured question should be coded. Codes are usually numbers, which are used to assist in organizing, quantifying and analysing data. The numbers can be arbitrary (e.g. '1' for those visiting Spain, and '2' for those visiting Greece). Coding makes the comparison process easier to understand if there are any gaps between the two destinations. Secondary data (metric data) of one destination are compared with those of another on the basis of months or years and nationality. Methods used for the analysis of primary data are explained below.

Reliability assessment

A reliability analysis is performed to test the reliability and internal consistency of each destination attribute given in a structured questionnaire instrument. A reliability score shows 'the degree to which measures are free from error and therefore yield consistent results' (Peter, 1979, p. 16). Coefficient α is one of the most useful approaches to assessing the reliability of measurement scales and is a measure of internal consistency reliability (Churchill, 1979; Peter, 1979). A low coefficient α indicates that the instrument performs poorly in capturing the anticipated outcomes, while a large coefficient α indicates that the instrument correlates well with the true items and scores (Churchill, 1979).

Validity assessment

Validity assessment examines whether the scale measures what it purports to measure (Czepiel *et al.*, 1974; Churchill, 1979). Concurrent and predictive validity tests are conducted to investigate the extent to which the instrument measured what it was intended to measure (Carmines and Zeller, 1979). Concurrent validity is assessed by correlating a measure and the criterion at the same point in time, provided that the criterion exists in the present. In this study, concurrent validity refers to the relationship between individual items (or the scale) and the measurement of overall tourist experiences or perceptions, as a sign of current performance. Predictive validity concerns a future criterion, which is correlated with the relevant measure, e.g. intention for word-of-mouth recommendation and repeat business, as a sign of future performance (Moser and Kalton, 1971).

Where quantitative research techniques are employed and the structured questionnaires with scales are used, both reliability and validity assessments will be significant in designing effective and valid destination benchmarking research in order to be sure that findings are accurate and to discuss further implications. No such reliability and validity test is statistically possible for open-ended questionnaires or face-to-face interviews.

Other statistical tests

With particular reference to the administration of external benchmarking, it is significant to see if there is any difference in the characteristics of the sample population visiting destinations. This type of assessment is helpful for identifying not only the profile of market segments but also partner destinations with which external benchmarking is to be conducted. Such an attempt could be significant for destination benchmarking research in order to have a better understanding of competitors involved in the same set in terms of a particular market and make a decision about who and what to benchmark. For instance, the sample destinations could select their benchmarking partners from countries in the Mediterranean basin because the majority of tourists visiting Spain tend to take their holidays around this region. A series of χ^2 tests are applied in order to investigate if there are any statistical differences between independent (nominal) variables such as sociodemographic and holiday-taking behaviour of each tourist group visiting different destinations. A series of χ^2 tests and regression analysis are also utilized to assess the expenditure patterns of sample groups.

The application of external benchmarking, with few exceptions (e.g. New and Szwejczewski, 1995; Boger *et al.*, 1999), generally lacks the use of statistical tools such as t-, χ^2 and analysis of variance tests, particularly while measuring the qualitative performance of samples observed and employing structured questionnaires. There may be no need to use statistical tools for the assessment of some quantitative measures, but it is necessary to do so for qualitative measures when a large sample popula- tion is involved in the study. Unlike most of the earlier benchmarking stud- ies, this book suggests that using statistical methods could be more valuable than self-selected methods, where simple mean values of organi- zation A are plotted against those of organization B on a chart. There may be some gaps, but it is difficult to perceive how significant and how large they are. The result (or the gap) will be either positive or negative. Attributes with larger *t*-values result in larger gaps than those with smaller mean values in terms of mean scores. This type of analysis also helps to concentrate on those attributes with larger or smaller *t*-values, depending upon the future objectives.

Factor analysis is then performed to identify the group of destination attributes. The consideration of factor analysis is a significant procedure while carrying out both internal and external benchmarking. Examining the correlation or relationships between items, factor analysis demonstrates the extent to which questions seem to be measuring the same variables and the degree to which they could be reduced to a more general and smaller set of factor attributes. Having been accepted as a helpful statistical tool for assessing the reliability and validity of empirical measures (Carmines and Zeller, 1979), factor analysis is a useful method in assessing tourist motiva- tions and measuring tourist satisfaction, as the tourism product or the holi- day experience is made up of many interrelated components such as accommodation, food and drink, recreation, and so on (Pizam *et al.*, 1978).

Multiple regression is used subsequently to determine the aggregate impact of certain destination attributes on various performance measures with respect to overall satisfaction, image perceptions and future behav- iour. This procedure was earlier suggested in this book as a measure of internal benchmarking. This method demonstrates the strength of any vari- able in the overall model, which aims to predict either overall satisfaction or the intention for the future behaviour in consumer research. One advan- tage of using multiple regression measures (R^2 values) is to assess the con- vergent validity of the performance-only based survey instrument (Crompton and Love, 1995). For each performance factor, the technique of least-squares is used to estimate the regression coefficients (b_i) in an equa- tion of the form:

$$Y = a + b_1 x_1 + b_2 x_2 + \ldots + b_n x_n$$

where Y is the predicted performance (dependent variable), a is the con- stant value, and b_i is the β coefficient value for each independent variable and shows the correlation between the dependent variable and each of the independent variables. It also represents the expected change in the perfor- mance indicator associated with a one-unit change in the *i*th independent variable when impacts of the other variables in the model are held constant.

x is the mean score of each independent variable. The dependent variables of the regression model are the level of tourists' overall satisfaction with their holiday experiences in the host and partner destinations, their intention of recommending their holidays to their friends and relatives, and their intention to revisit the same destinations. The orthogonal factors are the independent variables of each model.

Results of each process are reported in a table, along with the t-statistics, standardized regression coefficients and R^2 values. Each table presents the significant variables that remained in the equation and which explain tourist satisfaction in order of their importance based on standardized β coefficient values. The standardized estimate (β coefficients) of each variable reflects the relative importance of each independent factor variable. In other words, the larger the estimate, the higher the importance of variables in the overall model. The value of R^2 shows how well the model fits the population. The higher the value of R^2, the better the predictor of the model. Likewise, the lower the value of R^2, the worse the predictor. The tolerance values indicate the degree of standard error in the model. The large tolerance values refer to the low level of standard error, which is a credit to the success of the model.

This type of analysis may indicate the strength of each destination attribute (factor items) within a destination benchmarking investigation. In other words, the stronger an attribute, the better it is performing and is considered as a strength or competitive advantage. Findings may be useful to formulate some recommendations regarding a marketing strategy that destination authorities should consider in efforts to improve the performance of their facilities and services. Such types of summary questions, as suggested in Chapter 4, may ease the interpretation of attributes on the basis of destination benchmarking and the internal performance analysis of destinations, rather than capturing gaps between the two on the basis of 'apple with apple' comparison. At the stage of taking action, objectives could be revised based on findings, and the relevant people and organizations within the destination might be asked to share their opinions and experiences.

Analysis of Qualitative Data

Content analysis is a method for use in analysing open-ended questionnaire data as well as documents (Robson, 1993). It is therefore essential to use content analysis in benchmarking research to analyse qualitative data derived by distributing the open-ended questionnaire. The analysis of the open-ended questionnaire provides lists of words (or items) in the space provided for each question. These items are ordered according to the number of times that they appear. The frequency values are then calculated for each item by dividing each value by the total size of the sample population in each tourist group. Responses are ranked in order of the percentage value. The higher the percentage value, the better the factor (or item) is considered by respondents for the question designed to demonstrate how likely the destination was perceived to be better than other destinations. In contrast, the higher the percentage value, the worse the factor (or item) for the question designed to demonstrate how likely the destination is perceived to be worse than other destinations. A similar method is also used for the assessment of comments and the repeat tourists' perceptions of changes in sample destinations. Also, some direct quotations from the open-ended questionnaire may be helpful to emphasize some of the differences.

Overall Analysis

The outcome of overall analysis is expected to make a contribution to the overall performance analysis of competitiveness and destination management. The findings of primary research including observations could illustrate the areas where gap(s) appear and weaknesses and complaints can be addressed, whereas those of secondary research along with observations could identify the root causes of problems in one destination and examples of good practice in another, if any. Providing background to improve services and establish positioning strategies, all the results may be incorporated into one setting to produce an overall picture from the destination benchmarking perspective, and should be used to observe and document changes in the market structure because the tourist market is dynamic and competitiveness requires the deployment of continuous improvement programmes. Box 8.3 shows a comparison of the Balearic Islands and Turkey in terms of their governments' willingness to keep the records of annual changes in their tourism industry.

Summary

This chapter has aimed to demonstrate the design and approach to data collection for decision-making and problem-solving in destination benchmarking research. General guidelines for the application of qualitative and quantitative data collection methods have been provided and a structured approach to the formulation, estimation and interpretation of data analysis presented. The chapter has emphasized the importance of using both qualitative and quantitative research methods in tandem for carrying out an effective benchmarking study for tourist destinations. The next chapter is devoted to the discussion of how destination benchmarking differs from organization benchmarking, and of the limitations influencing the successful development and implementation of the destination benchmarking practice.

Box 8.3. Documentation of data. Source: Kozak (2000).

Personal observations reveal that both Mallorca and Turkey have well-docu-
mented quantitative measures such as the number of tourists per month
and per year, the distribution of tourists by nationality and socioeconomic
and sociodemographic clusters, the distribution of the length of stays by
nationality, destination, months and years, level of tourist expenditure, and
the capacity of accommodation stock by destination, type and years. In
terms of documenting qualitative measures, Turkey is not as successful as
Mallorca. The Department of Tourism in the Balearic Islands documents the
survey findings of qualitative measures to use as comparative instruments
for historical data kept in records on a seasonal and annual basis. The
availability of historical data and its extension to future periods will aid in
monitoring changes in the market structure, changes in the market's wishes
and motivations, and customer satisfaction and complaints. As a significant
practical implication of this study, Turkey needs to draw attention to the
importance of keeping records of qualitative measures and their potential
use in the industry, since the collection of these sorts of data is still either
missing or not well organized.

Destination Benchmarking: Characteristics and Limitations

9

Introduction

As emphasized earlier, this book considers two categories of benchmarking in terms of their applications: organization benchmarking and destination benchmarking. The former deals with the performance evaluation of only a particular organization and its departments. In contrast, the latter draws a broader picture including all elements of one destination such as transport services, airport services, accommodation services, leisure and sport facilities, hospitality and local attitudes, hygiene and cleanliness, and so on. Therefore, this chapter begins with identifying the main differences between organization benchmarking and destination benchmarking. It then considers the limitations arising from the structure of the travel and tourism industry and influencing the successful development and implementation of destination benchmarking practices.

Destination Benchmarking Versus Organization Benchmarking

Depending upon the analysis of the structure of previous benchmarking research and the findings of the case study, and the underlying features of tourist destinations mentioned in Chapter 3, the main differences between organization benchmarking and destination benchmarking can be identified as follows (see also Table 9.1).

1. Destination benchmarking does not yet need to establish legal agreements between hosts and partners.

It is a new concept and is insufficiently developed. There would be no need to obtain permission for using available quantitative or qualitative data

Table 9.1. Differences between organization benchmarking and destination benchmarking.

Cases	Organization benchmarking	Destination benchmarking
Legal agreements required	Yes	No
Context	More specific	Wider in scope
Number of attributes	Fewer	Greater
Time	Shorter	Longer
Repeat business	Higher	Lower
Distribution method	Indirect customer experience (limited contact with producers)	Direct customer experience at the destination
Management	More management oriented	More partnership oriented between central and local government, private industry, and international organizations
Performance measurement	Largely relies on quantitative measures	Largely relies on qualitative measures

Source: own elaboration.

from other destinations. Data such as overall occupancy rate of establishments, number of tourists, tourist revenues and tourists' complaints about the destination may be in the public domain. Nevertheless, due to confidentiality, it can be difficult for businesses to obtain useful data about partners (Cook, 1995). Because of the strong level of competition, businesses tend to keep their own data confidential. It is much easier to get access to tourist destinations in order to obtain feedback from customers. Anyone can carry out a survey among customers visiting a particular destination, whereas one may not be allowed access to private or public organizations to collect empirical data. In organization benchmarking, suppliers may be very reluctant to provide information about other businesses, which might be direct competitors for the same business. In destination benchmarking, tourism suppliers (tour operators and travel agents) may participate in sharing their experiences in other destinations. In future, the destination benchmarking process may be carried out more formally. If the application of this model is extended within the tourism industry and demand for it increases, there may be grounds for establishing legal agreements.

2. Destination benchmarking is wider in scope than organization benchmarking due to its multi-dimensional, heterogeneous and interrelated (multirelated) features.

The literature provides sufficient evidence to confirm that there are different dimensions related to both tangible and intangible aspects of destinations. For instance, intangible aspects include the quality of facilities, the attitude of local people towards tourists and a sense of personal safety. As one destination is made up of a combination of many facilities and services, the variety of tangible and intangible elements together means that the number of relevant attributes in destinations is likely to be greater than that for organizations, e.g. destination attributes regarding accommodation facilities, nightlife and entertainment, airport facilities and services, the local people, shopping facilities, and so on. Hence, it is crucial to decide which dimensions/attributes should be selected for measurement. This process may be more difficult than for individual organizations. As a result, it may take a longer time for a destination benchmarking study to identify what and how to benchmark.

3. Customer loyalty for destinations is lower than for organizations. Even in the situation where a customer may have visited the same destination several times, visits will have been at the rate of once or twice per year.

The research findings support the above statement, indicating that the majority of tourists visit a destination two or three times in their whole life (Beaman *et al.*, 2001). The same customers may have been using products and services provided by organizations much more frequently, e.g. supermarkets, department stores, and so on. Alternatively, they may have an experience with a tangible product until its life cycle ends, e.g. a TV or car. Actual customer experiences in tourism expire once the holiday ends. The tourist has to take a new holiday for a new experience. This would be the consideration of a new destination for every holiday they take (McDougall and Munro, 1994). As a result of the high level of customer turnover, there is a need in destination benchmarking to consider the needs, wants and demands of other potential customers who may arrange their first visits to a destination in the future, alongside the needs of those making repeat visits. This requires a continuous administration of benchmarking studies and continuous measurement of the current performance of the destination.

4. The method of distribution of tourism products is, to a certain extent, different from that in some other industries.

The literature review shows that a variety of supply- and demand-based reasons could influence customer decisions in the selection of a particular destination because they have to be physically present at a destination in order to have both psychological and physical holiday experiences (e.g. Gronross, 1978). Of these, tourists have the opportunity to receive information about the destination through multiple information sources such as word-of-mouth communication, brochures, TV and other media, and their own experiences with the destination. In organizations, customers do not have direct access to the location where goods and services are produced or provided; they can purchase goods and services from retailers. In some cases, they may have experience with only a few attributes provided by businesses. For example, customers can conduct all the business relating to their bank account without speaking to any of the bank staff. They can just use the automatic bank teller machines to complete the process. The significant point here will be the overall image of the business among its customers and the efficiency of the machines. Such marketing differences

make the importance of distance, and cultural differences between supply and demand, between destinations and between tourists factors influencing the investigation of external destination benchmarking.

5. In organization benchmarking, the executive management committee is
in charge of directing organization resources and making decisions to
administer any research and development studies in a particular field.

However, as success will depend on delivering the right mix of components to meet customer demand, the programme of destination benchmarking should involve consideration of all facilities and services that affect the
tourist experience. This indicates that the most distinctive part of destination
benchmarking is the identification of which comprehensive generic destination dimensions to measure. In destination benchmarking, it is important to
have coordination and cooperation between a set of organizations such as
local and central government, private industry and the related international
organizations (e.g. Kotler *et al.*, 1993; Gunn, 1997) as the public sector is in
charge of both releasing and approving plans and projects to design an
urban or rural setting in a suitable manner and the private sector has the
responsibility of running tourism or tourism-related businesses. The benefits
of such cooperation would be avoiding duplication and wasting financial
resources, and providing better communication channels to set plans, make
decisions and put them into practice. Being aware of its advantages, some
governments recently have begun to pay attention to the protection of natural resources and to upgrade and enhance the national heritage by developing an integrated approach involving collaboration between public and
private sector representatives, e.g. France and the Balearic Islands.

6. The methods of performance measurement in organization benchmarking and destination benchmarking differ significantly from one another.

The major indicators of performance measurement in organization benchmarking are largely based on industry-specific standards that are developed
and updated by considering what and how others are doing the same work.
For example, the production cost of each item, the labour cost per item, the
number of defects and returns in relation to the total production, speed of
delivery service, and net profit per annum are some of the major performance
indicators used in organization benchmarking. However, in destination
benchmarking, indicators of performance measurement should be regarded
as the level of repeat visits, the overall occupancy rate, the average time
spent on cleaning a hotel room, the average time spent on checking in and
out both at accommodation establishments and at the destination airport,
and so on. Establishing standard values for such measures seems to be rigid.

Principles of Destination Benchmarking

There exist several steps in terms of their effectiveness in delivering a
successful benchmarking study. Of these, Cook (1995) suggests eight steps

---

Box 9.1. Principles of destination benchmarking. Source: adapted from Cook (1995).

1. Linking benchmarking to the destination's mission statement (positioning strategy)
2. Setting measurable goals and objectives
3. Gaining public and private sector commitment
4. Creating a powerful team
5. Choosing the right time to benchmark
6. Focusing on the right issues
7. Focusing on the right partners
8. Willingness to change

---

for gaining success in a benchmarking process. Her framework can be modified to emphasize the major stages of benchmarking tourist destinations, as displayed in Box 9.1. These steps begin by linking benchmarking studies to the destination's mission statement, and go further by setting measurable goals and objectives, providing public and private sector commitment, establishing a powerful teamwork, choosing the right time, issues and partners to benchmark, and being open to change. Each is explained in detail below. It can also be argued that carrying out each task is the responsibility of destination management authorities.

Linking benchmarking to the destination's mission statement

As in every organization and industry, destination management authorities need to establish an effective mission statement that is feasible, motivating, distinctive, achievable and conforms to the general aims of management (Heath and Wall, 1992). In a competitive environment, each destination has to check the positions of its products and services on a regular basis. If necessary, older strategies may be replaced by newer ones. In the light of these guidelines, the mission statement of destinations can be set as, for example, 'to benchmark our performance levels against those of other destinations in order to seek better practices and gain a higher level of performance through a higher level of services, a better image and more effective word-of-mouth recommendation'. Different destinations have different objectives and expectations from the tourism industry. Some destinations tend to offer a variety of tourist facilities and activities and be a year-round destination that attracts top-class customer groups, whereas some others only want to offer seasonal facilities and services for middle- or low-class customer groups. All such objectives will be related to destination benchmarking as they will influence the extent to which authorities are ambitious in the international market. There could be different marketing mix concepts for different market segments relating to tourist destinations as customers may have different personalities, needs and desires. Hence, for example, destinations can focus only on specific tourism products to approach the specific segments of the tourism market. Heath and Wall (1992) draw attention to the benefits of a regional product portfolio approach in tourism marketing and competitiveness. This encompasses the analysis of mission statements of destinations and how likely a tourism product or strategy is to be related to the place's mission.

Setting measurable goals and objectives

Destination management should identify destination attributes that really need to be benchmarked and clear goals and objectives regarding what is expected to be gained at the end of the process. There is always a need to define clearly the goals of every plan and programme. Goals are the main vehicles for establishing plans and taking action. Objectives are the operational and measurable forms of goals. The goal stating that 'annual tourism revenues will be increased' can be transformed into an objective such as, for instance, 'a 10% increase in tourism revenues will be expected' (Heath and Wall, 1992). As such, objectives are more specific and clearly identified than reaching goals. Goals and objectives can be prepared as a part of short- and long-term planning procedures. Specifying objectives will help to define the process of qualitative or quantitative measurement methods. Depending upon the type and mission of destinations, objectives can be set to increase the number of arrivals and the level of tourist expenditure, to achieve increased satisfaction and a better image, and to maintain a sustainable form of tourism activity balancing supply and demand or focusing on attracting only some markets. Based on developments in the business environment and changes in tourism demand, destination management may define its goals and objectives for every new tourism season or term.

A list of goals is provided in Table 9.2. To achieve any of these or similar goals, the following issues could be taken into account from both the supply and demand point of view while formulating a benchmarking project and taking action afterwards. It is also a fact that there is no need for a destination to benchmark itself if it is content with its position or has no wish to earn more from tourism. While setting goals and establishing action plans, destination management can benefit from the findings of either internal or external benchmarking exercises depending upon which one has been followed. In the case of external benchmarking, methods used by other destinations and thought to be rational and applicable to one's own purposes can be considered. Attention needs to be paid to the factors that affect the success of practices and the overall performance of benchmarking studies, e.g. cultural differences between tourist-receiving and tourist-generating countries, and between different tourist-receiving countries. Types of customers visiting different destinations, the power of marketing channels and their restructuring, and differences in laws and legislation

Table 9.2. Goals in destination benchmarking.

Perspectives	Goals
Customer perspective	Increase customer satisfaction
	Decrease customer complaints
	Increase customer compliments
	Increase the share of repeat customers
	Attract new customers
Internal businesses	Identify and promote core competencies
	Deliver a better-quality service
	Facilitate an effective relationship among local businesses
Innovation and learning	Introduce new products
	Revise destination positioning
	Provide continuous improvement
	Search for good practices in other destinations or elsewhere
Financial perspective	Deliver a competitive price
	Deliver better value for money
	Increase revenue per tourist/group
	Increase average occupancy rates
	Increase total tourism receipts

Source: adapted from Kaplan and Norton (1993).

between tourist-receiving countries are also the subject of benchmarking research between destinations. It is highly likely that there are differences in managerial practices and services between destinations although they take place in the same competitiveness set in terms of the market structure and tourism products on offer, e.g. Turkey, Spain, Portugal and Greece.

The basic idea behind the benchmarking concept is to identify gaps in performance and close them by monitoring other organizations to get ideas about how they perform and achieve their targets. This refers to what 'process' benchmarking aims to achieve (Watson, 1993). If the objective is to investigate the strengths and weaknesses of one particular destination or differences between two destinations, in the case of external benchmarking, then it would be necessary to observe those attributes with higher or lower satisfaction levels in order to test if such differences really exist and explore their reasons. This stage may concentrate on monitoring the sample destination airports, road and traffic conditions, accessibility, cleanliness, sea and beaches, tourist attractions and the attitudes of local people.

Gaining public and private sector commitment

The tourism literature, to a large extent, suggests that coordination and cooperation between the public and the private sector is required (e.g. Gunn, 1997) as the public sector is in charge of both releasing and approving plans and projects to design an urban or rural setting in a suitable manner, and the private sector has the responsibility of running tourism or tourism-related businesses. Internal cooperation and coordination among government bodies (public sector) is required to use time and financial resources in a much more effective and productive manner because the private sector receives more profits and the public sector more tax revenue and a well-balanced economy (Timothy, 1998). In contrast to organization benchmarking, it would be advisable to collaborate with local authorities, departments of tourism and tourism businesses for destination benchmarking since many attractions, facilities and services are run by private businesses; others (zoos and museums) may be operated by private, voluntary or public organizations; and some others (roads and public services) are provided by local government (Goodall and Bergsma, 1990). For instance, the natural environment is a resource that tourism should benefit from and never ignore. Any failure in a place or organization spreads quickly and influences others in the industry. Collaboration between the tourism industry, local authorities and environmental agencies is therefore essential for offering a sustainable tourism product.

It must be stressed that achieving sustainable forms of tourism is not only the responsibility of stakeholders involved, governments at all levels, and representatives of the private industry and local community in tourism destination countries, but is also the responsibility of international organizations, environmental groups, tour operators, travel agents and potential tourists in the tourist-generating countries. Nevertheless, it is the responsibility of the destination and those who are involved in the destination management to enhance competitiveness. Thus, representatives of the local community should have the right to take part in a proposed benchmarking-based destination management model while taking action for improvement due to a high level of cross-cultural interaction and communication in tourism between hosts and guests, e.g. actual behaviour towards tourists. They are the people whose quality of life is influenced by the consequences of tourism development within the area, e.g. air pollution, traffic congestion and overcommercialization (Gunn, 1997). As far as mass tourism is concerned, tour operators or their local representatives could also take part in such cooperative and collaborative work to encourage local tourism businesses to improve the standards of their services and facilities. Some evidence can be seen in the tourism development of Mallorca where financial contributions and guidelines are provided by foreign tour operators, such as TUI and Thomson, to improve the quality of facilities and services. Similarly, airport management in Palma has collaborated with tour operators (e.g. TUI and NUR) to serve passengers visiting Mallorca in the high-peak season better by promoting staggered arrivals and departures.

The growth of mass tourism has led to significant environmental problems in a number of critical areas (e.g. polluted sea and beaches and noisy atmosphere). These areas could be a basis to underline why a destination benchmarking approach is required to minimize the negative consequences of tourism. According to the policy of the Fifth Environmental Action Programme established in 1992, the quality of planning, development and management of mass tourism particularly in coastal and mountainous areas needs to be improved. The programme gives priority to sustainable forms of tourism and encourages tourists' awareness of environmental issues. In response, a number of initiatives have been introduced. National governments are asked to prepare inventories of their tourism resources and develop new policies. Cooperation between practitioners working in different regions who have similar problems and practices is encouraged in order to share both their positive and negative experiences. These cooperative relationships reflect the idea of destination benchmarking proposed in this study.

Creating a powerful team

Organization benchmarking studies are directed by the establishment of a professional committee that is responsible solely for benchmarking procedures. Destination management should launch a powerful and expert team who will be familiar with the destination, the tourism industry and other destinations worldwide. The members of the committee should be selected from those who have a professional background and are capable of analysing current developments within the industry. As discussed above, benchmarking requires effective collaboration, cooperation and coordination not only between members of the tourism industry but also between members and external organizations. As in organization benchmarking, the implementation of a TQM programme may provide a means of cooperative decision-making, collaboration and communication. As Jafari (1983) suggests, tourism and other establishments need to be in harmony in the development and promotion of tourism activities in the destination. In this sense, destination management can be considered as the authority that will direct TQM programmes towards the implementation of the results. Therefore, this study suggests the establishment of a destination management organization (DMAO), which will be in charge of directing tourism supply resources and coordinating with local tourism establishments and destination marketing organizations (DMOs). Though DMOs are expected to have similar roles to DMAOs, their activities are focused solely on marketing communications. Box 9.2 provides a list of good practices that may be accomplished under the responsibility of DMAOs.

Choosing the right time to benchmark

Although a destination can decide on a benchmarking exercise at any time, there should be a specific reason for carrying out a benchmarking

Box 9.2. A checklist of good practices for tourist destinations.

In order for the management of tourist destinations (i) to give a distinctive appeal to such elements as leisure activities, sports, food, welcoming tourists, and natural and cultural heritage; and (ii) to meet the standards and quality labels formulated and implemented by national and/or international professional authorities, this study is based on the analysis of the following measures that seem to play a key role in the success of quality management in tourist destinations:

Undertake regular surveys obtaining feedback from tourists about their perceptions of the quality of the destination and how it changes.

Be aware that a dissatisfied tourist is a potential danger for the destination's success in the future, whereas a satisfied tourist is a marketing officer promoting the destination free of charge outside.

Ensure that the relevant aspects of a destination conform to both the national and international standards in eco-label systems.

Ensure that both local residents (hosts welcoming tourists) and tourists (guests) are well aware of the cultural differences between them.

Prepare an information pack for tourists to inform them about the local laws, regulations, traditions, ecology, and natural and social environment, e.g. Tongan Visitors Bureau prepared a leaflet in which all guidelines or tips are provided to visitors about what they should and should not do while on holiday in Tonga.

Be hospitable and helpful, discourage people from bothering tourists with hassle, particularly shopkeepers and restaurateurs calling customers in.

Bear in mind that a destination attracts tourists from different segments of a market (e.g. young people, elderly, low-income level, etc.) and ensure that the destination has the capacity of the variety to meet the needs and expectations of each group.

Ensure that developments in tourism do not bring any potential danger for other local or national institutions, e.g. agriculture, handicrafts, fishing, and so on.

Consult with other related bodies and be collaborative, as a direct result of establishing a TQM-based destination management approach.

Be family- and disabled-friendly. Provide parents and disabled people with access to use their pushchairs and wheelchairs in pedestrian areas, in toilets, public areas and accommodation facilities.

Conduct training programmes for local residents and those working in tourism to inform them about all aspects of tourism, how to preserve the local identity and heritage, and how to behave towards foreign tourists.

Provide visitors with access to frequent public transport such as trains, trams or bus services.

Locate tourism information offices at the centre of the destination where tourists have the opportunity to access them easily.

Provide access to networks on the Internet and central reservation systems via computer services.

All the useful information should be stored in a computer database and the results should be presented in a newsletter to those who are either interested in or in charge of the tourism industry. The results should also be integrated into the destination management's TQM programme.

An annual budget should be established for customer research and destination benchmarking research.

study. It should usually be carried out when (i) tourism demand for the destination or tourism revenues are in decline; (ii) there appears to be tourist dissatisfaction or a lower level of satisfaction; (iii) there is enthusiasm for following recent developments in the tourism and travel industry; (iv) findings of market research and destination performance measurements fail to meet expectations; and (v) destination management wants to maintain a competitive advantage and overtake competitors in the market.

A model of a destination life cycle was developed by Butler (1980) to examine the impacts of tourism development in an area and show how it moves from one stage to another. From the early stage when the place is explored as a tourist location, to the last stage when the place is about to fall, this model refers to the subsequent six stages: exploration, involvement, development, consolidation, stagnation and rejuvenation. Taking this model into consideration, each stage could be an indicator to show how the destination performs. Destinations in earlier stages could follow others that are regarded as being mature and at the next stage. For those that are at the stage of 'stagnation' and 'decline', the best benchmarking partners would be those who had had similar negative experiences in the past (Watson, 1997). Drawing conclusions from others' previous negative experiences may sometimes provide positive or better experiences or advantages.

In addition, depending on the type of destination, a benchmarking study can be carried out at the end of each season in order to set a performance measurement portfolio. If the destination has a year-round clientele, then it could be useful to prepare such a portfolio for particular periods to identify the main features of customer needs, wants and the structure of the local tourism industry and whether there are any seasonal fluctuations. These may help destination management review its strategies according to each period's features and particular requirements. Mass tourist destinations may conduct such data collection procedures at the end of each season. This will help destination management learn more about their seasonal performance levels, see whether they have recorded any improvements and make changes for the next season. The Department of Tourism in Mallorca has created a database with the findings of surveys carried out three times a year; these are published for the benefit of those who are interested in tourism on the island. Interpreting these findings, it is possible to see how much difference there is between the current year and previous years and between high and low seasons.

Focusing on the right issues

It is necessary to figure out what specific pieces of information need to be compared without wasting time, and financial and human resources. For instance, Barksy (1996) recommends that objectives focus on areas where expectations are not being met and where customer priorities are high. Although it seems easy to learn how people perceive destinations by employing a set of attributes, destination benchmarking has a problem in finding the most appropriate attributes to measure performance. Here, attention must be paid to both controllable (e.g. facilities and services) and uncontrollable attributes (e.g. weather and culture). The measurement of controllable attributes in destination benchmarking offers more potential for bringing about improvement. For instance, people can perceive climate, culture or natural attractions at one destination as being worse and better than another (see Box 9.3). This does not necessarily mean that these attributes should be considered as benchmark elements. They are unique to different destinations and it is hardly possible to change them in the short or even the long term. In benchmarking, variables are classified as being those that are changeable either in the short or long term. Depending on the destinations' policies, either of these variables can be taken into a benchmarking study. Watson (1993) highlights that the importance of benchmarking emerges from the reality of what measure or measures gives the best results in terms of what needs to be known and can potentially be changed. To accomplish this, there should be a prioritization process according to whether the element is important to customer dis/satisfaction, whether results are unexpected and whether there is a possibility of improvement (Balm, 1992).

Focusing on the right partners

Unlike those of organizations, the selection of partner destinations seems to be difficult at present due to the limited amount of published work about international tourist destinations, but publications such as statistics, industry reports, government sources and academic papers can be helpful in choosing a partner. Additionally, site visits arranged to other destinations can provide an opportunity to make observations regarding what and how they are doing. Upon completing observations, a decision can be made. Generally, it is expected that destinations that are performing better on a number of criteria and thought to be worth sharing ideas with can be approached as potential partners. The other method is to obtain feedback from customers visiting other destinations. All these methods would be helpful in evaluating the main features of other specific destinations and their performance levels.

Destination management should initially pay attention to the characteristics of destinations, to their similarities and differences when choosing the right partner. As the choice of partner varies with the objective, a categorization of destinations is required (Laws, 1995). These are: capital cities, developed traditional centres, touring centres, purpose-built resorts and mega holiday villages (Table 9.3). *Capital cities* are major places to which tourists are attracted not just for tourism but also for business and cultural

---

Box 9.3. Influence of culture-oriented factors.

One could point out the existence of other traditional cultural values. For instance, bargaining is one of the national trading habits in Turkey, whereas shopkeepers in Mallorca seem to be rather reluctant to reduce prices for shoppers. In terms of the availability of either local or familiar food, the Mallorcan cuisine is much closer to its markets' taste such as offering customers dishes with pork; but the Turkish cuisine is limited partly due to cultural reasons. A further example could be given from the availability of condom machines located in certain parts of resorts in Mallorca. The culture in Turkey is not ready to accept this yet. Briefly, any best practice that is working efficiently in one place or is found to be useful for its customers may not necessarily be transferred easily to another place if it is culture-oriented.

---

purposes, e.g. Athens, London and Paris. *Developed traditional centres* are places dominated by the tourism industry and where tourist facilities and services are either located on the basis of regular planning or separated speculatively, e.g. Mallorca, Hawaii and Bodrum. *Touring centres* are places with a high concentration of secondary tourist facilities and major transport links to both tourist-generating places and scenic and cultural attractions, e.g. Salzburg. *Purpose-built resorts* are mainly isolated places where infrastructure and tourist facilities are offered to attract tourists to a specific type of tourism, leisure or recreation activity, e.g. Disneyland (Paris). Finally, *mega holiday villages* are tourist complexes built away from centres of tourism and offering many facilities, activities and services so that all the customers' needs are met within the area, which is also the case for purpose-built resorts. The only disadvantage for customers choosing such complexes is that they will be isolated from the external sociocultural and socioeconomic environment. However, for benchmarking, it is an advantage to compare only these complexes because it is easy to survey all controllable items within the area, e.g. Club Med.

This classification provides basic information with regard to the features of each destination. While selecting a partner, relevance to operations, accessibility and others' innovative practices may be the most important elements (Rogers *et al.*, 1995). International tourist destinations differ depending upon the types of tourism activities and tourism demand they have. A Mediterranean destination may be dominated by mass holiday tourism, whereas for an eastern European destination it may be dominated by heritage tourism. It is also important to note that two destinations in the same country in terms of tourism supply and tourism demand may be very different, e.g. Blackpool and Edinburgh. Destination benchmarking should therefore consider the main characteristics of every destination. To some extent, benchmarking can be carried out between very different destinations (business tourism and winter tourism) when only limited types or

Table 9.3. Categorization of destinations.

Type	Target market	Examples
Capital cities	Business and culture	Athens, London, Moscow, Paris
Developed traditional centres	Mass tourism	Hawaii, Ibiza, Bali
Touring centres	Nature and culture	Salzburg
Purpose-built places	Leisure/recreation	Disneyland
Mega holiday villages	Leisure/recreation	Club Med

Source: Laws (1995).

service levels of accommodation or food and beverage facilities are the subject of the research. As customers are the main elements of the subject, there may be very little difference in terms of diversity and levels of service offered. Similarly, provision of infrastructure and superstructure as basic needs for tourism and travel might be the same for all destinations and customers. Nevertheless, it may be impossible to compare the overall performance of a destination dedicated to business tourism with that of another dedicated to mass holiday tourism due to the varying nature of tourism demand and tourism supply.

Willingness to change

Although the objective of organization benchmarking is to change either the structure of the organization or some of its operations in a way that increases its performance, it is not reasonable to expect that destination management should suggest that its members change all their products or the style of service they offer where any customer dissatisfaction may result or destination benchmarking research gives negative scores; but it can show ways in which to improve these areas. To do so, all elements of a destination should have a commitment to improvement. Moreover, the most distinctive part of destination benchmarking may be, as stated by Ahmed (1991), to suggest that sample destinations select a position in which they can gain a strong competitive advantage and link it to their target markets. There is no need for a destination to benchmark itself if it is content with its position or has no wish to earn more from tourism.

Limitations Influencing the Success of Destination Benchmarking

The following nine subheadings discuss the theoretical limitations arising particularly from the structure of the tourism and travel industry and main features of consumer psychology in tourism, and influencing a successful implementation of destination benchmarking. These limitations are of interest when considering the future research and further development of the benchmarking model presented in this study. A summary is provided in Box 9.4.

Industry-specific features

The existing organization benchmarking studies mentioned in the benchmarking literature follow a defined sequence of activities such as plan, do, check and act (Camp, 1989). These activities could also be relevant to benchmarking destinations to some extent. However, as discussed earlier in this book, it appears to be more difficult to benchmark service operations than to benchmark products. This is due to the difficulty of quantifying qualitative measures and the lack of fully accepted industry-wide standards and criteria on which to evaluate effective performance (Shetty, 1993). For instance, it is not clear to what extent customers should be regarded as satisfied or dissatisfied with a destination or whether they would come back.

Comparison research

Several conclusions have been drawn from customer-based comparative research (Smelser, 1973). Attitude scales including satisfaction and image measurement cannot be evaluated by playing with the scores, as numbers are just symbols indicating the direction of scales for each item (from negative to positive or vice versa). It may be impossible to reach a conclusion by multiplying or dividing scale values (Moser and Kalton, 1971). The interpretation of the strength of a scale, for example 'terrible', could vary from one tourist to another. One person's feeling could be weaker or stronger than another's. As tourist opinions are not fixed, changes in people's values and perceptions are evident over time (Mayo and Jarvis, 1981). This is defined by the marketing literature as 'temporal satisfaction' (Czepiel *et al.*, 1974). In a reference to the difficulty of comparison research, Deutscher (1973) claims that the structure of language and the meaning of words in two different cultures or nationalities can be different. Warwick and Osherson (1973) further suggest that what is important to one nationality may be less important to another or not important at all. Thus, results obtained and assessed by using methods such as gap analysis and using the same set of questions in the survey instrument could still be problematic and superficial in a comparative research activity.

Box 9.4. Limitations influencing the success of destination benchmarking.

Industry-specific features	It appears to be more difficult to benchmark service operations than to benchmark products. This is due to the difficulty of quantifying qualitative measures and the lack of fully accepted industry-wide standards and criteria on which to evaluate effective performance. For instance, it is not clear to what extent customers should be regarded as satisfied or dissatisfied with a destination or whether they would come back.
Comparison research	Several conclusions have been drawn from customer-based comparative research. Attitude scales including satisfaction and image measurement cannot be evaluated by playing with the scores, as numbers are just symbols indicating the direction of scales for each item. Thus, results obtained and assessed by using methods such as gap analysis and using the same set of questions in the survey instrument could still be problematic in a comparative research activity.
Destination-based features	There appears to be a problem in collecting the right kind of information upon which destination(s) are to be compared, what dimensions/elements are to be taken into account and the difficulty of implementing findings because of the cultural, legislative and geographical differences and of undertaking continuous measure-ment. There are many reasons, sometimes differing between nationalities, that affect what tourists want from a particular destination. Each group of customers might have a different set of expectations, needs and wants as a reflection of their culture.
Demand-based features	The different holiday-taking behaviour of two nationalities could influence the findings of comparative surveys. In other words, measuring the extent of tourists' first-hand experiences with several facilities, activities and services is limited in a cross-cultural comparison study as well as in a destination benchmarking study. One group stays in a hotel with full board whereas another stays in a self-catering apartment. This point therefore needs a considerable amount of attention when carrying out benchmarking studies.
Process benchmarking	The general proposition is that it is much easier to benchmark a process than to benchmark an output. Thus, it is recommended to focus further on applying solely process benchmarking, which aims to investigate operating systems, e.g. length of time to serve waiting customers, methods to keep beaches, sea and footpaths clean or reasons for high or low prices.

Box 9.4. *Continued.*

Tour operators	Within the context of mass tourism, tour operators are the only group able to reduce or increase the volume of tourism demand, not the destinations themselves. Sometimes holidaymakers may have bad experiences due to the services provided by their tour operators, e.g. mistakenly transferred to different accommodation, not being helpful for customer complaints, flight delays, overbooking and non-reliable brochures. This provides further insight into the involvement of tour operators in benchmarking mass tourist destinations.
Determinants of consumer behaviour	It is important to bear in mind the existence of other non-satisfaction determinants affecting consumer behaviour. Overall perceptions of tourists may depend on external factors that are not manageable or controllable by destination management or local tourism businesses. These may be economic, political or temporal features appearing in tourist-generating countries and tourist destinations, i.e. age, income, occupation, personality, cost, time, motivation, distance, risk and the existence of alternative destinations.
Tourist expenses	Although there may be no major problem in calculating the amount of spending for each category, it is necessary to examine possible reasons for differences in outlay between sample destinations. The calculation of spending on food and drink and its comparison creates some problems in the measurement of total tourist spending as it relies mostly on other factors such as the type of holiday and the number in the party. It is clear that pre-paid parts of package holidays create several problems when measuring an accurate level of tourist expenditure at the destination.
Physical and cultural distance	The analysis of the demand-based structure indicates differences between tourist-generating countries and tourist destinations. Factors such as accessibility (physical and cultural distance) and the level of similarities and differences in cultural and economic structure between supply and demand may become a significant issue in designing an effective and efficient methodology of destination benchmarking including 'taking action'.

Destination-based features

With reference to the above statement, there appears to be a problem in collecting the right kind of information upon which destination(s) are to be compared, what dimensions/elements are to be taken into account and the difficulty in implementing findings because of the cultural, legislative and geographic differences and of undertaking continuous measurement. There are many reasons, sometimes differing between nationalities, that affect what tourists want from a particular destination. Each group of customers might have a different set of expectations, needs and wants as a reflection of their culture. Destination benchmarking has to find a unique solution for this issue. There may be no major problem for measures such as the level of language communication or the availability of facilities; but there may be differences between how two different nationalities perceive the overall cleanliness and the level of prices. It may appear easy to learn how people perceive destinations by employing attributes; however, the selection of appropriate attributes that can be used to measure the performance of destinations, then be used to compare findings and finally decide what can be achieved and how it can be changed is highly complex. For instance, people can perceive climate, culture or natural environment in one destination better or worse than in another. This does not mean that such attributes could be considered as benchmark elements as these are unique dimensions in each different destination and it is impossible to change them in the short or even in the long term; but each destination can emphasize its unique resources.

Demand-based features

The different holiday-taking behaviour of two nationalities could influence the findings of comparative surveys. In other words, measuring the extent of tourists' first-hand experiences with several facilities, activities and services is limited in a cross-cultural comparison study as well as in a destination benchmarking study. One group stays in a hotel with full-board while another stays in a self-catering apartment. One has to use the hotel restaurant; another has to choose a restaurant outside or prepare something themselves. One group takes full advantage of the services on offer while another chooses to be as independent as possible. Alternatively, the two groups take holidays of different lengths, or one group has more repeat visits than another. One might speculate that the level of tourists' satisfaction may be coloured by their past experiences and, as a result, either higher or lower satisfaction scores might appear in comparison with those of first-time tourists (Crompton and Love, 1995). Past research confirmed that repeat customers are more likely than first-time customers to be satisfied (Westbrook and Newman, 1978). For instance, it is not reasonable to expect that both groups had experiences of the same depth or extent. This point therefore needs a considerable amount of attention while carrying out benchmarking studies.

Process benchmarking

The general proposition is that it is much easier to benchmark a process than to benchmark an output (Kaplan, 1993). A process is an activity of specific investigation, whereas output is rather complex and extensive. A process can be taken into account for benchmarking whenever any failure has been observed, but final data are needed to benchmark outputs. Outputs can be influenced by various factors, which may not be easily identified and controlled. The number of factors affecting processes might be more limited. Thus, it is recommended to focus further on applying solely process benchmarking that aims to investigate operating systems, e.g. length of time to serve waiting customers, methods to keep beaches, sea and footpaths clean, or reasons for high or low prices. As the domain of inquiry here concerns mostly the analysis of quantitative and statistical data, future research could be directed at a sample of qualitative data such as designing interview and focus group surveys with both customers and suppliers for activating process benchmarking. Benchmarking is related not only to the satisfaction levels of external customers but also to that of internal customers including local residents, employees, and tourism businesses and associations because these are affected by a destination's performance at different levels (Kotler *et al.*, 1993; Atkinson *et al.*, 1997). Further research should therefore focus on how to involve these groups in destination benchmarking and may extend the body of knowledge in designing a broader model of destination benchmarking.

Tour operators

Within the context of mass tourism, tour operators have an enormous power in marketing destinations even though the degree of dependence on the tour operator may vary from one destination to another depending on the amount of revenue. The prime purpose of tour operators is to create customer loyalty to themselves rather than to destinations they promote (Carey *et al.*, 1997). Destinations are speculated to become a commodity of tour operators and a substitute against each other (Laws, 1995). One tourist examines destinations from the point of the availability of price and convenience rather than attributes of each destination because brochures are used to display general benefits such as beaches, entertainment and accommodation. Hence, it could be claimed that tour operators are the only group able to reduce or increase the volume of tourism demand, not the destinations themselves. The image of a destination may be primarily affected by the tour operator's promotional activities in the tourist generating-country (Goodall, 1990). Moreover, sometimes holidaymakers may have bad experiences due to the services provided by their tour operators, e.g. mistakenly transferred to different accommodation, not being helpful for customer complaints, flight delays, overbooking and non-reliable brochures. This provides further insight into the involvement of tour operators in benchmarking mass tourist destinations.

Determinants of consumer behaviour

It is important to bear in mind the existence of other non-satisfaction determinants affecting consumer behaviour (Oliver, 1999). Overall perceptions of tourists may depend on external factors that are not manageable or controllable by destination management or local tourism businesses. These may be economic, political or temporal features appearing in tourist-generating countries and tourist destinations, i.e. age, income, occupation, personality, cost, time, motivation, distance, risk and the existence of alternative destinations. There are also some other uncontrollable external factors such as terrorism, spread of disease and natural disasters, which may have a more powerful effect when they happen; but it may be difficult to predict the impact these factors are likely to have on the tourism industry and control their consequences. It is extremely difficult for benchmarking studies to assess such factors. This leads to the link between quantitative and qualitative measures proposed in this study. Do satisfied customers really come back? Do they encourage their friends and relatives to visit the destination? Do high satisfaction scores or positive images increase tourism revenues in the future?

Tourist expenses

Although there may be no major problem in calculating the amount of spending for each category, it is necessary to examine possible reasons for differences in outlay between sample destinations. This study indicates that the calculation of spending on food and drink and its comparison creates some problems in the measurement of total tourist spending as it relies mostly on other factors such as the type of holiday and the number in the party. It is clear that pre-paid parts of package holidays create several problems when measuring an accurate level of tourist expenditure at the destination. For instance, if a tourist books accommodation with full-board, the problem here is to find how the money spent on food and drink can be reflected in the tourist's actual holiday expenditure. This also applies to the attempt to measure such expenditure per person (tourist). It may not be reasonable to expect or anticipate that each person in a party spends an equal amount, e.g. adults and children of different ages or with different interests. This part of the study therefore needs further consideration.

Physical and cultural distance

The analysis of the demand-based (market-based) structure indicates differences between tourist-generating countries and tourist destinations. Factors such as accessibility (physical and cultural distance) and the level of similarities and differences in cultural and economic structure between supply and demand may become a significant issue in designing an effective and efficient methodology of destination benchmarking including 'taking action'. First, the physical distance varies from one destination to another and from one market to another. There are many cases in practice displaying the physical distance as an effective factor for choosing one destination for taking holidays, e.g. the British tourist market to Spain. This advantage combined with the availability of direct flights all year round has led to Spain being promoted within the British market as a short-break holiday destination. Next, it is important to understand differences in tourists' and hosts' cultural background such as communication style, expressing feelings, establishing relationships and developing a positive tourist–host contact and enhancing tourist satisfaction and loyalty. It is not certain how much tourists want their national culture to be reproduced in other places that they visit. Some tourists may want to experience another culture (cultural motivations), whereas some others may dislike the culture of their holiday destination (e.g. harassment).

Summary

This chapter has set out a general discussion of the application of benchmarking in tourist destinations and its implications for benchmarking theory and practice. It has underlined the main differences between the terms 'organization benchmarking' and 'destination benchmarking', and then addressed the limitations arising from the structure of the travel and tourism industry and influencing the successful development and implementation of destination benchmarking practices. The discussion was based on the findings emerging from the case studies on Mallorca and Turkey, as two Mediterranean destinations competing with each other. As the concluding chapter, the next chapter summarizes the main arguments and considers some of the potential contributions and implications in light of the context of previous discussions.

Conclusion

10

Introduction

This concluding chapter summarizes the main arguments and considers some of the potential contributions and implications in light of the context of previous discussions. The chapter begins by giving an overview of the proposed model of destination benchmarking built upon internal and external benchmarking approaches. Contributions to the benchmarking literature are then explicitly pointed out. It then moves to the discussion of the practical application of destination benchmarking. The chapter ends with a brief summary emphasizing both the theoretical and practical contributions the book has provided.

A General Overview of Destination Benchmarking

The importance of benchmarking for destinations arises from the fact that motivations (psychographic attributes) are important factors for choosing a destination and, when they are not satisfied, tourists are unlikely to return and on return home are likely to discourage their relatives and friends from visiting. Similarly, positive experiences are expected to lead to customer satisfaction and positive word-of-mouth recommendation (Kozak, 2002c). The main feature of a destination benchmarking study may be to help all those concerned with destination management to think out of the box when they want to be aware of what their customers think, and to benefit from knowledge of activities in other destinations and their impact on tourist experiences and tourism receipts. Destination managers therefore should be aware of what they and their competitors provide and how they perform, due to the possibility of tour operators and customers exploring new destinations. They should also pay attention to developments in customer needs, wants and perceptions. Several examples can be given from the Balearic Islands and Greece where the changes in customers' sociodemographic and holiday-taking patterns are regularly monitored.

As discussed earlier, developing and using destination-specific measures helps to identify current performance and monitor the direction of changes over a period. Measures identified during the planning stage of benchmarking may also help to determine the magnitude of the performance gaps between destinations and select what is to be benchmarked, as they do in organization benchmarking. It is also possible to shape future strategies depending upon the measures and their findings obtained in a benchmarking project. For instance, it might be necessary to pay more attention to those areas where satisfaction scores indicated lower performance. In terms of the potential use of measures in destination benchmarking, the quantitative measures can only indicate where gaps exist, but are unable to provide any insight into why the selected areas perform well or poorly. This is what the use of qualitative measures aims to achieve. For instance, any problem with a low level of satisfaction with cleanliness could pinpoint the potential reason and arrive at the conclusion that it needs to be improved. It seems probable that there is also a potential link between both measures. Improvements in qualitative measures may lead to improvements in quantitative measures, e.g. the impact of the increased satisfaction over the number of tourist arrivals or increased tourist expenditure.

The applicability of benchmarking to tourist destinations was examined through testing internal and external benchmarking approaches on an individual basis. (Generic benchmarking is also considered as a part of external benchmarking.) The main difference between internal and external benchmarking is that the former designs benchmarking along the lines of the feedback obtained from one's own customers and members (internal data). This approach considers the measurement and improvement of performance on the basis of a comparison with earlier outcomes. A positive gap shows that the destination performs better than it used to in some respects. External benchmarking refers to identifying one's competitiveness level and obtaining information about new practices and methods by comparing the findings of both internal and external data, examining the potential reasons for gaps and assessing the utility of outcomes for the host destination. The destination with a superior score is believed to be performing better than the other in the sample area.

Following the benchmarking process, it is possible to learn about the present and future performance of destinations. Presenting the findings helps to elicit what strengths and weaknesses have emerged and what opportunities and threats exist to maintain a sustainable development. These data will be instrumental in setting goals and making recommendations. Upon completing all these stages in benchmarking, an action plan containing future goals and recommendations should be presented. Setting goals will consist of defining a destination's strengths and how to minimize weaknesses and threats in order to cope with the new applications and developments. Depending on the projected future performance of destinations, destination management may wish to change its marketing policies or markets. It may also attract similar groups of tourists by preserving its current image and by improving its existing performance.

As already stated earlier, although the objective of organization benchmarking is to change either the structure of the organization or some of its operations in a way that increases its performance, it is not reasonable to expect that destination management should suggest that its members change all their products or the style of service they offer where any customer dissatisfaction may result or destination benchmarking research gives negative scores; but it can show ways in which to improve these areas. To do so, all bodies in one destination should have a commitment to improvement. What quality management aims for is to sustain an ongoing improvement of the standard of facilities and services they provide. This is also what benchmarking aims to achieve. In the light of these two statements, it is possible to suggest benchmarking as a management technique to improve the quality of service provision. However, as the subsequent impact is expected to lead to an increase in the market share, benchmarking also helps to maintain the competitiveness of a destination by identifying methods for improving its performance and increasing its market share in the international arena.

Final Words

As noted in the introductory chapter, the prime aims and objectives of this book are to investigate and demonstrate how benchmarking could be used to identify required performance improvements of tourist destinations and develop an initial benchmarking methodology. Based upon the stated aims and objectives and the overview of previous research, the following four propositions have been developed.

Benchmarking can be applied to tourist destinations to identify their performance gaps and take action for improvement. This requires the establishment of destination-specific performance measures.
Both primary and secondary types of data collection methods have been employed to carry out destination comparison/competitiveness research. Secondary data collection methods have focused primarily upon the analysis of pre-collected figures (e.g. Edwards, 1993; Bray, 1996; Seaton, 1996). Primary research methods focus solely on the collection of qualitative measures and the investigation of customer attitudes towards or satisfaction perceptions of the attractiveness of several individual destinations (e.g. Goodrich, 1977, 1978; Haahti, 1986). There is an upward trend in the number of studies using primary research methodology over recent years. Some researchers have

attempted to use both quantitative and qualitative measures in a self-selected destination comparison survey such as the distribution of visits by seasons and tourists' likes or dislikes (Kozak and Rimmington, 1999).

As emphasized earlier, insufficient attention has been paid to the development of a particular destination benchmarking methodology. This statement is therefore developed in response to the basic idea of the benchmarking approach. When adapting the benchmarking approach to the tourism and hospitality fields, it is assumed that strengths and weaknesses of destinations could be compared with each other and destinations could have an opportunity to learn something from others' best practices, mistakes and failures. Briefly, destinations should be aware of what they and their competitors provide and how they perform, due to the possibility of tour operators and customers exploring new destinations. By analysing the customer feedback and the factors influencing the performance of a destination, it is possible to identify what attributes need to be benchmarked (Karlof and Ostblom, 1993; Zairi, 1996). Findings may be useful to establish an accurate positioning strategy that will make the destination unique in some particular ways by improving some aspects of its characteristics and introducing new ones (Choy, 1992).

Destination competitiveness is not an individual concept. Rather it is totally dependent on social, economic and political developments in the tourist-generating countries as well as in the tourist-receiving countries. Moreover, to be competitive, as Ritchie and Crouch (1993) point out, a destination periodically has to evaluate its resources such as hotels, events, attractions, transportation networks and its labour force, and add economic values to them. One definition of benchmarking is that it is a way of collecting information about customers and other organizations within the same industry (Lu *et al.*, 1994). To facilitate destination benchmarking, destination authorities have to search for information about what tourists like or dislike, what their socioeconomic and demographic profiles and motivations are and what other destinations are seeking to achieve and how to achieve the same results. This requires the establishment of destination-specific performance measures.

Depending upon the examination of their applications in the benchmarking literature, both qualitative and quantitative measures could be used for the purpose of undertaking research to identify internal and external performance of destinations. As a part of external benchmarking, tourist destinations could be benchmarked against each other by considering relevant destination attributes, as each destination has its own strengths and weaknesses, which may generate satisfaction and dissatisfaction and raise or lower tourism income. As a result, each destination has something to learn from the other as benchmarking is a two-way process. As a part of internal benchmarking, destinations could measure their performance levels either by using statistical tools or by comparing current measures with earlier ones.

Where tourists have visited multiple destinations, comparative surveys can be used to explore performance gaps.

As is widely known, as a part of the service industry, tourism differs from other industries in that it requires customers (or users) to participate directly in both the production and consumption stages of products and services. This highlights the importance of measuring the satisfaction levels of those who actually experience the performance of the organization. In other words, it is unreasonable in the tourism industry to avoid the experiences or the feedback of actual customers by asking outsiders about their ideas or feelings instead. As each destination may have its own admirers, tourists satisfied in one destination would be different from others at a different destination. This creates a problem in the measurement of external performance as well as carrying out external benchmarking research, whereas there is no problem for internal benchmarking. Nevertheless, with limited exceptions (e.g. King, 1994; Kozak and Rimmington, 1999), much of the research conducted using primary methods was undertaken without evidence that respondents had actually been to all sample destinations, and research to date does not therefore provide a full account of destination competitiveness. The proposed customer satisfaction models may not help evaluate a destination's comparative service performance although they may help identify the key determinants of self-assessment service performance. In today's competitive environments, it may not be reasonable to underestimate improvements in competitors and customers' opinions about them. In destination benchmarking, it is expected that sample populations have direct experience in order to respond accurately to all the questions regarding their actual holiday experiences in each destination. Otherwise, findings do not accurately reflect the performance of destinations on specific attributes.

There are cross-cultural differences between tourists from different countries visiting the same destination. This issue needs to be considered when performing a destination benchmarking study.

A cross-cultural analysis requires a systematic comparison of similarities and differences in values, ideas, attitudes, symbols, and so on (Engel and Blackwell, 1982). Thus, the possible differences could occur in qualitative measures (e.g. level of tourist satisfaction or tourist motivation) or quantitative measures (e.g. tourist expenditure or length of stay). The proposition in the statement is consistent with the findings of previous research in the tourism and hospitality fields and a reflection of the lack of sufficient research in general benchmarking considering cross-cultural differences among a particular organization's customers and between those visiting other competitor organizations. Karlof and Ostblom (1993), in a benchmarking research project, draw attention to the attempts to distinguish different markets if the organization (or the destination) serves more than one market.

A number of empirical studies have sought to explore the similarities and differences between multiple groups in relation to several vacation travel patterns and attitudes towards the selected destinations (Richardson and Crompton, 1988; Sussmann and Rashcovsky, 1997). The findings of past research confirmed that tourist perceptions of a destination or hospitality businesses or their satisfaction levels, demographic profiles and the activities in which they participated during their stay may vary according to their country of origin (Kozak and Nield, 1998). Despite this, as pointed out earlier in Chapter 2, past destination research in tourist satisfaction, motivation and tourist expenditure is limited to homogeneous sample populations and sample destinations. Sampling respondents represent only one country and those tourists visiting only one destination. This issue also applies to the context of the existing benchmarking literature.

A destination attracts customers from different cultures and countries, so tourists might be more or less satisfied or might have different motivations or different expenditure patterns depending on the countries from which they originate. The analysis of customer surveys sought to investigate whether any cross-cultural differences in tourists' perceived satisfaction levels with their holiday experiences at the same destination, their motivations and expenditure levels are important to the decision-making process of destination managers regarding the implementation of destination management and marketing strategies that are appropriate for each market, e.g. positioning and market segmentation. Those who come from other main generating countries therefore need to be included in benchmarking research. However, it is not clear what action to take when one group perceives a set of attributes to be better or has stronger motivations than another. Whose feedback will determine destination benchmarking? The former's or the latter's, or a combination of both? Destination benchmarking needs to address this question.

Due to the differences between tourists from different markets, as benchmarks for tourist destinations, measures could be examined in particular ways, e.g. by nationality and season or by comparison with other destinations. This type of assessment helps to measure the real performance of destinations for each market on the basis of, for example, the type of motivations, the level of tourist satisfaction, comments or complaints, the share of tourist arrivals, the volume of repeat tourists, the level of tourist expenditure and the length of stays. A separate benchmarking study should also be undertaken for each customer group representing a particular country (in both internal and external benchmarking). The findings of past studies confirmed the existence of differences in tourists' motivation, satisfaction, expenditure and the number of previous visits between British and German tourists (Kozak, 2000). For example, the level of spoken and written language at the destination may be very good for one group, but it may not seem so to those who speak another language. This study therefore suggests undertaking a separate benchmarking exercise for each national group. This type of analysis may assist destination authorities in establishing the positioning strategies and exploring their core competencies for each group. It may also assist in investigating reasons for differences between customer groups and enabling the establishment of effective strategies for improvement.

The comparison of international tourist destinations is impeded by their cultural, economic and geographical differences. These need to be considered when proposing a destination benchmarking study.

Some researchers in the field of benchmarking take a conceptual approach describing why benchmarking is important for organizations and for outlining the process of benchmarking (Camp, 1989). Others take an applied approach to identify gaps between organizations by using qualitative and quantitative measures and recommend ways of closing these gaps without much consideration of the impact of other factors that could probably affect the successful implementation of benchmarking findings (Zairi, 1998). As discussed earlier in Chapters 1 and 2, the widespread criticism of benchmarking stems from the notion that each organization or destination may have its own language system, which is used to set up objectives and policies, e.g. laws, regulations, economic structure, planning and management culture (Goldwasser, 1995; Codling, 1997). In the same way that every organization has a unique business culture and strategy, so might tourist destinations. The major issue covers cultural differences in management and marketing practices of two different international, or even national, tourist destinations (see Box 10.1). In the destination management context, Kotler *et al.* (1993) point out that different places should not be expected to develop similar approaches in adapting to change and making plans for their future because each destination may have its own history, culture, values, government and business institutions, and public and private systems. Moreover, customers and conditions are likely to change from one period to the next; therefore, products must be updated and refined, and, if necessary, new products must be designed to meet emerging needs. As a result of such differences, each place needs to develop its own unique decisions.

A further theoretical limitation of benchmarking emerges from the difficulty of translating external ideas that belong to a different culture. The tourism planning approach in developing countries differs significantly from that of developed countries (Tosun, 1998). Therefore, how to transfer such methods from developed countries to developing countries is a problem. Pointing out the negative consequences of development in mass tourism over natural environment and cultural heritage, Gunn (1997, p. 99) notes that 'every political and geographical area has a different historical background, different traditions, different ways of living and different means of accomplishing objectives'. In other words, each destination may have different community values and individual characteristics and may have unique ambitions for its future. Thus, models and techniques applied in one destination may not be applicable to another or may not give similar results even when applied.

Box 10.1. Political factors in destination benchmarking.

There are political factors that make the operationalization of destination benchmarking slow, such as passport, visa and custom control at the airport in Turkey. Resorts in Mallorca take more care over providing facilities for disabled people as a sign of commitment to the EU regulations. Turkish resorts seem to be careless about this as there is no formal sanction to be followed. The authorities and tourism organizations in Mallorca must continuously check the level of their facilities and services' performance in accordance with the EU standards and guidelines. Turkey, where the government wants to become an applicant for full membership of the EU, will have to revise its laws, regulations and practices. This could offer Turkey an opportunity to close some of the gaps between itself and other European destinations.

The identification of such factors is a critical step in the analysis of best practices emerging from benchmarking studies. Beretta *et al.* (1998) point out that environmental factors and organization structure are effective in the success of benchmarking studies. Transferring these factors to tourist destinations, environmental factors are designed by economic, political and social factors such as tax regulations, exchange rates, finance and banking management and culture, as well as geographical factors such as the size of land or the distribution of tourism activities in the country by regions. Organization structure refers to the feature of centralization or decentralization of the government, diffusion of authority and responsibility, and human resources. All these factors will be investigated within this subject. A summary of the related discussion about differences between centralization and decentralization is provided in Box 10.2.

Although it has been found that external benchmarking helps to show where a destination is stronger or weaker and to adapt some good practices from another, it is also obvious that each destination has its own regional differentiation and unique characteristics in some respects, e.g. attractiveness, attributes contributing to tourist satisfaction, tourist spending patterns, and regional political, cultural and economic structure. In line with these findings, this study suggests that certain aspects of service quality are unlikely to be considered as a proper benchmarking element against other destinations in the way that some aspects of physical or technical quality are. As a result, finding the most suitable destination as a partner and defining the attributes to benchmark is a major problem in external benchmarking.

Recommendations for Benchmarking in Practice

The recommendations for the practical applications of benchmarking include the stages of identifying measures to benchmark, the design of the

Box 10.2. Organizational structure of governments.

Differences could be observed among different international destinations with respect to the organizational structure of their governments. For instance, Turkey has a centralized government system where the central government has the power to set goals, take decisions and implement them, while Spain has a decentralized system where local government and city councils are given the power to take decisions and collaborate. The former model may create bureaucratic problems and delays in making efficient decisions since the central government deals with everything in the country. In the latter model, local institutions are given the responsibility of regulating tourism businesses and activities, inspecting and supervising them and developing their own promotion campaigns, locally and abroad, in order to renovate and revitalize the attractiveness of the destination. Briefly, such differences are another piece of evidence indicating that cross-cultural differences in managerial practices could hinder the successful implementation of benchmarking research findings, which a different political system could easily accomplish.

approach to follow, deciding how to collect data, and setting out strategies and their implementation. It is important to bear in mind that there is no best practice to observe and apply; therefore, benchmarking must be perceived as a method of learning from our own as well as others' successes and mistakes and assessing their utility to one's own culture and objectives, rather than accepting it as an attempt to copy what others are doing and providing. The application of destination benchmarking in practice comprises the following recommendations:

1. To achieve high standards, it is necessary to control and coordinate a variety of activities undertaken by various organizations and local groups, such as accommodation, restaurants and bars, recreation and sports, shopping facilities and local people. It needs top-level organization and teamwork to produce effective outcomes. This study therefore suggests launching a destination management department, either as a local committee or as a local council, where its director could be responsible for directing sources of tourism supply at the destination in order to serve customers better, evaluating customer needs and wants and carrying out destination benchmarking research to benefit from its applications. Introducing destination benchmarking as a new concept in benchmarking and tourism literature, this study regards it as a tool to obtain competitive advantage by assisting destination management to monitor the performance of its tourism products and services compared with that of previous years and that of other foreign destinations, and to review its positioning strategies.

2. Destination benchmarking could be a worthwhile technique to view the position of any destination on a league table of performance results.

Although there seems to be no major problem for quantitative measures, it is unlikely to identify criteria for qualitative performance measures for all destinations worldwide. Depending on the features of the destination, each destination management needs to clarify its own attributes to be measured and standards to be expected when setting up benchmarking research. A similar technique could be used for specific types of destinations offering similar products, such as ski resorts, urban tourism centres or mass tourist bathing resorts.

3. Authorities could attempt to understand the factors that have the greatest effect on the performance level of their destinations (internal benchmarking), and then to make further improvements to maximize their overall performance. This may be achieved by establishing new future-based strategies either by examining other destinations (external benchmarking) or by following the guidelines of some national and international grading schemes and awards (generic benchmarking). Taking generic benchmarking on board, destinations may look either at other destinations or at international standards in order to find effective solutions to their particular problems by having access to best practices recognized internationally. For example, one should not expect that problems such as insufficient quality of services, overcommercialization and environmental deregulation are limited to a particular destination.

4. Competition and customer satisfaction have a dynamic structure, and so does benchmarking. A database could therefore be formed including qualitative and quantitative measures about different national and international tourist destinations and their performance levels or applications. International organizations such as the WTO or WTTC could be in charge of this. A specific database could also be formed to collect data about the destination itself containing trends in the industry in comparison with previous years. The sample of customers might differ in profile, needs and attitudes over time, either at different times of the year or from one year to another, so all these processes may be repeated over different periods of time. The Department of Tourism in the Balearic Islands has done this very effectively by constantly monitoring all aspects of tourism, and keeping the results available in the archives.

5. External benchmarking, if properly carried out and implemented, could help both the management and marketing of a destination despite the fact that it has several limitations. It could compare one destination with others, quantify differences and document why those differences exist. The application of external benchmarking requires a two-way process. While the host destination is able to learn from another's best practices, implementation failures and problems, in return the partner is also given the opportunity to learn something from the host. This study proposes that national or international destinations must be aware of what others do, what features of destinations attract tourists and how likely these features are to be considered satisfactory. Destination authorities must review their own performance levels to bring about improvements in conjunction with developments, innovations in the travel and tourism industry and changes in consumer behaviour, needs and wants.

6. To some extent, benchmarking can be carried out between very different destinations (e.g. between business tourism and winter tourism) when only limited types of service levels of accommodation or food and beverage facilities are the subjects of the project. As customers are main elements of the subject, there may appear to be very little difference in terms of diversity and the levels of service provided. Similarly, the provision of infrastructure and superstructure as basic needs for tourism, travel and hospitality might be the same for all destinations and even for customers. Despite this, this recommendation holds one concern. This is not to compare the overall performance of one destination dedicated to business tourism with that of another dedicated to mass tourism due to the varying nature of tourism demand and supply between the two.

7. As a part of internal benchmarking, tourism businesses could benchmark themselves against their counterparts in the same destination. Internal benchmarking could be undertaken among hotels, restaurants and cafes to identify whether any gap exists in terms of providing a certain level of service. The same task could be undertaken in other destinations in the same country. Thus, this study suggests that each service experience be measured and counted just before or after it has taken place. For example, surveys could be conducted by each business such as hotels, restaurants, travel agents or museums individually among their own customers to investigate how well they are satisfied or if they are dissatisfied with the services offered, and learn their likes and dislikes and their opinions on how to lessen the dissatisfaction.

8. Another recommendation must be that individual businesses at the destination could pass on to destination management their own customers' complaints as well as compliments. Complaints would encourage destination management to find better solutions for those who have similar problems. Similarly, compliments would be used to help those who want to improve their service standards and deal with their customers' complaints but who do not know how to do so. It is clear that both complaints and compliments could be sources of internal destination benchmarking, a type of benchmarking undertaken in a single destination. Along with the regular administration of questionnaire surveys, destination management could be advised to place comment boxes at hotels, the destination airport or perhaps at museums, historical sites or even in the streets to maximize feedback in which customers can make suggestions or complain. Moreover, free customer hot lines could be established.

9. In external benchmarking, the overall performance of destinations can be benchmarked against the other(s) either in the same or in a different country. Measuring the external performance aims to compare the tourism position of one destination with the position of a similar one, e.g. trends in tourism, human resources, customer satisfaction. The destination to be nominated as the partner should be perceived as offering superior performance in some respects. Likewise, in competitive benchmarking, as a part of external benchmarking, destinations can be compared with their direct competitors operating in different countries or even geographic areas. For example, it can be one of the purposes of benchmarking to include those in the Mediterranean basin as summer as well as short-haul holiday destinations for the European market.

10. In external benchmarking, it is significant to see if there is any difference in the characteristics of the sample population visiting destinations. This type of assessment is helpful for identifying not only the profile of market segments but also partner destinations with whom external benchmarking is to be conducted. Such an attempt could be significant for destination benchmarking research in order to have a better understanding of competitors involved in the same set in terms of a particular market and make a decision about whom and what to benchmark. For instance, the sample destinations could select their benchmarking partners from countries in the Mediterranean basin because the majority of tourists visiting Mallorca and Turkey tend to take their holidays around this region.

The results of the case studies demonstrate how priority could be given to different aspects of destinations. The main feature of the destination benchmarking approach explained in this book is that it should start with understanding the motivations and perceptions of consumers visiting destinations in terms of demand and end with taking further actions for related destination attributes in terms of supply. This means that destination benchmarking has two main steps when conducting the actual benchmarking process: supply and demand. Demand refers to the process of converting consumer perceptions into quantitative measures by employing numeric scales such as Likert or semantic differential scales in order to identify gaps, make comparisons and take actions. Though it may be impossible to regard tourist motivations as a part of quantitative measures, they will be very helpful in understanding the types of tourist groups choosing the destination and features of pull factors at the destination attracting tourists. Having completed collecting data and identifying gaps, there is a need to arrange site visits to destinations in order to carry out deeper investigations. This stage will be very helpful for learning about the performance of destinations and applications within. All the collected data will then be used to make recommendations for both destinations. In terms of supply, tourism development trends, marketing and promotion, tourism policies and the contribution of tourism to the local economy, and so forth are analysed. All these supply-related research items are expected to be helpful for supporting the findings of empirical research in relation to tourism demand. The strategy to be followed can differ depending upon the type of benchmarking approach employed.

Summary and Review

As a method of seeking best practices by comparing one's own performance with others', the concept of benchmarking emerged in business management in the 1980s. Benchmarking, thinking and looking out of the box, has been adopted by a variety of national and international businesses in order to improve their performance levels, and has been used to evaluate products, services and processes in a number of industries, e.g. car production, food and drink production, health care, public services, education, mail delivery, transportation, water supply, travel and hotels. Benchmarking has traditionally involved inter-organization comparison. This allows the development of improved levels of performance through exposure to the ideas and practices of those organizations acknowledged to have high levels of expertise. As competitiveness forces businesses to improve productivity and quality, many have begun to look externally for new ideas rather than spend time re-inventing the same practices within the organization. However, to date, there have been far more conceptual papers on why benchmarking is important and how to operationalize it than empirical research focusing on methodological issues such as how to measure performance gaps.

This book takes the benchmarking approach a step further in a broader context. There are literally thousands of micro-benchmarks that might apply to many individual elements of a destination, such as accommodation establishments, food and beverage facilities, recreation and sports facilities, and the destination airport, e.g. average time spent in cleaning a room, average time spent in providing a service for the customers, revenues or cost per guest. However, this book is an attempt to apply benchmarking to destinations only for broad functional areas such as accommodation, food and beverages, hospitality, physical environment and the destination airport. Some of their attributes, regarded as an element of qualitative measures, are overall cleanliness, attitude towards tourists, overall value for money, and so on. There are also various quantitative measures, which can be useful either while conducting a benchmarking study or while evaluating its performance.

With the objective of evaluating the relevance of the benchmarking method to international tourist destinations, their development and management, this study has proposed a framework based upon an extensive review of the literature both in benchmarking and in tourism fields. Three types of benchmarking are adopted to destination benchmarking: internal, external and generic. Both qualitative and quantitative measures are revised to operationalize internal and external destination benchmarking procedures. Internal benchmarking is aimed at measuring the internal performance of destinations by analysing the impact of individual attributes on tourist satisfaction and future behaviour and repeat tourists' perceptions of changes compared with preceding years. Some quantitative measures are also evaluated in the context of comparison with past years and national economic figures. The external benchmarking sought to investigate in what respect one destination was more competitive or was performing better than others using self-generated data on tourist satisfaction, motivation and expenditure scores and statistical figures. Generic benchmarking has been introduced to measure own performance using several national or international quality or eco-label standards and to follow these guidelines to accelerate Improvement.

To conclude, tourism and hospitality benchmarking is still in its infancy and there are also some deficiencies in earlier benchmarking studies. For example, benchmarking should be regarded as a learning experience rather than a copying activity. Moreover, benchmarking is not only a management approach but also directly influences marketing strategies. Qualitative and quantitative measures must be interrelated as any change in the former is expected to have an impact on the latter. Therefore, this study has the potential to draw several significant theoretical and practical conclusions. From the theoretical point of view, the contribution of this study exists in the methods and techniques used to identify the factors influencing selected destination performance variables and in the methods to be employed for comparison between the two destinations. The analysis of these findings could be helpful for indicating the way in which the existing benchmarking approach could be adapted to tourist destinations and areas where there are weaknesses to be considered. From the practical point of view, the analysis of these findings might be helpful for pointing out the level of competitiveness, attributes in which destinations need to be improved and positioning strategies each destination has to establish by following the guidelines of either internal or external benchmarking. Benchmarking, if properly implemented, could help the management of a destination by comparing itself either with its earlier performance levels or with other destinations so as to learn from their past or current practices. This book also makes a substantial contribution to knowledge through gaining knowledge of performance and the reasons for any difference, and implications for the further development of tourism in tourist destinations.

References

Ahmed, Z.U. (1991) The influence of the components of a state's tourist image on product positioning strategy. *Tourism Management* 12(4), 331–340.

Almanza, B.A., Jaffe W. and Lin, L. (1994) Use of the service attribute matrix to measure consumer satisfaction. *Hospitality Research Journal* 17(2), 63–75.

American Productivity and Quality Center (1999) What is best practice? http://www.apqc.org retrieved on 12 January.

Andersen, B. (1995) Benchmarking in Norwegian industry and relationship benchmarking. In: Rolstadas, A. (ed.) *Benchmarking: Theory and Practice*. Chapman & Hall, London, pp. 105–109.

Ashworth, G. and Goodall, B. (1988) Tourist images: making considerations. In: Goodall, B. and Ashworth, G. (eds) *Marketing in the Tourism Industry: the Promotion of Destination Regions*. Routledge, Wiltshire, UK, pp. 213–238.

Ashworth, G.J. and Voogd, H. (1994) Marketing of tourism places: what are we doing? In: Uysal, M. (ed.) *Global Tourist Behavior*. The Haworth Press, New York, pp. 5–19.

Atkinson, A.A., Waterhouse, J.H. and Wells, R.B. (1997) A stakeholder approach to strategic performance measurement. *Sloan Management Review* Spring, 25–37.

Balm, G.J. (1992) *Benchmarking: a Practitioner's Guide for Becoming and Staying Best of the Best*, 2nd Edn. Quality and Productivity Management Association, Illinois.

Baloglu, S. (1998) An empirical investigation of attitude theory for tourist destinations: a comparison of visitors and nonvisitors. *Journal of Hospitality and Tourism Research* 22(3), 211–224.

Baloglu, S. and McCleary, K.W. (1999) U.S. international pleasure travelers' images of four Mediterranean destinations: a comparison of visitors and nonvisitors. *Journal of Travel Research* 38(November), 144–152.

Bareham, J. (1995) *Consumer Behaviour in the Food Industry: a European Perspective*. Butterworth-Heinemann, Oxford.

Barsky, J.D. (1996) Building a program for world-class service. *Cornell Hotel and Restaurant Administration Quarterly* February, 17–27.

Baum, T. and Odgers, P. (2001) Benchmarking best practice in hotel front office: the Western European experience. *Journal of Quality Assurance in Hospitality and Tourism* 2(3/4), 93–110.

Beaman, J., Huan, T.C. and Kozak, M. (2001) Estimating a Markov model that incorporates first visit decisions and varying repeat frequency. *Tourism Analysis* 6(2), 81–97.

Beeho, A.J. and Prentice, R.C. (1997) Conceptualising the experiences of heritage tourists: a case study of New Lanark and World Heritage Village. *Tourism Management* 18(2), 75–87.

Bell, R. and Morey, R. (1994) The search for appropriate benchmarking partners: a macro approach and application to corporate travel management. *Omega* 22(5), 477–490.

Bendell, T., Boulter, L. and Kelly, J. (1993) *Benchmarking for Competitive Advantage*. Financial Times–Pitman Publishing, London.

Beretta, S., Dossi, A. and Grove, H. (1998) Methodological strategies for benchmarking accounting processes. *Benchmarking for Quality Management and Technology* 5(3), 165–183.

Bitner, M.J. and Hubbert, A.R. (1994) Encounter satisfaction versus overall satisfaction versus quality. In: Rust, R.T. and Oliver, R.L. (eds) *Service Quality: New Directions in Theory and Practice*. Sage, California, pp. 72–93.

Bloom, J. (1996) Optimising the use of national tourism statistics in strategic performance measurement. In: *The 27th TTRA Annual Conference*, 16–19 June, Las Vegas, Nevada, pp. 396–407.

Bogan, C.E. and English, M.J. (1994) *Benchmarking for Best Practices: Winning Through Innovative Adaptation*. McGraw-Hill, New York.

Boger, C.A., Cai, L.A. and Li, L. (1999) Benchmarking: comparing discounted business rates among lodging companies. *Journal of Hospitality and Tourism Research* 23(3), 256–267.

Bonifield, R.L., Jeng, L.M. and Fesenmaier, D.R. (1996) Comparison of approaches for measuring traveler motivations. *Tourism Analysis* 1(1), 39–47.

Bray, R. (1996) The package holiday market in Europe. *Travel and Tourism Analyst* 4, 51–71.

Breiter, D. and Kline, S.F. (1995) Benchmarking quality management in hotels. *FIU Hospitality Review* 13(2), 45–52.

Brignall, S. and Ballantine, J. (1996) Performance measurement in service businesses revisited. *International Journal of Service Industry Management* 7(1), 6–31.

Brotherton, B. and Shaw, J. (1996) Towards an identification and classification of critical success factors in UK Hotels PLC. *International Journal of Hospitality Management* 15(2), 113–135.

Bryman, A. (1988) *Quantity and Quality in Social Research, Contemporary Social Research: 18*. Unwin Hyman, London.

Bryman, A. and Cramer, D. (1990) *Quantitative Data Analysis for Social Scientists*. Routledge, London.

Bull, A. (1995) *The Economics of Travel and Tourism*. Pitman, Australia.

Butler, R.W. (1980) The concept of a tourist area cycle of evolution: implications for management of resources. *Canadian Geographer* 24(1), 5–12.

Butler, R. and Mao, B. (1997) Seasonality in tourism: problems and measurement. In: Murphy, P.A. (ed.) *Quality Management in Urban Tourism*. John Wiley & Sons, Chichester, UK, pp. 9–23.

Cadotte, E.R., Woodruff, R.B. and Jenkins, R.L. (1987) Expectations and norms in models of consumer satisfaction. *Journal of Marketing Research* 24(August), 305–314.

Callan, R.J. (1994) Hotel classification and grading schemes: a paradigm of utilisation and user characteristics. *International Journal of Hospitality Management* 14(3–4), 271–284.

Callan, R.J. (1996) Attributional analysis of customers' hotel selection criteria by grading scheme categories. In: *Proceedings of the Fifth CHME Conference.* Nottingham, UK, pp. 116–143.

Camp, R.C. (1989) *Benchmarking: the Search for Industry Best Practices that Leads to Superior Performance.* ASQC Quality Press, Milwaukee, Wisconsin.

Campbell, A. (1999) Tailored, not benchmarked: a fresh look at corporate planning. *Harvard Business Review* March–April, 41–50.

Canon, D.F. and Kent, W.E. (1994) What every hospitality educator should know about benchmarking. *Hospitality and Tourism Educator* 6(4), 61–64.

Carey, S., Gountas, Y. and Gilbert, D. (1997) Tour operators and destination sustainability. *Tourism Management* 18(7), 425–431.

Carmines, E.G. and Zeller, R.A. (1979) *Reliability and Validity Assessment.* Sage Publications, Beverly Hills.

CBI News (1995) Room for improvement in Britain's hotel sector. November–December, p. 24.

CBI News (1997) Travellers checked? January, p. 13.

Cheshire, M. (1997) Introducing the concept of best practice benchmarking into the Portsmouth heritage area. *Tourism* Summer, 6–7.

Chisnall, G.A. (1992) *Marketing Research,* 4th edn. McGraw-Hill, London.

Cho, B. (1998) Assessing tourist satisfaction: an exploratory study of Korean youth tourists in Australia. *Tourism Recreation Research* 23(1), 47–54.

Choi, T.Y. and Chu, R. (2000) Levels of satisfaction among Asian and Western travellers. *International Journal of Quality and Reliability Management* 17(2), 116–131.

Chon, K.S. (1989) Understanding recreational traveler's motivation, attitude and satisfaction. *Tourist Review* 1, 3–6.

Choy, D.J.L. (1992) Life cycle models for Pacific Island destinations. *Journal of Travel Research* 30(3), 26–31.

Churchill, G.A. (1979) A paradigm for developing better measures of marketing constructs. *Journal of Marketing Research* 16(February), 64–73.

Codling, B.S. (1997) Dynamics of best practice: a multidimensional perspective. *Benchmarking for Quality Management and Technology* 4(2), 96–103.

Codling, S. (1992) *Best Practice Benchmarking: a Management Guide.* Gower, Hampshire, UK.

Cohen, E. (1974) Who is a tourist? A conceptual clarification. *Sociological Review* 22, 527–555.

Coker, C. (1996) Benchmarking and beyond. *Insights* March, 139–144.

Coltman, M.M. (1989) *Tourism Marketing.* Van Nostrand Reinhold, New York.

Cook, S. (1995) *Practical Benchmarking: a Manager's Guide to Creating a Competitive Advantage.* Kogan Page, London.

Cortada, J.W. (1995) How to do benchmarking. In: Cortada, J.W. and Woods, J.A. (eds) *The Quality Yearbook.* McGraw-Hill, London, pp. 733–737.

Court, B. and Lupton, R.A. (1997) Customer portfolio development: modeling destination adopters, inactives and rejecters. *Journal of Travel Research* 36(1), 35–43.

Cox, A. and Thompson, I. (1998) On the appropriateness of benchmarking. *Journal of General Management* 23(3), 1–20.

Cox, J.R., Mann, L. and Samson, D. (1997) Benchmarking as a mixed metaphor: disentangling assumptions of competition and collaboration. *Journal of Management Studies* 34(2), 285–314.

Crompton, J.L. and Love, L.L. (1995) The predictive validity of alternative approaches to evaluating quality of a festival. *Journal of Travel Research* 34(1), 11–25.

Cross, R. and Leonard, P. (1994) Benchmarking: a strategic and tactical perspective. In: Dale, B.G. (ed.) *Managing Quality*, 2nd edn. Prentice Hall, New Jersey, pp. 497–513.

Crouch, G.I. and Ritchie, J.R.B. (1999) Tourism, competitiveness and societal prosperity. *Journal of Business Research* 44, 137–152.

Czepiel, J.A., Rosenberg, L.J. and Akerele, A. (1974) Perspectives on consumer satisfaction. In: Curhan, R.C. (ed.) *1974 Combined Proceedings Series No. 36.* American Marketing Association, pp. 119–123.

Danaher, P.J. and Arweiler, N. (1996) customer satisfaction in the tourist industry: a case study of visitors to New Zealand. *Journal of Travel Research* 34(1), 89–93.

Danaher, P.J. and Haddrell, V. (1996) A comparison of question scales for measuring customer satisfaction. *International Journal of Service Industry Management* 7(4), 4–26.

Danaher, P.J. and Mattsson, J. (1994) Customer satisfaction during the service delivery process. *European Journal of Marketing* 28(5), 5–16.

Dann, G.M.S. (1996) Tourists' images of a destination: an alternative analysis. *Journal of Travel and Tourism Research* 5(1–2), 41–45.

Dann, G.M.S., Nash, D. and Pearce, P. (1988) Methodology in tourism research. *Annals of Tourism Research* 15, 1–28.

Davidson, R. and Maitland, R. (1997) *Tourism Destinations.* Hodder and Stoughton, London.

Davies, P. (1990) Benchmarking. *Total Quality Management* December, 309–310.

Day, R.L. and Ash, S.B. (1978) Consumer response to dissatisfaction with durable products. In: Wilkie, W.L. (ed.) *Advances in Consumer Research*, Vol. 6, *Proceedings of the Association for Consumer Research Ninth Annual Conference.* Florida, pp. 438–444.

Deming, W.E. (1982) *Quality, Productivity and Competitive Position.* Center for Advanced Engineering Study, Massachusetts Institute of Technology, Cambridge, Massachusetts.

Department of National Heritage (1996) *Benchmarking for Smaller Hotels: Competing with the Best.* London.

Derby City Council (2001) Derby City Destination Benchmarking Survey, Executive Summary.

Deutscher, I. (1973) Asking questions cross-culturally: some problems of linguistic comparability. In: Warwick, D.P. and Osherson, S. (eds) *Comparative Research Methods.* Prentice Hall, New Jersey, pp. 163–185.

Dorfman, P.W. (1979) Measurement and meaning of recreation satisfaction: a case study in camping. *Environment and Behavior* 11(4), 483–510.

Dorsch, J.J. and Yasin, M.M. (1998) A framework for benchmarking in the public sector. *International Journal of Public Sector Management* 11(2–3), 91–115.

Duke, C.R. and Persia, M.A. (1996) Consumer-defined dimensions for escorted tour industry segment: expectations, satisfactions and importance. *Journal of Travel and Tourism Marketing* 5(1–2), 77–99.

Echtner, C.M. and Ritchie, J.R.B. (1991) The meaning and measurement of destination image. *Journal of Tourism Studies* 2(2), 2–12.

Edgett, S. and Snow, K. (1996) Benchmarking measures of customer satisfaction, quality and performance for new financial service products. *Journal of Services Marketing* 10, 6–17.

Edwards, A. (1993) *Price Competitiveness of Holiday Destinations: Costs from European Travellers (No. 2).* The Economist Intelligence Unit, London.

Elmuti, D. and Kathawala, Y. (1997) An overview of benchmarking process: a tool for continuous improvement and competitive advantage. *Benchmarking for Quality Management and Technology* 4(4), 229–243.

Engel, J.F. and Blackwell, R.D. (1982) *Consumer Behavior*, 4th edn. The Dryden Press, New York.

European Commission (1998) Research in the field of integrated quality management of tourism destinations. http://www.wttc.org retrieved on 14 November, 2002.

Evans, J.R. and Lindsey, W.M. (1993) *The Management and Control of Quality*, 2nd edn. West Publishing Company, St Paul, Minnesotta.

Fakeye, P.C. and Crompton, J.L. (1991) Image differences between prospective, first-time and repeat visitors to the lower Rio Grand valley. *Journal of Travel Research* 30(Autumn), 10–16.

Ferdows, K. and DeMeyer, A. (1990) Lasting improvements in manufacturing performance: in search of a new theory. *Journal of Operations Management* 9(2), 168–184.

Fishbein, M. and Ajzen, I. (1975) *Belief, Attitude, Intention and Behavior: an Introduction to Theory and Research.* Addison-Wesley, USA.

Fornell, C. (1992) A national customer satisfaction barometer: the Swedish experience. *Journal of Marketing* 56, 6–21.

Fournier, S. and Mick, D.G. (1999) Rediscovering satisfaction. *Journal of Marketing* 63(October), 5–23.

Fuchs, M. and Weiermair, K. (2001) Development opportunities for a tourism benchmarking tool: the case of Tyrol. *Journal of Quality Assurance in Hospitality and Tourism* 2(3/4), 71–92.

Gardini, A. and Bernini, C. (2002) Benchmark in the conference hospitality industry. *Journal of Quality Assurance in Hospitality and Tourism* 3(1/2), 1–18.

Geber, B. (1990) Benchmarking: measuring yourself against the best. *Training* November, 36–44.

Gitelson, R.J. and Crompton, J.L. (1983) The planning horizons and source of information used by pleasure vacationers. *Journal of Travel Research* Winter, 2–7.

Goh, S. and Richards, G. (1997) Benchmarking the learning capability of organisations. *European Management Journal* 15(5), 575–583.

Goldwasser, C. (1995) Benchmarking: people make the process. *Management Review* June, 39–43.

Goodall, B. (1988) How tourists choose their holidays: an analytical framework. In: Goodall, B. and Ashworth, G. (eds) *Marketing in the Tourism Industry: the Promotion of Destination Regions.* Routledge, London, pp.1–17.

Goodall, B. (1990) Opportunity sets as analytical marketing instruments: a destination area view. In: Ashworth, G. and Goodall, B. (eds) *Marketing Tourism Places.* Routledge, London, pp. 63–84.

Goodall, B. and Bergsma, J. (1990) Destinations as marketed in tour operators' brochures. In: Ashworth, G. and Goodall, B. (eds) *Marketing Tourism Places.* Routledge, London, pp. 170–192.

Goodrich, J.N. (1977) Differences in perceived similarity of tourism regions: a spatial analysis. *Journal of Travel Research* 16(Summer), 10–13.

Goodrich, J.N. (1978) The relationship between preferences for and perceptions of vacation destinations: application of a choice model. *Journal of Travel Research* 17(Autumn), 8–13.

Govern Balear (1999) *El Turisme a les Illes Balears: Dades Informatives, any 1998.* Palma de Mallorca, Spain.

Grabler, K. (1997) Perceptual mapping and positioning of tourist cities. In: Mazanec, J.A. (ed.) *International City Tourism: Analysis and Strategy.* Pinter, London, pp. 101–113.

Graburn, N.H. and Jafari, J. (1991) Introduction: tourism social science. *Annals of Tourism Research* 18, 1–11.

Gronross, C. (1978) A service-oriented approach to marketing of services. *European Journal of Marketing* 12(8), 588–601.

Gunn, C.A. (1997) *Vacationscape: Developing Tourist Areas,* 3rd edn. Taylor and Francis, Washington, DC.

Gyte, D.M. and Phelps, A. (1989) Patterns of destination repeat business: British tourists in Mallorca, Spain. *Journal of Travel Research* 28(Summer), 24–28.

Haahti, A.J. (1986) Finland's competitive position as a destination. *Annals of Tourism Research* 13, 11–35.

Hair, J.F., Anderson, R.E., Tatham, R.L. and Black, W.C. (1995) *Multivariate Data Analysis with Readings,* 4th edn. Prentice-Hall, New Jersey.

Hauser, J. and Katz, G. (1998) Metrics: you are what you measure. *European Management Journal* 16(5), 517–528.

Heath, E. and Wall, G. (1992) *Marketing Tourism Destinations: a Strategic Planning Approach.* John Wiley & Sons, Canada.

Hill, B.J., McDonald, C. and Uysal, M. (1990) Resort motivations for different family life cycle stages. *Visions in Leisure and Business* 8(4), 18–27.

Holloway, J., Francis, G., Hinton, M. and Mayle, D. (1998) Best practice benchmarking: delivering the goods? *Total Quality Management* 9(4–5), 121–125.

Hunt, J.D. (1975) Image as a factor in tourism development. *Journal of Travel Research* 13(3), 1–7.

Hurst, F. (1994) En route surveys. In: Ritchie, J.R.B. and Goeldner, C.R. (eds) *Travel and Hospitality Research: a Handbook for Managers and Researchers,* 2nd edn. John Wiley & Sons, New York, pp. 453–471.

Hutton, R. and Zairi, M. (1995) Effective benchmarking through a prioritisation methodology. *Total Quality Management* 6(4), 399–411.

Illum, S. and Schaefer, A. (1995) Destination attributes: perspectives of motorcoach tour operators and destination marketers. *Journal of Travel and Tourism Marketing* 4 (4), 1–15.

Inskeep, E. (1991) *Tourism Planning: an Integrated and Sustainable Development Approach.* Van Nostrand Reinhold, New York.

Jackson, M.S., White, G.N. and Schmierer, C.L. (1996) Tourism experiences within an attributional framework. *Annals of Tourism Research* 23, 798–810.

Jafari, J. (1983) Anatomy of the travel industry. *Cornell Hotel and Restaurant Administration Quarterly* 24(May), 71–77.

Johns, N. and Lee-Ross, D. (1995) Profile accumulation: a quality assessment technique for hospitality SMEs. In: Teare, R. and Armistead, C. (eds) *Services Management: New Directions and Perspectives*. Cassell, London.

Johns, N., Lee-Ross, D., Graves, M.R. and Ingram, H. (1996) Quality benchmarking in the small hotel sector using profile accumulation: a new measurement tool. *Proceedings of the Fifth Annual Hospitality Research Conference*, 10–11 April, Nottingham, UK, pp. 192–207.

Johns, N., Lee-Ross, D. and Ingram, H. (1997) A study of service quality in small hotels and guesthouses. *Progress in Hospitality and Tourism Research* 3(4), 351–363.

Jorgensen, D.I. (1989) *Participant Observation: a Methodology for Human Studies*. Sage Publications, London.

Kaplan, R.S. (1993) Implementing the balanced scorecard at FMC Corporation: an interview with Larry D. Brady. *Harvard Business Review* September–October, 143–149.

Kaplan, R.S. and Norton, D.P. (1992) The balanced scorecard: measures that drive performance. *Harvard Business Review* January–February, 71–79.

Kaplan, R.S. and Norton, D.P. (1993) Putting the balanced scorecard to work. *Harvard Business Review* September–October, 134–142.

Karlof, B. and Ostblom, S. (1993) *Benchmarking: a Signpost of Excellence in Quality and Productivity*. John Wiley & Sons, Chichester, UK.

Kasul, R.A. and Motwani, J.G. (1995) Performance measurements in world-class operations: a strategic model. *Benchmarking for Quality Management and Technology* 2(2), 20–36.

King, B. (1994) Australian attitudes to domestic and international resort holidays: a comparison of Fiji and Queensland. In: Seaton, A.V. *et al.* (eds) *Tourism: the State of the Art*. John Wiley & Sons, London, pp. 347–358.

Klaus, P. (1985) Quality epiphenomenon: the conceptual understanding of quality in face-to-face service encounters. In: Czepiel, A., Solomon, M.R., Suprenant, C.L. and Guttman, E.G. (eds) *The Service Encounter: Managing Employee Customer Interaction in Service Business*. Lexington Books, Lexington, Massachusetts, pp. 17–33.

Kleine, B.M. (1994) Benchmarking for continuous performance improvement: tactics for success. *Total Quality Environmental Management* Spring, 283–295.

Klenosky, D. and Gitelson, R.E. (1998) Travel agents' destination recommendations. *Annals of Tourism Research* 25(3), 661–674.

Kotler, P. (1994) *Marketing Management: Analysis, Planning, Implementation and Control*, 8th edn. Prentice Hall International Editions, New Jersey.

Kotler, P., Haider, D. and Rein, I. (1993) *Marketing Places: Attracting Investment, Industry and Tourism to Cities, States and Nations*. The Free Press, New York.

Kotler, P., Bowen, J. and Makens, J. (1996) *Marketing for Hospitality and Tourism*. Prentice Hall, New Jersey.

Kozak, M. (2000) Destination benchmarking: facilities, customer satisfaction and levels of tourist expenditure. PhD thesis, Sheffield Hallam University, UK.

Kozak, M. (2001) Comparative assessment of tourist satisfaction with destinations across two nationalities. *Tourism Management* 22(3), 391–401.

Kozak, M. (2002a) Comparative analysis of tourist motivations by nationality and destinations. *Tourism Management* 23(2), 221–232.

Kozak, M. (2002b) Destination benchmarking. *Annals of Tourism Research* 29(2), 497–519.

Kozak, M. (2002c) Measuring tourist satisfaction with multiple destination attributes. *Tourism Analysis* 7(3–4), 229–240.

Kozak, M. (2004) Introducing destination benchmarking: a conceptual approach. *Journal of Hospitality and Tourism Research* (in press).

Kozak, M. and Nield, K. (1998) Importance-performance analysis and cultural perspectives in Romanian Black Sea resorts. *Anatolia: an International Journal of Tourism and Hospitality Research* 9(2), 99–116.

Kozak, M. and Nield, K. (2001) An overview of benchmarking literature: strengths and weaknesses. *Journal of Quality Assurance in Tourism and Hospitality* 2(3–4), 7–23.

Kozak, M. and Rimmington, M. (1998) Benchmarking: destination attractiveness and small hospitality business performance. *International Journal of Contemporary Hospitality Management* 10(5), 74–78.

Kozak, M. and Rimmington, M. (1999) Measuring destination competitiveness: conceptual considerations and empirical findings. *International Journal of Hospitality Management* 18(3), 273–283.

Kozak, M. and Rimmington, M. (2000) Tourist satisfaction with Mallorca, Spain as an off-season holiday destination. *Journal of Travel Research* 39(3), 260–269.

Krishnan, S. and Valle, V.A. (1978) Dissatisfaction attributions and consumer complaint behavior. In: Wilkie, W.L. (ed.) *Advances in Consumer Research*, Vol. 6, *Proceedings of the Association for Consumer Research Ninth Annual Conference*. Florida, pp. 445–449.

Laws, E. (1995) *Tourist Destination Management: Issues, Analysis and Policies.* Routledge, New York.

Leslie, D. (2001) Serviced accommodation, environmental performance and benchmarks. *Journal of Quality Assurance in Hospitality and Tourism* 2(3/4), 127–148.

Lewis, B. and Owtram, M. (1986) Customer satisfaction with package holidays. In: Moores, B. (ed.) *Are They Being Served?* Philip Allan Publishers, Oxford, pp. 201–213.

Lewis, R.C. (1984) Theoretical and practical considerations in research design. *Cornell Hotel and Restaurant Administration Quarterly* February, 25–35.

Liverpool City Council (2000) Liverpool City Destination Benchmarking Survey, Executive Summary.

Lu, M.H., Madu, C.N., Kuei, C. and Winokur, D. (1994) Integrating QFD, AHP and benchmarking in strategic marketing. *Journal of Business and Industrial Marketing* 9(1), 41–50.

Madigan, J.M. (1993) Measures matrix chart: a holistic approach to understanding operations. *Quality Management Journal* 1(1), 77–86.

Mak, J., Moncur, J. and Yonamine, D. (1977) How or how not to measure visitor expenditures. *Journal of Travel Research* 16, 1–4.

Mann, R., Adebanjo, O. and Kehoe, D. (1999a) An assessment of management systems and business performance in the UK food and drinks industry. *British Food Journal* 101(1), 5–21.

Mann, R., Adebanjo, O. and Kehoe, D. (1999b) Best practices in the food and drinks industry. *British Food Journal* 101(3), 238–253.

Mansfeld, Y. (1992) From motivation to actual travel. *Annals of Tourism Research* 19, 399–419.

Martinuzzi, A. (2000) *ÖkoBusinessPlan.* Evaluationsbericht, Vienna.

Matzler, K. and Pechlaner, H. (2001) Guest satisfaction barometer and benchmarking: experiences from Austria. *Journal of Quality Assurance in Hospitality and Tourism* 2(3/4), 25–48.

Mayo, E.J. and Jarvis, L.P. (1981) *The Psychology of Leisure Travel: Effective Marketing and Selling of Travel Services.* CBI Publishing Company, Boston.

McDougall, G.H.G. and Munro, H. (1994) Scaling and attitude measurement in travel and tourism research. In: Ritchie, J.R.B. and Goeldner, C.R. (eds) *Travel and Hospitality Research: a Handbook for Managers and Researchers,* 2nd edn. John Wiley & Sons, New York.

McIntyre, G. (1993) *Sustainable Tourism Development: Guide for Local Planners.* World Tourism Organisation, Madrid.

McNair, C.J. and Leibfried, K.H.J. (1992) *Benchmarking: a Tool for Continuous Improvement.* Harper Business, New York.

Meade, B. and Pringle, J. (2001) Environmental management systems for Caribbean hotels and resorts: a case study of five properties in Jamaica. *Journal of Quality Assurance in Hospitality and Tourism* 2(3/4), 149–159.

Melcher, A., Acar, W., DuMont, P. and Khouja, M. (1990) Standard-maintaining and continuous improvement systems: experiences and comparisons. *Interfaces* 20(3), 24–40.

Mentzer, T., Bienstock, C. and Kahn, K. (1995) Benchmarking satisfaction. *Marketing Management* Summer, 7, 40.

Mihalic, T. (1998) Ecological labelling in tourism. In: Briguglio, L., Archer, B., Jafari, J. and Wall, G. (eds) *Sustainable Tourism in Islands and Small States Issues and Policies.* Pinter, London, pp. 197–205.

Mill, R.C. and Morrison, A.M. (1992) *The Tourism System: an Introductory Text,* 2nd edn. Prentice Hall International Editions, New Jersey.

Min, H. and Min, H. (1997) Benchmarking the quality of hotel services: managerial perspectives. *International Journal of Quality and Reliability Management* 14(6), 582–597.

Morey, R.C. and Dittman, D.A. (1995) Evaluating a hotel GM's performance. *Cornell Hotel and Restaurant Administration Quarterly* October, 30–35.

Morrison, A.M. (1989) *Hospitality and Travel Marketing.* Albany, New York.

Moser, C.A. and Kalton, G. (1971) *Survey Methods in Social Investigation,* 2nd edn. Gower, Andover, UK.

Mudie, P. and Cottam, A. (1993) *The Management and Marketing of Services.* Butterworth-Heinemann, London.

Mules, T. (1998) Decomposition of Australian tourist expenditure. *Tourism Management* 19(3), 267–271.

Murphy, P.E. and Pritchard, M. (1997) Destination price-value perceptions: an examination of origin and seasonal influences. *Journal of Travel Research* 35(Winter), 16–22.

Nadkarni, R.A. (1995) A not-so-secret recipe for successful TQM. *Quality Progress* November, 91–96.

New, C.C. and Szwejczewski, M. (1995) Performance measurement and the focused factory: empirical evidence. *International Journal of Operations and Production Management* 15(4), 63–79.

Nolan, J.J. and Swan, J.E. (1984) Rising expectation: do expectations increase with experience? In: Hunt, H.K. and Day, R.L. (eds) *Combined Proceedings of the Eighth Conference and the Ninth Conference. Louisiana and Arizona 1984–1985*. Indiana University, Indianapolis, pp. 17–22.

Ohinata, Y. (1994) Benchmarking: the Japanese experience. *Long Range Planning* 27(4), 48–53.

Oliver, R.L. (1999) Whence consumer loyalty. *Journal of Marketing* 63, 33–44.

Oppermann, M. (1999) Predicting destination choice: a discussion of destination loyalty. *Journal of Vacation Marketing* 5(1), 51–65.

Osgood, C.E., Suci, G.J. and Tannenbaum, P.H. (1971) *The Measurement of Meaning*. University of Illinois Press, Urbana, Illinois.

Parasuraman, A., Zeithaml, V.A. and Berry, L.L. (1985) A conceptual model of service quality and its implications for future research. *Journal of Marketing* 49, 41–50.

Pearce, D.G. (1997) Competitive destination analysis in Southeast Asia. *Journal of Travel Research* 35(4), 16–24.

Pearce, P.L. (1982) Perceived changes in holiday destinations. *Annals of Tourism Research* 9, 145–164.

Pearce, P.L. and Caltabiano, M.L. (1983) Inferring travel from traveller's experiences. *Journal of Travel Research* Autumn, 16–20.

Perez, E.A. and Sampol, C.J. (2000) Tourist expenditure for mass tourism markets. *Annals of Tourism Research* 27(3), 624–636.

Peter, J.P. (1979) Reliability: a review of psychometric basics and recent marketing practices. *Journal of Marketing Research* 16 (February), 6–17.

Peters, G. (1994) *Benchmarking Customer Service*. Financial Times–Pitman Publishing, London.

Peterson, R.A. and Wilson, W.R. (1992) Measuring customer satisfaction: fact and artifact. *Journal of the Academy of Marketing Science* 20(1), 61–71.

Phillips, P. and Appiah-Adu, K. (1998) Benchmarking to improve the strategic planning process in the hotel sector. *The Service Industries Journal* 18(1), 1–17.

Pizam, A. (1994a) Monitoring customer satisfaction. In: David, B. and Lockwood, A. (eds) *Food and Beverage Management: a Selection of Readings*. Butterworth-Heinemann, Oxford, pp. 231–247.

Pizam, A. (1994b) Planning a tourism research investigation. In: Ritchie, R.B. and Goeldner, C.R. (eds) *Travel and Hospitality Research: a Handbook for Managers and Researchers*, 2nd edn. John Wiley & Sons, New York, pp. 91–104.

Pizam, A. (1999) Cross-cultural tourist behavior. In: Pizam, A. and Mansfeld, Y. (eds) *Consumer Behavior in Travel and Tourism*. The Haworth Press, New York, pp. 393–411.

Pizam, A. and Milman, A. (1993) Predicting satisfaction among first-time visitors to a destination by using the expectancy disconfirmation theory. *International Journal of Hospitality Management* 12(2), 197–209.

Pizam, A. and Reichel, A. (1979) Big spenders and little spenders in US tourism. *Journal of Travel Research* 18 (Summer), 42–43.

Pizam, A., Neumann, Y. and Reichel, A. (1978) Dimensions of tourist satisfaction area. *Annals of Tourism Research* 5, 314–322.

Plog, S.C. (1974) Why destination areas rise and fall in popularity. *Cornell Hotel and Restaurant Administration Quarterly* 14(4), 55–58.

Porter, M.E. (1985) *Competitive Advantage: Creating and Sustaining Superior Performance.* Free Press, New York.

Porter, M.E. (1996) What is strategy? *Harvard Business Review* November–December, 61–78.

Pyo, S., Mihalik, B.J. and Uysal, M. (1989) Attraction attributes and motivations: a canonical correlation analysis. *Annals of Tourism Research* 16, 277–282.

Quelch, J.A. and Ash, S.B. (1981) Consumer satisfaction with professional services. In: Donnely, J.H. and George, W.R. (eds) *Marketing of Services.* American Marketing Association, Illinois, pp. 82–85.

Reilly, M.D. (1990) Free elicitation of descriptive-adjectives for tourism image assessment. *Journal of Travel Research* 28(4), 21–26.

Reisinger, Y. and Turner, L. (1998) Cross-cultural differences in tourism: a strategy for tourism marketers. *Journal of Travel and Tourism Marketing* 7(4), 79–105.

Richardson, S.L. and Crompton, J. (1988) Vacation patterns of French and English Canadians. *Annals of Tourism Research* 15(4), 430–448.

Richins, M.L. (1979) Consumer perceptions of costs and benefits associated with complaining. In: Hunt, H.K. and Day, R.L (eds) *Refining Concepts and Measures of Consumer Satisfaction and Complaining Behavior. Fourth Annual Conference on Consumer Satisfaction, Dissatisfaction and Complaining Behavior.* Bloomington, Indiana, pp. 50–53.

Ritchie, J.R.B. and Crouch, G.I. (1993) Competitiveness in international tourism: a framework for understanding and analysis. *Aiest Publications* 34, 23–71.

Roberts, E.B. (1995) Benchmarking the strategic management of technology: I. *Research Technology Management* January–February, 44–56.

Robson, C. (1993) *Real World Research: a Resource for Social Scientists and Practitioner-Researchers.* Blackwell, Oxford.

Rogers, D.S., Daugherty, P.J. and Stank, T.P. (1995) Benchmarking programs: opportunities for enhancing performance. *Journal of Business Logistics* 10(2), 43–63.

Ross, G.F. (1993) Destination evaluation and vacation preferences. *Annals of Tourism Research* 20, 477–489.

Rust, R.T., Zahonik, A.J. and Keiningham, T.L. (1996) *Service Marketing.* Harper Collins, New York.

Saleh, F. and Ryan, C. (1992) Client perceptions of hotels. *Tourism Management* June, 163–168.

Sandbach, M. (1997) *International Competition and Structural Changes in Tourism Markets. WTO/CEU-ETC Joint Seminar: Faced with Worldwide Competition and Structural Changes, What are the Tourism Responsibilities of European Governments?* 9–10 April, Salzburg, Austria, p. 26.

Schroeder, D.M. and Robinson, A.G. (1991) America's most successful export to Japan: continuous improvement programs. *Sloan Management Review* Spring, 67–80.

Seaton, A.V. (1996) *The Competitive Evaluation of Tourism Destination Performance: Scotland and European Tourism 1985–1994.* Report for the Scottish Tourist Board.

Seaton, A.V. and Bennett, M.M. (1996) *Marketing Tourism Products.* International Thomson Business Press.

Selby, M. and Morgan, N.J. (1996) Restructuring place image. *Tourism Management* 17(4), 287–294.

Shetty, Y.K. (1993) Aiming high: competitive benchmarking for superior performance. *Long Range Planning* 26(1), 39–44.

Singh, J. (1991) Understanding the structure of consumers' satisfaction evaluations of service delivery. *Journal of the Academy of Marketing Science* 19(3), 223–244.

Smelser, N.J. (1973) The methodology of comparative analysis. In: Warwick, D.P. and Osherson, S. (eds) *Comparative Research Methods.* Prentice-Hall, New Jersey, pp. 42–86.

Smith, G.A., Ritter, D. and Tuggle, W.P. (1993) Benchmarking: the fundamental questions. *Marketing Management* 2(3), 43–48.

Spachis, N.E. (1997) The Greek hotel classification system: should quality grading be incorporated in it? MSc dissertation, University of Surrey, UK.

Spendolini, M.J. (1992) *The Benchmarking Book.* American Management Association, New York.

Spotts, D.M. and Mahoney, E.M. (1991) Segmenting visitors to a destination region based on the volume of their expenditures. *Journal of Travel Research* 29(Spring), 24–31.

Stephens, S. (1997) Eco grading for Scots. *Leisure Week,* 13 June.

Stronge, W.B. (1992) Statistical measurements in tourism. In: Khan, M., Olsen, M. and Var, T. (eds) *VNR's Encyclopaedia of Hospitality and Tourism.* Van Nostrand Reinhold, New York, pp. 735–745.

Struebing, L. (1996) Measuring for excellence. *Quality Progress* December, 25–28.

Sussmann, S. and Rashcovsky, C. (1997) A cross-cultural analysis of English and French Canadians' vacation travel patterns. *International Journal of Hospitality Management* 16(2), 191–208.

Swan, J.E. and Combs, L.J. (1976) Product performance and consumer satisfaction: a new concept. *Journal of Marketing* 40(April), 25–33.

Swift, F.W., Gallwey, T. and Swift, J.A. (1995) Benchmarking – the neglected element in total quality management. In: Rolstadas, A. (ed.) *Benchmarking: Theory and Practice.* Chapman & Hall, London, pp. 42–50.

Syriopoulos, T.C. and Sinclair, M.T. (1993) An econometric study of tourism demand: the aids model of US and European tourism in the Mediterranean countries. *Applied Economics* 25, 1541–1552.

Tang, K.H. and Zairi, M. (1998) Benchmarking quality implementation in a service context: a comparative analysis of financial services and institutions of higher education II. *Total Quality Management* 9(7), 539–552.

Thomason, L., Colling, P. and Wyatt, C. (1999a) Benchmarking: an essential tool in destination management and the achievement of best value. *Insights* January, A111–A117.

Thomason, L., Colling, P. and Wyatt, C. (1999b) Destination benchmarking II: the 1998 pilot. *Insights* May, A173–A180.

Timothy, D.J. (1998) Co-operative tourism planning in a developing destination. *Journal of Sustainable Tourism* 6(1), 52–68.

Tosun, C. (1998) Roots of unsustainable tourism development at the local level: the case of Urgup in Turkey. *Tourism Management* 19(6), 595–610.

Um, S. and Crompton, J.L. (1990) Attitude determinants in tourism destination choice. *Annals of Tourism Research* 17, 432–448.

UNEP (1997) *Guidelines for Carrying Capacity Assessment for Tourism in Mediterranean Coastal Areas. Split,* pp. 23–24.

Uysal, M. and Hagan, L. (1993) Motivations of pleasure travel and tourism. In: Khan, M., Olsen, M. and Var, T. (eds) *Encyclopaedia of Hospitality and Tourism.* Van Nostrand Reinhold, New York, pp. 798–810.

Vaziri, K. (1992) Using competitive benchmarking to set goals. *Quality Progress* October, 81–85.

Veal, A.J. (1992) *Research Methods for Leisure and Tourism: a Practical Guide.* Pitman Publishing, Glasgow.

Vogt, C.A. and Fesenmaier, D.R. (1995) Tourists and retailers' perceptions of services. *Annals of Tourism Research* 22(4), 763–780.

Vrtiprah, V. (2001) Managing quality in Hotel Excelsior. *Journal of Quality Assurance in Hospitality and Tourism* 2(3/4), 111–126.

Walleck, A.S., O'Halloran, J.D. and Leader, C.A. (1991) Benchmarking world-class performance. *McKinsey Quarterly* 1(1), 3–24.

Warwick, D.P. and Osherson, S. (1973) Comparative analysis in the social sciences. In: Warwick, D.P. and Osherson, S. (eds) *Comparative Research Methods.* Prentice-Hall, New Jersey, pp. 3–41.

Watson, G.H. (1993) *Strategic Benchmarking: How to Rate Your Company's Performance Against the World's Best.* John Wiley & Sons, Canada.

Watson, G.H. (1997) Strategic benchmarking. In: Carnall, C.A. (ed.) *Strategic Change.* Butterworth-Heinemann, London, pp. 91–101.

Weller, L.D. (1996) Benchmarking: a paradigm for change to quality education. *TQM Magazine* 8(6), 24–29.

Westbrook, R.A. and Newman, J.W. (1978) An analysis of shopper dissatisfaction for major household appliances. *Journal of Marketing Research* 15(August), 456–466.

Wetzel, D.K. and Maul, G.P. (1996) How to measure continuous improvement. *Quality Progress* December, 41–47.

Wober, K.W. (2001) A heuristic model for benchmarking SME hotel and restaurant businesses on the Internet. *Journal of Quality Assurance in Hospitality and Tourism* 2(3/4), 49–70.

Wober, K.W. (2002) *Benchmarking in Tourism and Hospitality Industries: the Selection of Benchmarking Partners.* CAB International, Wallingford, UK.

Woodside, A.G. and Lysonski, S. (1989) A general model of traveler destination choice. *Journal of Travel Research* 27(4), 8–14.

Woodside, A.G. and Sherrell, D. (1977) Traveler evoked, inept and inert sets of vacation destinations. *Journal of Travel Research* 16(1), 14–18.

World Tourism Organization (1993) *Awards for Improving the Coastal Environment: the Example of Blue Flag.* Madrid.

Yin, R.K. (1994) *Case Study Research: Design and Methods,* 2nd edn. Applied Social Research Methods Series 5. Sage, California.

Young, S. and Ambrose, T. (1999) Benchmarking visitor attractions: Hampshire pilot project. *Insights* November, A71–A80.

Zairi, M. (1992) The art of benchmarking: using customer feedback to establish a performance gap. *Total Quality Management* 3(2), 177–188.

Zairi, M. (1994) Benchmarking: the best tool for measuring competitiveness. *Benchmarking for Quality Management and Technology* 1(1), 11–24.

Zairi, M. (1996) *Benchmarking for Best Practice: Continuous Learning through Sustainable Innovatio*n. Butterworth-Heinemann, Oxford.

Zairi, M. (1998) Benchmarking at TNT Express. *Benchmarking for Quality Management and Technology* 5(2), 138–149.

Zairi, M. and Hutton, R. (1995) Benchmarking: a process driven tool for quality improvement. *TQM Magazine* 7, 35.

Zhao, X., Maheshwari, S.K. and Zhang, J. (1995) Benchmarking quality practices in India, China and Mexico. *Benchmarking for Quality Management and Technology* 2(3), 20–40.

Index

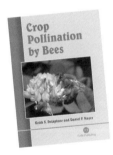
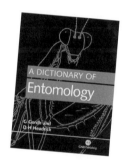
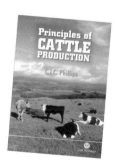